MW01009824

For current pricing information,
or to learn more about this or any Nextext title,
call us toll-free at **1-800-323-5435**
or visit our web site at www.nextext.com.

A NEXTEXT COURSEBOOK

Civics

IN AMERICA

Authors

Michael Barry   Stephen Feinstein   Mary Kathleen Flynn

Ann Sherman   Judith Lloyd Yero

nextext

Authors

Michael Barry is social studies chairman at Loyola Academy, Wilmette, Illinois.

Stephen Feinstein writes educational materials, specializing in social studies and language arts, from his home in Sausalito, California.

Mary Kathleen Flynn, formerly of CNN and MSNBC, is a writer and editor based in New York City and Dummerston, Vermont.

Ann Sherman is a lawyer and journalist living in New York City.

Judith Lloyd Yero, formerly of Carl Sandburg High School, Orland Park, Illinois, is currently director of Teacher's Mind Resources, Hamilton, Montana.

Consultant

Paul Finkelman is the Chapman Distinguished Professor of Law, University of Tulsa College of Law, Tulsa, Oklahoma.

Cover and interior illustrations: Eric Larsen

Printed in the United States of America

ISBN 0-618-22198-0

1 2 3 4 5 6 7 — DCI — 08 07 06 05 04 03 02

Table of Contents

Chapter 9
STATE GOVERNMENT

140

Chapter 10
LOCAL GOVERNMENT

158

American Citizenship

In this chapter, you will learn about:

- what citizenship means
- why we have government
- what values the citizens of the United States hold
- the duties and responsibilities of United States citizens

"Yesterday the greatest question was decided which ever was debated in America; and a greater perhaps never was, nor will be, decided among men. A resolution was passed without one dissenting colony that those United Colonies are, and of right ought to be, free and independent States."

John Adams, a leader in the movement for American independence from England and, later, the second president of the United States, wrote these words in a letter to his wife Abigail on July 3, 1776. The following day, July 4, America began a new and uncertain adventure, becoming a free and independent nation. A great experiment in democracy had begun.

What does it mean to be a citizen of this great nation? Citizens of the United States enjoy rights that many people in the world do not share. In this book, you'll learn about the rights and responsibilities of American citizens. These values are the principles that guide both the government and our lives as members in this society. The Declaration of Independence and the Constitution are built on and support these American values.

The Meaning of Citizenship

The Pledge of Allegiance was written by Francis Bellamy and was originally published in the September 8, 1892, issue of *The Youth's Companion*. It has been memorized by generations of schoolchildren and adults. Have you ever stopped to consider what the words mean?

I pledge allegiance to the Flag of the United States of America, and to the Republic for which it stands, one Nation under God, indivisible, with liberty and justice for all.

The Pledge is an unofficial oath or statement of loyalty. It sums up what it means to be a United States citizen.

Allegiance

Think about what loyalty means in your own life. To whom and to what are you loyal? Your family? Friends? Teachers? Perhaps you belong to a club, team, or other organization to which you feel loyal.

Loyalty, or **allegiance**, means devotion, affection, and attachment. Loyalty to your country is the basis of citizenship. A **citizen** is a person who:

* Owes allegiance to a government.
* Is entitled to government protection in exchange for that allegiance.
* Has certain rights and privileges, as well as responsibilities, that come with citizenship.

Citizenship is a contract or agreement in which both parties provide something. The citizen provides loyalty. The government provides protection and guarantees rights.

Primary Source

Oath of Allegiance

The oath below is taken by every person who becomes a citizen of the United States. It is a spoken contract made by new citizens to their new country.

"I hereby declare, on oath, that I absolutely and entirely renounce and abjure [give up] all allegiance and fidelity to any foreign prince, potentate, state, or sovereignty of whom or which I have heretofore been a subject or citizen; that I will support and defend the Constitution and laws of the United States of America against all enemies, foreign and domestic; that I will bear true faith and allegiance to the same; that I will bear arms on behalf of the United States when required by the law; that I will perform noncombatant service in the Armed Forces of the United States when required by the law; that I will perform work of national importance under civilian direction when required by the law; and that I take this obligation freely without any mental reservation or purpose of evasion; so help me God."

Becoming a Citizen

A person can generally become a citizen in one of **two** ways. You may be a citizen by birth, or you can become a naturalized citizen.

1. **Native Citizenship.** If you are born in a country, you are recognized as a **native**. If you are born in the United States, you are automatically a United States citizen. Children of American parents born outside of the United States may also be citizens.

2. **Naturalized Citizenship.** If you are born elsewhere and want to become a citizen, you must complete a process to become a **naturalized** citizen. To begin the naturalization process, you must be:

* At least 18 years old.
* A lawful, permanent resident of the United States for five years (or for three years if your spouse has been a United States citizen for at least three years).
* Willing to swear loyalty to the United States.
* Of good moral character.
* Able to read, write, and speak simple English.
* Knowledgeable about U.S. government and history.

A person begins the naturalization process by filling out an application from the Immigration and Naturalization Service (INS). Each applicant must also successfully complete an interview and oral exam on U.S. government and history, given by the INS. The naturalization process ends with a ceremony in which new citizens recite an oath of allegiance.

Membership in a Society

As a citizen, you are a member of a **society**—a community bound together by common interests and standards. Do you belong to a club or a team? As a member of that group or society, you agree to follow its rules. In the same way, as a citizen of the United States, you must obey the laws or rules of the country. **Civics** is the name given to the social science that deals with the rights and duties of citizens.

▲
New citizens take the oath of allegiance.

American Citizenship

The Test

In 2000, nearly 900,000 people were naturalized as U.S. citizens. All of them passed the oral test given by the Immigration and Naturalization Service (INS) about U.S. government and history.

To pass, you have to get 70 percent of the answers correct.

How would you do on an oral exam given by the INS? Take this sample test and see if you can correctly answer at least nine of the questions.

Questions:

1. Why did the Pilgrims come to America? _____
2. Who helped the Pilgrims in America? _____
3. What ship brought the Pilgrims to America? _____
4. What do the stripes on the flag mean? _____
5. What were the original 13 states? _____
6. What was the 50th state to join the union? _____
7. What country did the United States fight during the Revolutionary War? _____
8. Who was the first president of the United States? _____
9. Who was the president during the Civil War? _____
10. What do we call a change to the Constitution? _____
11. How many branches are there in our government? _____
12. Who was Martin Luther King, Jr.? _____

Answers: 1. Religious freedom. 2. Native Americans. 3. The *Mayflower*. 4. Colonies. 5. Connecticut, Delaware, Georgia, Maryland, Massachusetts, New Hampshire, New Jersey, New York, North Carolina, Pennsylvania, Rhode Island, South Carolina, Virginia. 6. Hawaii. 7. England (Great Britain). 8. George Washington. 9. Abraham Lincoln. 10. Amendment. 11. Three; legislative, executive, and judicial. 12. A civil rights leader.

Government and Society

Government is the organization that establishes and executes the policies, including the laws and rules, used by members of a society or community of people. However, setting up rules is only part of a government's job.

Reasons for Government

Generally, government serves a society by protecting and maintaining:

* The nation's security.
* Law and order.
* Public services.
* Other institutions necessary for the good of the society.

Security

The most important purpose of government is to protect its people. Protection is the government's half of the bargain in the contract of citizenship. You give allegiance to a country, and the country gives you its protection. The U.S. government protects you from:

* Foreign nations (through the Armed Forces).
* Other people (through laws against assault and battery, theft, murder, and so on, and through law-enforcement agents, such as police officers).
* Corporations and businesses (through consumer protection laws and other regulations).
* Yourself (through seatbelt laws, helmet laws, laws against suicide, and so on).

Law and Order

Laws provide order in a society. People in a society need order so that they can do the things they want or need to do every day—going to school, doing a job, or shopping at the mall. It is the government's job to make and enforce laws that will provide order. Without law and order, we would live in a state of **anarchy**—complete disorder and confusion that result from the absence of government.

Public Services

The government also provides public services that make society run more smoothly. These services help promote order and health in society. Some public services provided by government in the United States include:

* Street cleaning and garbage removal in most urban and suburban areas (through local sanitation departments).
* Letter and parcel delivery (through the U.S. Postal Service).
* Water purification (through city, county, and state agencies).

Maintaining Other Institutions

Since a wide variety of services are necessary for the good of any community, the government is responsible for establishing and maintaining important service institutions, such as:

* Public schools, to provide an education.
* Jails, to keep communities safe.
* Some types of hospitals, to provide health care.

Should Illegal Aliens Get Reduced Tuitions?

In many states, citizens and legal immigrants who live in that state get a discounted tuition, or a tuition "break," at state universities. In California in early 2002, the University of California's governing board voted to allow undocumented (illegal) immigrants who have lived in California for at least three years to pay the same tuition as other California residents. The financial benefit is substantial: In-state students paid an average of $3,859, while out-of-state and international students paid $14,933.

Should illegal state residents receive the in-state tuition discount at state universities, or should they pay the same tuition as out-of-state students? How might granting illegal aliens the rights of legal residents and citizens affect society? You decide.

Arguments for a Tuition Break

The students are residents of the state and should share the same benefits as other residents.

These tuition breaks make a college education possible for students who otherwise couldn't afford one.

Providing a college education for these students will allow them to be a more productive part of society. They will be able to contribute to the state's economy as workers.

Students should not be blamed for their parents' actions. They did not choose to live in the United States illegally.

Arguments against a Tuition Break

These students are not citizens and should not receive the same benefits as citizens.

The tuition break is unfair to U.S. citizens who live out-of-state and still must pay full tuition.

This benefit puts an additional tax burden on California citizens who must pay for the costs.

Extending benefits to undocumented immigrants encourages people from other countries to live in this country illegally.

Types of Government

Not all governments are the same. Different countries around the world have different types of governments. These governments may be:

* Monarchies.
* Dictatorships.
* Democracies.

Monarchy

In a **monarchy**, a single person, such as a king, queen, or emperor, is the ruler, or symbolic ruler. A monarch's right to rule is usually hereditary, handed down from generation to generation within a family. Generally, a monarch remains in power for life. His or her power may be complete, total, and absolute, or it may be limited by custom or by law. Monarchs in the world today include:

* The queen of England.
* The emperor of Japan.
* The king of Saudi Arabia.

Dictatorship

In a **dictatorship,** the head of government is a ruler who has absolute power and unlimited authority. Many dictators seize power by **coup**—the sudden, violent overthrow of a government by a small group. Other modern dictators achieved office legally, then later ignored the laws to seize more power and take control.

EXAMPLES: Benito Mussolini in Italy and Adolf Hitler in Germany gained public office legally, but later took total control of their countries. Many Latin American nations have been governed by dictators who were previously military leaders. Cuban dictator Fidel Castro led armed attacks against the government of Cuba from 1956 to 1959. He forced the government's leader, Fulgencio Batista, from power in 1959 and seized power himself.

Democracy

In a **democracy,** citizens share in guiding the activities of the government, usually by voting for their representatives. The concept of democracy, which began in ancient Greece, has expanded in modern times. Today, the term describes a belief that the people, acting either directly or through representatives (such as elected officials), must control their government.

Democracy values the equality of individuals, and it aims to free people from unnecessary rules imposed by government. In a modern democracy like our own country, governments make laws that limit behavior only when a majority of the people agrees.

What Unites America?

Americans are united by a common ideal or vision, sometimes known as the "American Dream." What does the American Dream mean to you? Perhaps it means being able to own a car or a home one day. Maybe it means going to college, getting the ideal job, or becoming the president of the United States.

Because you live in America, you have the *opportunity* to see your dreams come true. No dreams are guaranteed, of course, but you have the right to *pursue* your dreams. Many people come to America from other countries to be able to do so. However, to understand the dream more fully, you need to understand our roots as a nation. We are a varied nation bound together by common values.

Did You Know?

The Statue of Liberty

For more than a century, the Statue of Liberty has been a symbol of freedom throughout the world.

A gift from the people of France, "Lady Liberty" was unveiled in October 1886. Since then, she has stood overlooking New York's harbor, greeting immigrants and announcing that their journey to the "land of the free" has finally come to an end. Her official name is *Liberty Enlightening the World.*

Diversity in America

America is a country made up of **immigrants**—people who were born elsewhere, but who came here in order to settle permanently. From 1820 to 1930, the United States received about 60 percent of the world's immigrants. In the last century, the United States welcomed over 17 million new, naturalized citizens through immigration.

The American population is becoming more and more **diverse,** or varied. According to the 2000 U.S. census, about 11 percent of the United States population was born in another country. Since its founding in 1776, and even before then when most immigrants were British, the United States has become home for people from around the world, including approximately 250,000 Africans who came as slaves. As these immigrants have made America their home, our country has become a wonderful mixture of people, culture, and hope.

"Wake up, Tom. You're having the American dream again."

Census 2000—Racial Diversity in America

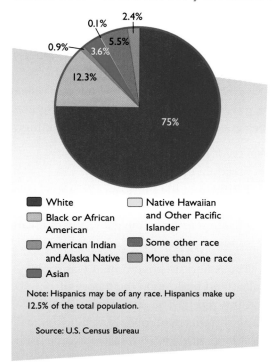

Legend:
- White
- Black or African American
- American Indian and Alaska Native
- Asian
- Native Hawaiian and Other Pacific Islander
- Some other race
- More than one race

Note: Hispanics may be of any race. Hispanics make up 12.5% of the total population.

Source: U.S. Census Bureau

With all this diversity, no one should be surprised that our national motto is *E Pluribus Unum*, a Latin phrase meaning "From Many, One."

How do the many become one? People have answered that question by making comparisons.

* ***Melting Pot.*** Just as different metals are fused together in the heating process, people from different countries blend into the American culture over time, and the final product is stronger as a result.

Critics have objected to the image of the melting pot, pointing out that the image suggests that immigrants must give up their own cultures to be part of American culture.

* ***Salad Bowl.*** Recently, some people have begun describing the country as a salad bowl or a mosaic to suggest that people don't have to give up their native culture to be an American.

Whatever image you prefer, America is a better place because so many different cultures have joined together in one nation.

Did You Know?

Snapshot of America

The most complete study of the American population is the **census**, or survey to count the population, taken by the U.S. Census Bureau every 10 years. Information from the 2000 Census shows that:

* The population is growing older, due to the aging of so-called **baby boomers** (people born in the post-World War II period from 1946 through 1964).
* Households are shrinking slightly. The average household size in 2000 was 2.59 people, down slightly from 2.63 in 1990.
* Single-mom households increased three times as quickly as married-couple families.
* More Americans are Hispanic. The number of Hispanics rose by nearly 13 million between 1990 and 2000, a 53 percent increase. Hispanics now make up about 12.5 percent of the United States population.

American Values

The values that define our country help to unite this land of immigrants. These values are the foundation of our government and legal system. They include:

* *Equality.* All citizens are treated equally by government.
* *Freedom.* Certain basic human rights are guaranteed by our government.
* *Justice.* Laws are applied fairly and equally to everyone.

Equality

Equality of people before the law is an ideal that we try to achieve, and Americans have made great progress. In 1776, when the Declaration of Independence stated that "all men are created equal," white people—men, women, and children—were recognized as citizens. In six states, free blacks were also citizens. However, for many years, slaves were not recognized as citizens and were not regarded by law as people, but as property. Today, slavery is not an issue, but many people feel that wealth can still make some people "more equal" than others. Because we value equality, we will continue to get closer to the idea of perfect equality among all people. Perhaps you will be part of the changes that will make that happen.

Freedom

The Declaration of Independence was written to announce that the United States was a free and separate country, no longer subject to the restraints of the British government. The Founders built our system of government on guaranteed basic rights designed to promote freedoms, including:

* Freedom of religion.
* Freedom of speech.
* Freedom of the press.
* Freedom to meet in groups peacefully.
* Freedom to make the government aware of ideas and concerns.

The American government was established and built upon the theory of **natural rights.** This theory says that the natural rights of all people *aren't given to them by government,* but instead come from nature or God. Because of that, they are **inalienable**—they cannot be taken away by people or government.

Justice

No person can be punished for a crime unless government officials follow certain rules and processes. The American justice system protects the rights of citizens:

* To a speedy and public trial.
* To have an attorney when accused of a crime.
* To have witnesses testify in court.
* To trial by jury in specific cases.
* To protection from cruel punishment.

Edwards v. South Carolina (1963)

Sometimes being a good citizen means speaking out against laws that you feel are unfair or bad. The freedoms guaranteed to you as a citizen protect your rights to say what you think, even if you criticize the government, as long as you do so peacefully. Late in the morning of March 2, 1961, a group of African-American high school and college students met at a local church and walked in groups of about 15 to the South Carolina State House grounds. Their purpose was to protest discrimination against African Americans.

The same small groups of students walked in a peaceful and orderly way through the grounds. They carried signs with messages, such as "I am proud to be a Negro" and "Down with segregation." When ordered by police to leave the site, they remained where they were. Many were arrested and convicted of the crime of disturbing the peace.

The Supreme Court, however, ordered the students' release and ruled that South Carolina infringed on the students' rights of free speech, free assembly, freedom to petition, and their rights to express their views peacefully.

The Supreme Court decision stated that, "[A] function of free speech under our system of government is to invite dispute. It may indeed best serve its high purpose when it induces a condition of unrest, creates dissatisfaction with conditions as they are, or even stirs people to anger. . . . It may . . . have profound unsettling effects as it presses for acceptance of an idea. That is why freedom of speech . . . is . . . protected against censorship or punishment, unless shown likely to produce a clear and present danger of a serious substantive evil that rises far above public inconvenience, annoyance, or unrest. . . . There is no room under our Constitution for a more restrictive view."

Striving Toward an Ideal

Ideals are noble. However, in the real world, we don't find perfect equality, perfect freedom, or perfect justice in our (or any other) country. Perhaps you know someone who was treated unfairly by the government or by law officers. Maybe you find some

laws unfair. Maybe you're concerned that some people have been put in jail for crimes they didn't commit.

The real world isn't perfect, but by working together as citizens toward this common dream, we can get closer to achieving our country's ideals. President

George W. Bush summarized this dream in his 2002 State of the Union address:

"America will lead by defending liberty and justice, because they are right and true and unchanging for all people everywhere. No nation owns these aspirations, and no nation is exempt from them. We have no intention of imposing our culture—but America will always stand firm for the non-negotiable demands of human dignity: the rule of law . . . limits on the power of the state . . . respect for women . . . private property . . . free speech . . . equal justice . . . and religious tolerance.

"America will take the side of brave men and women who advocate these values around the world . . . because we have a greater objective than eliminating threats and containing resentment. We seek a just and peaceful world beyond the war on terror."

The Duties and Responsibilities of Citizenship

Becoming a good citizen is one way to participate actively in the American Dream. As an American citizen, you enjoy many rights. However, your rights come with duties required by law, as well as responsibilities.

Duties of Citizens

In return for your rights and for your government's protection, you are asked to fulfill certain duties as a citizen. Your duties include:

* Obeying the laws of local, state, and national governments.
* Defending the nation.
* Paying taxes.
* Serving on a jury.
* Attending school.

Obeying the Laws

As part of their Oath of Allegiance to their new country, naturalized United States citizens promise to "support and defend the Constitution and laws of the United States of America." Obeying the laws of our land is part of the contract of citizenship. People who break the law break the contract, and so they may face penalties including fines, imprisonment, and, for some crimes, even death.

Defending the Nation

As a citizen, you may be asked to fight for your country. In the Oath of Allegiance, naturalized citizens swear to "bear arms on behalf of the United States when required by the law." (However, the government may allow people with religious objections to serving in the military to promise to perform non-military service.)

We need the military to defend our country and protect our way of life. Defending your country—through military or nonmilitary service—is a necessary part of citizenship.

Paying Taxes

An old saying goes: "There are only two certainties in life: death and taxes." In this country, you must pay your taxes—or risk fines and possibly imprisonment.

The government uses taxes to raise money to provide services for the good of the people. These services include public schooling, garbage removal and recycling, mail delivery, operating the military, and so on. Society benefits from the services provided by the government, so everyone should help pay for them.

Serving on a Jury

Juries play an important role in our legal system. In the United States, most people accused of a crime are allowed to have their case heard by a **jury**—a group of citizens called upon to decide the guilt or innocence of a person accused of a crime. Jury members base their decision on the evidence presented in a trial.

As an American citizen, you will probably receive a call to serve on a jury at least once in your life. This will be your opportunity to participate in the legal processes of our country. Failure to report for jury duty can be punished with fines.

Attending School

As a student, you know that attending school (or being home-schooled) from the age of 5 until the age of 16 is required by law. While reading, writing, and math are important, your education is about more than that. Did you realize that your education benefits your country? Your education prepares you to play an active, intelligent, and helpful role in society when you are an adult.

Responsibilities of Citizens

Citizens must do more than just obey the law. Citizens have other responsibilities, including:

* Protecting each other's rights.
* Voting.
* Helping to make society better.

Respecting the Rights of Others

The Declaration of Independence lists specific rights, including "Life, Liberty, and the pursuit of Happiness." However, your personal pursuit of happiness doesn't mean you can do anything you want, any-where you want, to anyone you want. Your personal rights are always balanced against the rights of others and the good of the community as a whole.

Voting

The right to vote is a central value of democracy. Voting either for a candidate or for a new law gives you the opportunity to influence the direction of government and, therefore, to change your community and your country.

Often, people don't vote because they believe that their one vote cannot make a difference. If you ever feel this way, remember that, throughout history, people have fought and even died to gain the right to vote.

Volunteering

In his 2002 State of the Union address, President George W. Bush emphasized the importance of volunteers.

America's youth have the volunteer spirit. Thirteen million teens, more than half of America's teenagers, did volunteer work in just one year during the 1990s. They gave an estimated 3.5 hours per week, totaling 2.4 billion hours of volunteer time.

One volunteer can make a big difference in someone's life, as a tutor, a mentor, or a friend to someone in need. As a volunteer, you help make your community a better place to live.

Chapter 1 Wrap-up
AMERICAN CITIZENSHIP

Citizenship is an understood agreement, or contract, between a citizen and a government. The citizen pledges allegiance or loyalty to the government, and the government promises to protect the citizen. Citizens may be born in a country, or they may be naturalized.

There are many different types of government in our world today, including dictatorships, monarchies, and democracies. Because the United States is a democracy, the people have a say in guiding their government, primarily by voting to elect their representatives.

The American population is diverse, made up of many immigrants and descendants of immigrants from many countries. This diverse population is united by a shared belief in the American Dream. American values of equality, freedom, and justice are all part of this dream.

Citizenship involves many rights, duties, and responsibilities. Duties of American citizens include obeying the law, defending the nation, paying taxes, serving on a jury, and attending school. Responsible citizens respect the rights of others, vote, and work actively for society's good.

allegiance—devotion or loyalty owed by a citizen to a government. *p. 2*

anarchy—state of political disorder resulting from the absence of government. *p. 5*

baby boomers—people born in the post-World War II period from 1946 through 1964. *p. 9*

census—count of the population. *p. 9*

citizen—person who owes allegiance to a government and who is entitled to government protection. *p. 2*

civics—social science dealing with the rights and duties of citizens. *p. 3*

coup (KOO)—sudden, violent overthrow of a government by a small group. Coups are nonpeaceful ways of changing a government's leaders. *p. 7*

democracy—government in which power is held by the people and exercised either directly or through representation, usually determined by elections. *p. 7*

dictatorship—government in which the ruler has absolute power and unlimited authority. *p. 7*

diverse—made up of different parts. *p. 8*

government—organization that controls and directs the making and administration of a society's policies. *p. 5*

immigrant—person born in one country who goes to another country to live. *p. 8*

inalienable—impossible to be taken away by people or government, such as are natural rights. *p. 10*

jury—group of ordinary citizens chosen to decide the guilt or innocence of the person accused in a trial. *p. 13*

loyalty—allegiance, affection, devotion, and attachment. *p. 2*

monarchy—government in which the ruler is a hereditary head of state who rules for life. *p. 7*

native—person born in a particular place or country. A native citizen is someone who receives citizenship by being born in a country. *p. 3*

naturalize—to admit to or grant citizenship to someone who was born in another country. *p. 3*

natural rights—theory that certain inalienable rights of all people come from nature or God. *p. 10*

society—voluntary association of people bound together by common interests and standards. *p. 3*

CHAPTER 2

The Foundations of American Government

In this chapter, you will learn about:

- the roots of our government
- how the American colonies were governed
- why the colonies moved toward independence
- how our nation's early governments worked

The American Revolution ended England's control over the American colonies, with its unfair trade rules, abusive kings, and hated British soldiers. What would come next? How should the new country be governed?

The Founders, the men who set out to create America's new government, knew their history well. Ancient Greece and Rome, as well as England, provided models for ways to govern. Exciting ideas from European philosophers guided them. Their experiences as legislators in the colonial governments helped them. Yet, the challenge of creating a new government was great. It would take two attempts to set up a government system that they could use. What they created has influenced governments the world over ever since.

The Roots of Citizenship

The ideas about government that guided America's first leaders came from their knowledge of history and their own recent experiences.

The Heritage of Ancient Greece and Rome

Two very important ideas came from the classic period in world history. These were the concepts of:

1. **Direct Democracy.**
2. **Republic.**

Direct Democracy

The Ancient Greeks were the first people to develop a democracy. In some of their city states, such as Athens, all the adult male citizens formed the government. We call this kind of government **direct democracy**, because every citizen voted for the laws they followed. Women and slaves were not citizens, so they had no voice in government. Democracy worked well for the Greeks because their city states were small, and citizens could meet and discuss issues face to face. (A **city state** is a nation that consists of a single city and its surrounding area.)

Republic

Like the Greeks, the ancient Romans believed that citizens should run their own government. The Romans also didn't want a rule by kings. But the Roman Empire stretched over thousands of miles. Direct democracy was not possible. So, Rome developed a **republic**—a representative form of government. In a republic, citizens elect representatives to make the rules and laws for them.

When the representatives meet in a group to discuss and pass laws, that body, or group, is called a **legislature**. In the Roman Republic, the legislature was the Roman Senate.

"The Athenians are here, Sire, with an offer to back us with ships, money, arms, and men—and, of course, their usual lectures about democracy."

How Should Representatives Vote?

In any representative form of government, a representative has to balance responsibility to voters' opinions with what the representative believes is right personally. A representative must choose when to vote the way he or she believes the constituents want him or her to vote and when to vote according to conscience, if the two are in conflict.

Let's look at this problem: A bill has been proposed that will limit handgun ownership by citizens, and Representative Smith must decide how to vote.

How should Representative Smith vote? Why?

A Vote for the Bill

Representative Smith is personally opposed to handgun ownership. He feels he should vote for the bill.

* Rep. Smith thinks crime rates are high because too many people own handguns. He believes the anti-handgun bill would help reduce crime.
* He believes that too many people are hurt or killed by guns in accidents.
* Rep. Smith feels there would be fewer accidents if there were not so many guns available.

A Vote against the Bill

Representative Smith knows that most of his constituents would want him to vote against the bill.

* The crime rate in his district is fairly high and people in his district are afraid. They want to be able to protect themselves.
* A survey mailed to his constituents showed that seven out of ten who responded were in favor of private handgun ownership.
* Rep. Smith received and accepted a campaign donation from the National Rifle Association (NRA). The NRA is a group that supports and defends citizens' rights to responsible handgun ownership. Rep. Smith supports some, but not all, of the NRA's policies.
* The leaders of Rep. Smith's party have said they will oppose the bill. They have asked all loyal party members to vote against the bill, too.

The United States is a republic. The advantages of a republic include:

* **Workability.** The representative system works for a large, widespread population.
* **Accountability.** People can elect new representatives if they feel their representatives aren't making good laws.
* **Expertise.** Citizens can choose representatives who have the education and experience to make good laws. They aren't stuck with people who were born into certain ruling families.
* **Participation.** Citizens can take part in the system by voting for and influencing their representatives.
* **Leadership.** People who want to be more involved can work to be elected as representatives.

The English Tradition

England, the country that colonized much of America, had a history of freedom for its citizens and limits on the power of its monarchs. **Four** important developments in English history shaped the way that England was ruled and governed. These were:

1. The signing of the Magna Carta.
2. The development of the English Bill of Rights.
3. The development of England's unwritten constitution.
4. The use of common law.

The Magna Carta

In 1215, a group of powerful nobles forced England's King John to sign the Magna Carta. This historic document stated that the king would respect certain basic rights, including trial by jury and **due process** of law, which meant the king could not have someone jailed or executed without a proper trial. At first, these rights applied only to the nobles. Over time, all people were covered.

The English Bill of Rights

In 1689, after years of wars and bitter power struggles between English kings and their subjects, **Parliament**—the English legislature—invited William III to become king and agree to a Bill of Rights.

English Bill of Rights	
Who Was Protected	**Safeguards Addressed in the Bill**
Rights for Parliament	* Parliament had the right to select a ruler. * The ruler had to follow laws passed by Parliament. * The ruler couldn't make up new laws, or cancel or suspend laws that Parliament had already passed, without Parliament's consent. * Rulers could not order new taxes without the approval of Parliament. * Rulers could not keep an army during times of peace without Parliament's permission. * Parliament was required to meet often to develop and amend laws as needed. * Members of Parliament could speak and debate freely in Parliament without fear of punishment for what they said. * The ruler couldn't interfere with Parliamentary elections or the freedom of election of members.

Rights for Citizens	* The government could not set excessive **bail** for prisoners just to keep them in prison.
	* Government could not fine or punish someone who had not been found guilty in a trial.
	* Punishments for convicted criminals could not be cruel or unusual.
	* Citizens could petition (send requests to) government without any chance of being punished for doing so.
	* The earlier Habeas Corpus Act of 1679 guaranteed that anyone who was arrested had the right to ask to be brought, within a reasonable time, before an impartial judge. That judge would then decide:
	    – if authorities had a legal reason to charge the prisoner and hold him for trial, or
	    – if the prisoner should be set free.
	* This right of citizens prevented rulers from "making people disappear" by keeping them locked up without just cause and for as long as the ruler wanted. **Habeas Corpus** means "bring the body to us" in Latin. A writ, or written order, of habeas corpus from a judge, legally forces authorities to bring an imprisoned person to a judge for a hearing.

Ex Parte Merryman (1861)

John Merryman, a civilian, was arrested by the Union army during the American Civil War. He was suspected of treason and of plotting against the North, and was imprisoned by the army without a trial or hearing.

Merryman complained to the Chief Justice of the Supreme Court, claiming that his rights as a citizen to a court hearing and trial had been violated. Chief Justice Roger Taney issued a writ of habeas corpus, demanding that the army bring Merryman before him for a hearing to determine if there was cause for the prisoner to remain in custody.

The army officers involved refused to obey Justice Taney's writ, or written order. They claimed that they were obeying President Lincoln's decision to suspend the right of habeas corpus at the start of the war. The president had done so to give his officials the power they needed to imprison suspected traitors to the Union during the war.

Justice Taney used an ex parte hearing to respond as quickly as he could. "Ex parte" means that he was responding in a legal dispute to the arguments of one party, or side, only, without waiting to hear the arguments of the other party. Taney stated that, even during a war or emergency, only Congress, not a president, had the power to suspend habeas corpus. He said that Lincoln's actions were beyond the power of the presidency, and therefore unconstitutional.

The Merryman dispute was never considered by the Supreme Court itself, and Merryman stayed in custody. However, the Supreme Court and other courts have heard several cases involving government suspension of the right of habeas corpus, arbitrary arrest, and whether military trials (instead of more open civilian trials) can be used to try civilians during times of war or crisis. Because national security is involved at such times, the issues are very complicated. However, the courts have generally made it clear that they consider the privilege of habeas corpus and related rights fundamental to democratic freedom.

An Unwritten Constitution

The English constitution is not a single, written document. It consists of all the formal laws, legal customs, and traditions—some written, some not—that have shaped English government. Parliament interprets the constitution.

This was one English tradition that the founders of our country did not follow. All American constitutions, state and national, are written.

Common Law

Governments and laws have traditions. These rules and customs aren't written down. In most countries, they have been created over many years. Like family traditions, people know them and follow them.

British **common law** is the tradition of laws created from the history of court cases and law-related customs that developed over the centuries in England. British common law:

* **Guides Great Britain's legal system.** Judges look to the legal tradition in deciding what is legal and what is illegal.
* **Influenced the American system.** The colonists brought this tradition to the new land.

Even after the colonies became independent, British common law remained part of American law.

The Colonial Heritage

The Founders got useful ideas for setting up a government from the history of the colonies. Two important early models were the Mayflower Compact and the House of Burgesses.

The Mayflower Compact

Some people consider the **Mayflower Compact** to be America's first written constitution. The *Mayflower* left England in 1620, full of settlers heading for Virginia, but the ship strayed off course and landed at Plymouth, Massachusetts. There were no colonial laws or colonial charters in Massachusetts to provide law and government for them. So, the men on board decided to write a plan for governing the new colony. The result was the Mayflower Compact, which was guided by the Greek ideas of:

* Direct democracy.
* Using majority agreement at public town meetings to make laws.

Primary Source

Mayflower Compact

". . . We, whose names are underwritten . . . combine ourselves together into a civil Body Politic. . . . and by Virtue hereof to enact, constitute, and frame such just and equal Laws, Ordinances, Acts, Constitutions and Offices, from time to time, as shall be thought most meet and convenient for the General good of the Colony; unto which we promise all due submission and obedience."

The House of Burgesses

The governor was the representative of the British king in a colony. He approved any and all laws passed by the colonists.

One governor of the Virginia colony, Sir George Yeardley, didn't like to travel to every village in the colony to approve laws passed by local assemblies. Instead, he asked each of the assemblies to select someone who would speak for them. He invited those representatives to meetings in Williamsburg.

This group, now called the **House of Burgesses**, met to discuss and debate issues, make laws, and pass taxes for the Virginia colony. This representative system became widely used in other American colonies before independence.

Did You Know?

The House of Burgesses

The House of Burgesses was also the name of the building where the Virginia representatives met. The original building was destroyed many years ago, but the site has been restored to its original form in Williamsburg, Virginia. It is part of the much larger colonial village of Williamsburg and a popular tourist stop.

English Colonial Governments

By the time of the Revolution, the colonies had certain elements of government.

* *Charter*—a document from the English king. It set up the colony.
* *Legislature*—an elected branch of government that made laws and controlled the money.
* *Governor*—an official who represented the English king in the colony. All laws made by the legislature had to be approved by the governor.

Many of the colonies provided **three** basic rights to their citizens:

1. **The Right to Vote.**
2. **Freedom of Religion.**
3. **Freedom of the Press.**

The Right to Vote

The right to vote did not extend to all adults in the colonies. The common belief was that only the people who owned land in their community deserved the responsibility of making its rules and laws. Usually, therefore, only landowners could vote. Furthermore, as in many other earlier societies, only male adults could vote.

The Right to Vote

The right to vote is one of the most important rights Americans have. As times and beliefs changed, our country allowed more and more groups of people to vote.

* By the 1840s, most states had dropped the rule that only people who owned property could vote.
* African Americans received the right to vote with the ratification of the 15th Amendment in 1870, although it took many years for this right to take effect in all communities.
* Women were given the right to vote with the passage of the 19th Amendment in 1920.
* Finally, the voting age was lowered to 18 with the ratification of the 26th Amendment in 1971.

Freedom of Religion

Some of the colonies were set up by people seeking a place to live out their religious beliefs.

The Puritans founded a colony in Massachusetts and ruled their colony by their religious ideas. Only church members could vote in elections.

Other colonies were established by people with different beliefs. Roger Williams, a former Puritan minister, challenged his leaders about religious freedom and was driven out of the Massachusetts colony. He started a new settlement in Rhode Island, where his people could follow their conscience. One of the earliest Jewish settlements in the Americas was also established there.

Freedom of the Press

In 1735, a publisher named John Peter Zenger wrote some rather nasty comments about the New York governor. The governor got angry and had Zenger arrested and charged with **libel**—the crime of publishing statements intended to harm someone else's reputation.

Andrew Hamilton defended Zenger as his lawyer. Hamilton argued that, as long as the comments were not false, libel had not occurred. The jury agreed with Hamilton, overruled the judge's directions, and established the right of freedom of the press in the colonies.

Did You Know?

The Origin of Great Britain

England and Scotland united in 1707 and became Great Britain. We use the term British to describe the government, people, and culture after that date.

Steps Toward Independence

Most of the colonists in America were proud to be British and valued their rights as British subjects. Ironically, their belief in these rights gradually led to revolution.

Taxation Without Representation

By the mid-1700s, Great Britain had a large, worldwide colonial empire to defend. After a long and costly war with France (that included the French and Indian War in North America), Britain needed to raise money. Parliament felt that since the colonies benefited from British rule and protection, a tax on them was fair. They passed the Stamp Act.

Stamp Act

How would you feel if suddenly you had to pay extra for something you used and needed? Most colonists got angry when, in 1765, the British government passed the **Stamp Act**, which taxed documents. They had to pay the stamp tax whenever they bought anything made of paper—newspapers, calendars, legal documents. The colonists reacted by:

* Protesting and petitioning.
* Boycotting British goods.
* Establishing *Committees of Correspondence*, citizen groups that shared information.
* Forming *Sons of Liberty* associations, radical patriot groups that frightened British officials.

Their protests and boycotts worked. Britain **repealed**, or cancelled, the Stamp Act. Unfortunately, the peace didn't last. Parliament passed more taxes. They, too, were protested and repealed—but not the tax on tea.

Boston Tea Party

In 1773, ships with tea from British merchants were in Boston Harbor. The American workers, aware of the tax, refused to unload the tea from the ships.

In a famous action that was more of a prank than a protest, members of a Sons of Liberty group disguised themselves as Native Americans. They boarded the ships and dumped the tea into the bay.

Intolerable Acts

To punish Massachusetts for the Boston Tea Party, Parliament passed the Coercive Acts. The colonists called them **Intolerable Acts**. These were:

* ***The Boston Port Bill,*** which closed Boston Harbor until the colonists paid for the tea.
* ***The Massachusetts Government Act,*** which shut down the Massachusetts legislature and gave the royal governor authority to make all decisions in the colony.
* ***The Administration of Justice Act,*** which ruled that any trial involving a British official or soldier would be held in England.
* ***The Quartering Act,*** which forced the colonists to house British soldiers in their barns and houses.

Growing Rebellion

The Intolerable Acts had an unplanned result. When the other colonies saw how Britain punished Massachusetts, they worried that they could be next. Now the 13 separate colonies had a single cause—changing how Britain ruled the colonies.

First Continental Congress

Leaders in Massachusetts organized a meeting of representatives of the colonies. This became the First Continental Congress. Knowing they had no authority in law, the representatives:

* Made up a list of the colonies' complaints against Britain.
* Proposed that colonists stop buying British goods.
* Agreed to meet again if their complaints were not addressed.

Second Continental Congress

Their next meeting, the Second Continental Congress, was in the spring of 1775. By then, skirmishes between colonists and British troops had already broken out, and war was likely.

The delegates were not sure how many colonists supported them. John Adams estimated that:

* One-third of the people supported revolution.
* One-third of the people supported Britain.
* One-third were unsure or didn't care.

Feelings changed, however, when Thomas Paine published a pamphlet called *Common Sense*. Using very emotional but convincing language, Paine explained why America had to rebel against British rule.

Declaration of Independence

By 1776, more and more colonists wanted independence. The Second Continental Congress made a historic decision on June 7, 1776. Richard Lee of Virginia introduced the following resolution:

Primary Source

Common Sense by Thomas Paine

"It is the violence which is done and threatened to our persons; the destruction of our property by an armed force; the invasion of our country by fire and sword, which conscientiously qualifies the use of arms.

". . . But the most powerful of all arguments is that nothing but independence . . . can keep the peace of the continent and preserve it inviolate from civil wars. I dread the event of reconciliation with Britain now, as it is more than probable that it will be followed by a revolt somewhere or other, the consequences of which may be far more fatal than all the malice of Britain."

"That these United Colonies are, and of Right ought to be, Free and Independent States; that they are absolved from all Allegiance to the British Crown, and that all political connection between them and the State of Great Britain, is and ought to be totally dissolved . . ."

The delegates chose Thomas Jefferson, one of the youngest among them, to write a statement that would clearly explain America's position to its own people, to Britain, and the world.

Influence of the Enlightenment

Jefferson was a scholar. He had read the writings of many of the **Enlightenment** thinkers in Europe, including Thomas Hobbes and John Locke. The Enlightenment was a movement among philosophers in Europe that:

* Stressed the rights of individuals.
* Questioned older ideas.
* Argued that people could use reason to solve problems.

Jefferson used many ideas from both Hobbes and Locke in crafting the Declaration.

Basic Ideas

The Declaration of Independence that Jefferson wrote has **three** parts.

1. Beliefs about government, including ideas from Hobbes' **social contract** theory.
2. A list of grievances that showed how the British king had violated the social contract.
3. The formal declaration stating that the colonies were now independent from Britain. To Britain, this last section was a declaration of war.

The Declaration of Independence was officially adopted on July 4, 1776.

All people have certain "natural rights," including life, liberty, and the right to own property. These are never given to a ruler, even in a social contract.

All governments rule only with the consent of the people they govern. If rulers become cruel or unfair, citizens have a duty to stop them.

John Locke

A social contract or unspoken agreement exists between the government or ruler and the people.

In that contract, the people agree to give the ruler certain powers. In return, the government ruler promises to keep society safe from lawlessness.

Thomas Hobbes

The Nation's Early Governments

Once the country had declared itself independent, most of the colonies replaced their earlier charters with constitutions and became self-governing states.

State Constitutions

One by one until 1780, 11 of the 13 colonies each wrote a new state constitution. Connecticut and Rhode Island kept their older charters until 1818 and 1842, respectively.

Different states set up different types of governments. Some gave more power to their state executives or governors. Others gave more power to their legislatures.

EXAMPLES: Pennsylvania set up a group to watch over government actions. Only New York and Massachusetts had powerful elected governors. Most states let their legislatures elect their judges.

Massachusetts State Constitution

Massachusetts used a **two-step** approach that was different from the other colonies.

1. **State leaders arranged a meeting of specially elected representatives** to write the new state constitution. Unlike other colonies, in Massachusetts the legislature did not write the state constitution.

2. **The new constitution drafted by the convention was then put to a vote** by the people.

The Massachusetts constitution created a government that balanced some new executive powers with existing legislative powers:

* **Legislative powers** included the elected assembly's responsibility to debate and make laws, pass taxes, regulate trade within its borders, and raise a militia.

* **Executive powers** included the right of a state leader to approve laws, **veto** laws—have the power to prevent bills that have been passed by lawmakers from becoming laws—make appointments, and ensure that laws are properly carried out.

When other states saw what Massachusetts had done, some of them used the same process to rewrite their own constitutions.

The Articles of Confederation

The Second Continental Congress recognized that it needed a system that would allow the new, independent states to act as a group.

In November 1779, after 17 months of hard work and debate, the Congress approved a plan for a new **confederation**—alliance, league, or friendly union—of the states, called the **Articles of Confederation**. It took until March 1781, when the Revolutionary War was almost over, for all 13 states to approve the Articles.

The Articles of Confederation tried to balance **two** very different ideas:

1. **A central government.** The states needed a government with enough power that it could represent all the states on such issues as coordinating war efforts or negotiating treaties with other countries.
2. **State sovereignty.** Every state wanted to protect its own **sovereignty**—the power to make decisions within its own borders.

It was no surprise, then, that the Articles created a government that had little power and was very weak.

* The central government had no executive or judicial branches.
* The Confederation legislature was **unicameral**. (It had only one house, or congress, of elected representatives.) Each state had only one vote, regardless of how many people lived there—the states with smaller populations could not be outvoted by a few larger states.
* Laws required agreement from representatives of 9 of the 13 states to be passed.
* Amendments—changes or additions—to the Articles needed the approval of all 13 states.

Problems with the Articles

The new Confederation worked well enough to allow the states to win the war and sign a peace treaty with Britain, and to pass the Northwest Ordinance in 1787. However, the Articles created a central government that was too weak to do everything the new alliance of states needed. It had **six** crucial problems:

1. **It had no taxation power.** Fresh from their problems with Britain over taxes, the founders did not give the legislature the power to collect taxes. This meant the government had no way to raise money to provide services.
2. **It created no national court.** The Articles did not provide a central court system. The Confederation had no authority to settle differences among different states.
3. **The states used different currencies.** Each state had its own money system, so doing business between states was difficult. Some states accepted other states' currencies, while others did not. EXAMPLE: Rhode Island kept printing money to pay off its debts. No one wanted Rhode Island money because it was virtually worthless.

4. **There was no executive.** Without a president or any national executive, no one was responsible for carrying out the laws passed by the Congress.
5. **Interstate commerce was not regulated.** Congress could not set rules for trade between states. Each state was free to put taxes on products coming in from other states. The states competed with one another in ways that hurt them all.
6. **Each state had veto power on amendments.** Just one state, for any reason, could oppose a change and stop an amendment that most other states wanted.

Most leaders realized that the Articles didn't work, but the states took several years to decide to address the problems. The event that finally made the states deal with the issue was Shays's Rebellion.

Shays's Rebellion

Daniel Shays was a farmer in Massachusetts. In 1786, Shays and his neighbors were about to lose their farms because they couldn't afford to pay their taxes. In protest, Shays and a group of farmers took over the Massachusetts courthouse at gunpoint. They believed that, if the state court judges could not meet, they could not order Shays and the others to give up their farms.

Massachusetts asked the Confederation Congress for help. The Congress replied that it would like to assist but, since it had almost no money and therefore no army, Massachusetts would have to deal with the uprising itself.

The states and the Congress saw that their government was too weak—too weak even to protect its own citizens! Giving protection to its citizens is perhaps the most important role of government. It was time for a change.

▲
A group of angry farmers take over the Massachusetts courthouse at gunpoint.

The roots of American government lie in world history. The Greeks and Romans provided ideas of a representative democracy and a republic. The settlers brought British traditions of certain rights and of common law. The Puritans on board the Mayflower made them a part of their Compact. The governments in the colonies before the Revolution incorporated these traditions.

Ideas from Enlightenment thinkers in Europe gave the colonists the understanding that there was an unspoken contract between a government and its people. So, when the British tried to force the colonists to accept laws that most colonists felt were unfair, they chose revolution.

After independence was declared, the colonies needed new governments. The states wrote constitutions. The Second Continental Congress set up a new central government under the Articles of Confederation, but they did not give it enough power to meet the country's needs.

Civics in America

Articles of Confederation—plan for government approved by the states in 1781. It proved to be too weak and was replaced by the U.S. Constitution. *p. 29*

bail—money supplied as a guarantee that an arrested person will return for trial after he or she is released. *p. 20*

charter—authority granted to an organization, such as a colony, to operate. *p. 23*

city state—nation that consists of a single city and its surrounding area. *p. 17*

common law—law based on custom and usage. British common law is the basis of much American law. *p. 22*

confederation—alliance or loose union of independent states. *p. 29*

direct democracy—system of government in which citizens vote directly for the laws by which they will be ruled, as opposed to a representative democracy in which laws are made by elected representatives. *p. 17*

due process—way of administering justice that is established by law. The right to due process includes the right of an accused person to a trial, a lawyer, and other protections of the law. *p. 19*

Enlightenment—philosophical movement in 18th-century Europe that stressed individualism, questioned traditional values, and argued that humans could use reason to solve problems. *p. 27*

executive powers—governing powers given to the executive or administrative branch in a government. These can include the right to appoint officials, to veto laws, and to set up and run departments to make sure the laws are carried out. *p. 28*

habeas corpus—right of an arrested person to be brought before a judge who determines if his imprisonment is legal. This right protects people from arbitrary arrest and imprisonment. *Habeas corpus* means "show us the person" in Latin. *p. 20*

House of Burgesses—first representative assembly in the American colonies. It helped govern the Virginia colony. *p. 23*

interstate commerce—trade between two or more states. *p. 30*

Intolerable Acts—name given by the colonists for the series of British laws, officially named the Coercive Acts, that were passed by Parliament to punish Massachusetts after the Boston Tea Party. *p. 25*

legislative powers—governing powers given to the legislature or law-making branch of government. These can include the power to tax, to declare war, and to regulate trade. *p. 28*

legislature—branch of government that makes the laws. *p. 17*

libel—written or published statement that damages another person's reputation; false or damaging statement; also, the crime of making such a statement. *p. 24*

Mayflower Compact—America's "first written constitution," it was a plan for governing the Pilgrim colony written on board the *Mayflower*. It featured direct democracy and a pledge by all to follow the rules passed by the majority. *p. 22*

Parliament—bicameral (two-chamber) national legislature of Great Britain, consisting of the House of Commons and the House of Lords. *p. 19*

repeal—withdraw or cancel an existing law. *p. 25*

republic—form of government run by elected representatives; it does not have a king or queen. *p. 17*

social contract—unspoken agreement by which people are joined to their government. People agree to give up rights and powers to the government in exchange for security, law, and order. The social contract theory was originally developed by Enlightenment philosopher Thomas Hobbes. *p. 27*

sovereignty—power of a government to make decisions for itself within its own territory or jurisdiction; freedom from foreign control. *p. 29*

Stamp Act—1765 British tax on publications and legal documents in the American colonies. *p. 25*

unicameral—having a single legislative body or house. The U.S. Congress is bicameral; it has two houses: the Senate and the House of Representatives. *p. 29*

veto—right or power to prevent a bill that has passed the legislature from becoming law. *p. 28*

CHAPTER 3

The Constitution

In this chapter, you will learn about:

- **how a meeting to revise the Articles of Confederation became the Constitutional Convention**
- **what principles of government were built into the Constitution**
- **how the Founding Fathers structured the Constitution**
- **how the Constitution can be amended**

On the day the Constitution was signed, September 17, 1787, none of the delegates considered the plan perfect. But most of the signers believed it was as perfect a document as could possibly be agreed upon. Some delegates refused to sign, believing the federal government was being given too much power at the expense of the states. However, the majority had recognized the need for a strong central government, especially after Shays's Rebellion the year before. Now that the delegates had drafted a Constitution, the states would have to individually approve the document. Only with those ratifications could it become the plan for a new American government and the law of the land.

The Constitutional Convention

On May 25, 1787, **delegates**—official representatives—from the states arrived at the Pennsylvania State House in Philadelphia, now called Independence Hall, to revise the Articles of Confederation.

The delegates came from all of the states except Rhode Island, which sent no delegates because it opposed any changes to the Articles that might weaken its state powers. At the time, no one called the meeting a **constitutional convention**, and many delegates did not arrive intending to write a whole new plan for a national government.

The Founding Fathers

The delegates who gathered at the **convention**, or assembly, would become what we now call the **Founding Fathers**, the writers and framers of our Constitution. By the time the convention ended, they had drawn up a brand new **constitution**—a plan of government—for the United States.

Who Were the Founding Fathers?

As you would expect, the 55 delegates were some of the best and most respected leaders in the states, including such political "all-stars" as:

* *George Washington* (1732–1799).
* *James Madison* (1751–1836).
* *Alexander Hamilton* (1757–1804).
* *Benjamin Franklin* (1706–1790).
* *George Mason* (1725–1792).
* *Robert Morris* (1734–1806).

Most of the delegates were businessmen, lawyers, bankers, shippers, gentleman farmers, and plantation owners. Some owned slaves. A few were the "elder statesmen" of the new nation: Benjamin Franklin was 81, George Mason was 62, and George Washington and Robert Morris were in their 50s. But most of the delegates were younger than that, many in their 20s or 30s. All had political experience.

* Nearly three-fourths had sat in the Continental Congress.
* Many had helped write their state constitutions and had served in their state legislatures.
* Eight had signed the Declaration of Independence.
* Seven had been state governors.
* Twenty-one had fought in the Revolutionary War.

Did You Know?

Three Who Did Not Attend the Convention

Thomas Jefferson, author of the Declaration of Independence, was in Paris serving as America's ambassador to France. John Adams, America's ambassador to Britain, was in London. And Patrick Henry, who had spoken the inspiring words "give me liberty or give me death," refused to attend. He was afraid that the delegates would take away the rights of the individual states.

Washington as Leader

General George Washington, the hero of the Revolutionary War, was among those Americans who knew that unless the government had more power, the alliance of states could not work. The delegates elected him to lead the Convention.

The Convention's Rules

The delegates agreed to the following **three** rules during the meetings:

1. **One State, One Vote.** The voting on all issues would be by state, with only one vote per state, no matter how big or small the population of the state was or how many delegates it had sent. This satisfied the smaller states.

2. **Majority Decides.** Proposals would be decided according to how the majority, seven or more states, voted.

3. **Keep the Proceedings Secret.** Have you ever needed privacy to get something important done? The delegates agreed that all details of the proceedings of the Convention should be closed, meaning not shared with the public, the press, or anyone outside in any way without permission, because:
   * The delegates didn't want the public to know how divided they were as a group.
   * Public scrutiny would have made it more difficult for delegates to modify their opinions without being criticized or to focus on getting the job done rather than on what their states might say about them.

Oops!

On one occasion, a delegate dropped his copy of an important proposal called the Virginia Plan on the ground outside the meeting hall. Somebody found it and returned it to the hall. An angry Washington gave a stern lecture to the delegates, pointing out that the plan could have become known to the press and ended up in the newspapers. Washington warned the delegates to take the secrecy rule seriously.

Virginia Plan vs. New Jersey Plan

Generally, the delegates sided with one of the following groups:

* *Nationalists.* Some delegates, representing both large and small states, were known as **nationalists**. They favored a national government that was significantly more powerful than what the Articles of Confederation had created.
* *Confederationists.* Representatives of the states who wanted more power for the states were called **confederationists**. These pro-states' rights delegates wanted the individual *states* to continue to hold most of the powers of government, as they did under the Articles. They hinted that they would leave if their views were not respected.

The Virginia Plan

On May 29, Edmund Randolph, the governor of Virginia, presented the **Virginia Plan**, which represented the interests of the nationalist delegates. The plan, drafted by James Madison, proposed to significantly strengthen the central government by giving it real power. It also proposed representation based on state populations. The Virginia Plan would earn Madison the title "Father of the Constitution" because it contained the basic ideas of government that would later appear in the Constitution.

▲
Portrait of James Madison, author of the Virginia Plan.

The New Jersey Plan

On June 15, William Paterson of New Jersey submitted an alternate plan. The **New Jersey Plan** represented confederationist views—a weaker executive and state equality in the Congress, similar to that in the Articles of Confederation. Although the New Jersey Plan strengthened the confederation government created in the original Articles, it limited the national government's power over the states.

Unlike the Virginia Plan, the New Jersey Plan addressed the national treasury. Its essential idea was that state tax contributions to the Confederation treasury would not be based on the value of land in each state, but on the number of free people and "three-fifths of all others" (by counting three-fifths of the slave population as people).

	Virginia Plan	New Jersey Plan
Legislative	* Bicameral—two separate "houses." * Members of the lower house (**House of Representatives**) elected by the people. * Members of the upper house (**Senate**) nominated by the state legislatures and elected by the lower house. * Number of votes from each state, at least in the lower house, based on its free population.	* Unicameral—only one "house." * Members elected by the people. * Each state has an equal vote. * Congress would have additional powers, such as levying import duties and regulating trade with foreign countries and among states. * Laws passed and treaties made by Congress would be the supreme law in all the states.
Executive	* Could be one or more persons. * Elected by Congress. * Has the right to review laws passed by national legislature and state legislatures. * Has the right to veto laws in some cases. * Has jurisdiction over specific kinds of cases, including any case involving "the national peace and harmony."	* Could be more than one person. * Elected by Congress. * Serves only one term. * Federal executive can be removed from office by a majority of state executives.
Judiciary	* Made up of a supreme court and council. * Along with the national executive, has the right to review and veto laws passed by Congress.	* Supreme court appointed by the executive.

Supreme Court Case

McCulloch v. Maryland (1819)

In the early 1800s, the states and the federal government debated who had the power to charter, or set up, banks. The state of Maryland passed a law prohibiting banks from issuing bank notes unless they were issued on special, state-stamped paper. The federal government objected. In the resulting Supreme Court case, lawyers for Maryland argued that the federal government did not have the power to regulate banks because this power was not listed specifically in the Constitution.

Chief Justice John Marshall wrote the opinion—formal decision—of the court, ruling that chartering banks is an *implied* power. The Constitution states that Congress can make "all laws which shall be necessary and proper" for carrying out the powers that are listed in the Constitution. Since the federal government needs a bank to collect and deposit tax money, among other things, Marshall ruled that Maryland was interfering in Congress's ability to carry out its powers. You will read more about this important clause when you learn about the legislative branch.

Compromises

Both plans offered some good ideas. Both contained ideas that other states would never accept. The delegates debated and argued about the rival plans, especially over whether they should use **proportional representation**. This method of deciding how many voting representatives each state would have is based on state populations—each representative speaks for about the same number of people.

* States with larger populations would get more representatives using this method.
* States with smaller populations were against it. They feared that the large states would hold all the power.
* The states with larger populations felt that it was unfair to give the same number of votes to a state with a small population as to one with a large population.

As part of this argument, the Convention delegates also debated if the count of a state's population should include slaves.

Slave-holding states wanted to include slaves in population counts to determine the number of representatives a state would have in Congress.

The Great Compromise

On July 6, Roger Sherman of Connecticut proposed the Great Compromise to break the impasse over proportional representation and the number of houses in the legislative branch. His compromise said:

* The national Congress would have both proportional and equal representation.
* Each state would elect members to the House of Representatives based on the population of that state.

* Each and every state legislature would also choose two people to represent their state in the Senate, so representation in the upper house would be the same for every state.

The Three-Fifths Compromise

James Wilson of Pennsylvania proposed that the number of representatives elected to the House from each state be based on the total free population *plus* three-fifths of the number of slaves in the state. This addition of three-fifths was designed to benefit the southern states, who would get less representation in the House if slaves were not counted.

It was agreed, too, that slaves would also be counted as three-fifths for determining taxes. This meant that slave owners would pay more taxes.

Commerce and Slavery Compromise

Delegates from the northern states wanted the national Congress, not the individual states, to have the power to regulate trade and commercial activities:

* Between states.
* Between a state and other countries.

Regulating trade includes the power to collect taxes on **exports**—goods sold to other countries—and to set tariffs on **imports**, goods purchased from other countries.

Delegates from southern states, which exported tobacco, rice, and other products to foreign countries and imported slaves, did not want the national government to have this important power. These agricultural, slave states feared that Congress might use this power to regulate and collect taxes on:

* Their farm exports to other countries.
* The importing of the slaves they needed.

The delegates worked out another important compromise:

* Congress would not do anything to stop the import of slaves for 20 years.
* Congress would have the power to regulate international and interstate commerce for all states.

Other Important Decisions

The Convention delegates were now clearly creating a much more detailed plan than most of them had intended. As one decision led to another, a smaller group of delegates, called a Committee of Details, was appointed to settle details in the plan.

In August and again in September, the committee presented details of a constitution. The plan contained important new ideas in several areas:

President

* A president would carry out the laws passed by Congress.
* The president would have the power to veto an act of Congress.
* A vote of two-thirds of the members of each of two houses of Congress would be required to override, or undo, a presidential veto.

Courts

* The president would nominate judges for a **Supreme Court**, which would be the highest court in the country.
* The Senate would have to approve them.
* Congress would have authority to establish lower courts.

Congress

* Congress would have the power to impose taxes and collect them directly from the people.
* By comparison, under the Articles of Confederation, only the states had power to tax the people.

Electoral College

* The president would be elected, but neither directly by the voters nor by Congress.
* Electors would vote for the president.
* State legislatures would choose the electors. (In most states, the voters soon got to choose their electors.)
* The person getting the most electoral votes would become president. The person with the second highest number of votes would become vice president, even if he differed from the president on all major issues.

Who Can Vote

* Some delegates believed that only white, male **freeholders**—property owners—should have a vote. However, most states already let people other than freeholders vote in state elections. The delegates agreed that those qualified in each state to vote for members of the larger house of their state legislature would also be eligible to vote for federal representatives. This meant each state would decide what people could vote in national elections, not the federal government.

The Signing

On September 17, 1787, a majority of the delegates to the Constitutional Convention signed the Constitution document. Many of the signers still weren't sure if the Constitution could work. But as Benjamin Franklin said, he was signing it "because I expect no better, and because I am not sure that it is not the best."

The Struggle for Ratification

The Constitution could not become the law of the land until at least *nine* states voted to **ratify**—officially approve—it. Two groups quickly argued its merits—the Federalists and the Anti-Federalists.

The Federalists

Those who supported the Constitution were called **Federalists**. They supported the plan's strong central or *federal* government that would share certain powers with the states.

The Anti-Federalists

The **Anti-Federalists** opposed ratification of the Constitution. In general, they wanted to keep the Articles of Confederation, perhaps adding some items from the New Jersey Plan. Anti-Federalists did not want a powerful central government at the expense of state powers.

Influence of the *Federalist Papers*

Federalists and Anti-Federalists waged a bitter struggle in New York, where there was strong opposition to the Constitution. Alexander Hamilton, with the help of James Madison and John Jay, published a series of 85 articles that explained the Constitution and argued for ratification. The pro-Constitution forces hoped that the *Federalist Papers* would sway New Yorkers and people from other states to ratify the Constitution.

Primary Source

Federalist Paper, No. 51

This paper was written by Alexander Hamilton or James Madison, and was printed in the *New York Packet*, Friday, February 8, 1788. In these excerpts, the writer argues why a system of checks and balances in government is necessary.

"In order to lay a due foundation for that separate and distinct exercise of the different powers of government, which to a certain extent is admitted on all hands to be essential to the preservation of liberty, it is evident that each department should have a will of its own . . . .

"But what is government itself, but the greatest of all reflections on human nature? If men were angels, no government would be necessary. If angels were to govern men, neither external nor internal controls on government would be necessary. In framing a government which is to be administered by men over men, the great difficulty lies in this: You must first enable the government to control the governed; and in the next place, oblige it to control itself."

Racing to Ratify

Delaware quickly ratified the Constitution on December 7, 1787, and is now known as the "First State." Pennsylvania ratified on December 12. A few weeks later, New Jersey and Georgia voted for ratification. By May 23, 1788, Connecticut, Massachusetts, Maryland, and South Carolina had all voted in favor, bringing the number of states ratifying the Constitution to eight. The Federalists needed one more vote to reach the necessary nine state approvals.

Although the Federalists focused a lot of effort on New York, New Hampshire voted to ratify next, on June 21, 1788, just before Virginia. The Constitution became the law of the land before New York had even voted. However, on July 26, 1788, New York *did* vote for ratification in a close vote. By 1790, North Carolina had also ratified the Constitution, and that year Rhode Island finally did so, too.

On March 4, 1789, the Congress that had been set up by the Articles of Confederation declared the Constitution in effect. On April 30, George Washington was inaugurated as the first president of the United States.

Government Principles in the Constitution

The framers based the Constitution on **five** basic principles:

1. **Popular Sovereignty.**
2. **Limited Government.**
3. **Federalism.**
4. **Separation of Powers.**
5. **Checks and Balances.**

Popular Sovereignty

When the people consent to be governed and spell out the rules by which they will allow that governing to happen, this is called **popular sovereignty**. Our Constitution is a realization of this principle. The people—not a king, dictator, or president—are supreme.

Limited Government

In the Constitution, the people grant the government limited powers to act on their behalf. Article I of the Constitution identifies the powers that the government has and has not been granted. This established citizen rights, as opposed to government rights.

Federalism

The Founding Fathers established a system of shared power called **federalism**. In this system, the states keep certain powers while giving up other powers to a strong central government.

National Government Alone May:	State Governments Alone May:
Regulate interstate and foreign trade.	Regulate trade within the state.
Raise (or recruit) and support armed forces.	Write business and corporation laws.
Declare war and make peace.	Establish and maintain public schools.
Coin and print money.	Set up local governments.
Grant patents and copyrights to protect new products and works.	Pass marriage and divorce laws.
Establish federal courts.	Conduct elections.
Govern territories.	Ratify constitutional amendments.
Admit new states.	
Set weights and measures.	
Establish a postal system.	
Regulate immigration.	

Both National and State Governments May:
Collect taxes.
Borrow money.
Make and enforce laws.
Establish and maintain courts.
Charter (set up) banks.
Provide for public welfare.

Checks and Balances of the Federal Government Branches

Executive Branch Checks on the Legislative Branch
- ☑ Can propose laws to Congress.
- ☑ Can veto laws passed by Congress.
- ☑ Can call special sessions of Congress.
- ☑ Makes appointments to federal posts.
- ☑ Negotiates foreign treaties.

Executive Branch Checks on the Judicial Branch
- ☑ Appoints federal judges to the judicial branch.
- ☑ Can grant pardons to federal offenders sentenced by courts.

Legislative Branch Checks on the Executive Branch
- ☑ Can override presidential veto.
- ☑ Must approve executive appointments.
- ☑ Must approve treaties negotiated by the executive.
- ☑ Can declare war.
- ☑ Can appropriate or withhold funds.
- ☑ Can impeach and remove the president.

Legislative Branch Checks on the Judicial Branch
- ☑ Creates lower federal courts.
- ☑ Can impeach and remove judges.
- ☑ Can propose amendments to the Constitution.
- ☑ Must approve appointments of federal judges.

Judicial Branch Checks on the Executive Branch
- ☑ Can declare executive actions unconstitutional.

Judicial Branch Checks on the Legislative Branch
- ☑ Can declare acts of Congress unconstitutional.

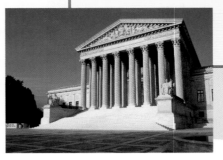

Separation of Powers

To prevent any group in government from gaining too much authority, the Constitution divides the federal government into **three** branches:

1. The legislative branch, or Congress, makes the laws. Congress consists of a House of Representatives and a Senate.
2. The executive branch, headed by the president, carries out the laws.
3. The judicial branch, consisting of the Supreme Court and other federal courts, interprets the laws as it decides cases.

Checks and Balances

The Founders were very smart. They set up the federal government in a way that lets the three branches keep an eye on each other's powers and authority, in a system of **checks and balances**.

The Structure of the Constitution

The Constitution consists of an introductory paragraph called the **Preamble**, seven articles, and 27 amendments that were added over time. The full text of the Constitution begins on page 334.

The Preamble

The Preamble lists **six** goals for the United States government:

1. To form a more perfect union.
2. To establish justice.
3. To ensure domestic tranquility, or peace.
4. To provide for the common defense.
5. To promote the general welfare.
6. To secure the blessings of liberty.

LEGISLATIVE   EXECUTIVE   JUDICIAL

The Articles

The seven Articles describe how the
government is organized and how it works.

The Seven Articles of the United States Constitution	
Article	**What It Defines**
Article I	**The Legislative Branch** ✳ Section 1. The Congress ✳ Section 2. The House of Representatives ✳ Section 3. The Senate ✳ Section 4. Elections and Meetings of Congress ✳ Section 5. Rules of Procedure for Congress ✳ Section 6. Privileges and Restrictions of Members of Congress ✳ Section 7. How Laws Are Made ✳ Section 8. Powers Granted to Congress ✳ Section 9. Powers Denied to Congress ✳ Section 10. Powers Denied to the States
Article II	**The Executive Branch** ✳ Section 1. Office of President and Vice President ✳ Section 2. Powers Granted to the President ✳ Section 3. Duties of the President ✳ Section 4. Removal from Office
Article III	**The Judicial Branch** ✳ Section 1. Federal Courts ✳ Section 2. Powers of Federal Courts ✳ Section 3. The Crime of Treason
Article IV	**Relations Among the States** ✳ Section 1. Recognition by Each State of Acts of Other States ✳ Section 2. Rights of Citizens in Other States ✳ Section 3. Treatment of New States and Territories ✳ Section 4. Guarantees to the States
Article V	**Amending the Constitution**
Article VI	**Debts, Federal Supremacy, Oaths of Office** ✳ Section 1. Prior Debts of the United States ✳ Section 2. The Supreme Law of the Land ✳ Section 3. Oaths of Office
Article VII	**Ratification of the Constitution**

Amending the Constitution

The **amendment process** allows lawmakers to change or add to the Constitution, but not easily. Since 1788, several thousand **amendments**—formal changes or additions—have been proposed, but only 27 have passed. The first 10 amendments, which protect the rights of citizens from the power of the federal government, are called the **Bill of Rights**.

Formal Process

The amendment process is a power shared between the federal and state governments.

Proposing an Amendment

The amendment process lists **two** different ways by which an amendment to the Constitution may be proposed.

1. **Two-thirds of the members of both houses of the federal Congress must vote** to propose an amendment.
2. **Two-thirds of the state legislatures must vote** to ask Congress to hold a special convention. The states have never chosen to propose an amendment.

Ratifying an Amendment

The Constitution also specifies **two** different ways that states can ratify amendments.

1. **Three-fourths of the state legislatures must vote** to approve the amendment.
2. **Conventions in three-fourths of the states** must approve the amendment.

Informal Processes

An amendment is the most formal way to revise the Constitution. There are, however, other ways to bring about change in our government.

EXAMPLE: Political parties, not mentioned in the Constitution, formed shortly after the Constitution was ratified.

American Citizenship

The Passage of the 26th Amendment

In 1970, during the Vietnam War, "Old enough to fight, old enough to vote" was a popular slogan. That year, Congress passed the Voting Rights Act of 1970, which lowered the voting age to 18 in all federal *and* state elections. When the Supreme Court later struck down, or declared illegal, the state-election provisions of the Voting Rights Act (because the Constitution gives the states, not Congress, the right to decide who can vote), Congress proposed the 26th Amendment. The amendment was ratified by the states on June 30, 1971. The lower voting age that the public largely favored, and that Congress had tried to pass as a law, finally made its way into the Constitution.

Proposed Flag-Burning Amendment

The Supreme Court has ruled that the Constitution's protection of free speech extends to actions that are meant as a form of protest. Specifically, the Court has ruled twice that flag burning is a protected expression of opinion.

Once the Supreme Court has decided, its ruling has the force of law. Even a law against flag burning would not be legal, because it would go against the Constitution. The only way to change the Constitution is to pass an amendment.

Would you be for or against an amendment to the Constitution that would make burning the American flag unlawful?

Arguments **for** an Amendment

The flag is a symbol of our country. When you attack the flag, you attack our country.

Many brave people have died to defend our flag. When you burn our flag, you symbolically join their killers.

The Supreme Court was in error in ruling that flag burning is a protected form of speech. It is treason.

Arguments **against** an Amendment

The flag represents our government, and when our government's policies are extremely wrong, burning it expresses extreme outrage.

Flag burning is intended to express great rage, but it does not hurt anyone. It does not kill our brave people.

Flag burning is an act of good citizenship. It seeks to change government through peaceful protest. It is the opposite of treason.

During the summer of 1787, delegates from all of the 13 states except Rhode Island were hard at work at the Constitutional Convention in Philadelphia. They came together because the central government created by the Articles of Confederation was too weak to work properly.

After long debates and a series of compromises, the Founding Fathers succeeded in drafting a Constitution. There was a struggle over ratification between the Federalists, supporters of ratification, and the Anti-Federalists, who opposed it. By the summer of 1788, the Constitution had been ratified.

The basic principles in the Constitution have created a balance between a strong central government, state powers, and individual liberties. Because the Constitution can be amended, it is a living document that can change with the times.

Civics in America

amendment—change or addition to a document or plan, such as the Constitution. *p. 47*

amendment process—rules for amending the Constitution. These are specified in the Constitution. *p. 47*

Anti-Federalist—opponent of the central government as defined by the Constitution; against its ratification. *p. 41*

Bill of Rights—first 10 amendments to the Constitution. *p. 47*

checks and balances—system in which the power of each branch of government is balanced and checked by the powers of the other branches. *p. 45*

confederationists—in the late 1700s, supporters of the Articles of Confederation who wanted states to hold most of the power in a loose alliance or confederation. *p. 36*

constitution—plan of government. In the United States, the Constitution is the supreme law and plan of the national government, adopted in 1789. *p. 34*

constitutional convention—meeting of delegates who draft a constitution. *p. 34*

convention—formal meeting of a group for a particular purpose. *p. 34*

delegate—official representative of some larger group or body, like a state assembly. *p. 34*

executive branch—part of government, headed in the United States by a president or governor, that carries out the laws. *p. 45*

exports—goods shipped to other countries for sale or use. *p. 39*

federalism—system of government in which power is shared between the central government and the state governments. *p. 43*

more Words to Know

Federalist—supporter of ratification of the Constitution. *p. 41*

Founding Fathers—writers and framers of the Constitution; the founders. *p. 34*

freeholders—property holders. *p. 40*

House of Representatives—"lower" house of Congress in which the number of each state's representatives is based on its population. *p. 37*

imports—goods brought in from other countries for sale or use. *p. 39*

judicial branch—part of government that interprets the laws through its decisions in legal cases. *p. 45*

legislative branch—law-making part of government. *p. 45*

nationalists—those who favored a strong national government in the late 1700s. *p. 36*

New Jersey Plan—plan presented by several states at the Constitutional Convention to give an equal number of representatives in Congress to all the states and establish a relatively weak central government. *p. 37*

popular sovereignty—consent of the governed; power to govern comes from the people. *p. 42*

Preamble—introductory part of the Constitution. *p. 45*

proportional representation—way of determining how many representatives a state can have, based on its population. The larger a state's population, the more representatives it gets. *p. 38*

ratify—approve and make official. *p. 41*

Senate—"senior" or "upper" house of Congress in which each state has two representatives, called Senators, regardless of its population. *p. 37*

Supreme Court—highest level of the judicial branch of the federal government; the highest court in the country. There are also state supreme courts. *p. 40*

Virginia Plan—plan presented by Edmond Randolph at the Constitutional Convention. It provided a basis for the Constitution. *p. 36*

Bill of Rights

In this chapter, you will learn about:

- why additions were made to the original Constitution
- how constitutional amendments protect the rights of citizens
- what rights and freedoms are protected by the Bill of Rights

In 1999, a Tennessee public school board approved a dress code for all students. Students from kindergarten to grade 12 were required to wear black pants or skirts, and white shirts or blouses. Other public schools adopted similar codes, and some students and their parents protested. They didn't believe schools funded by the government have the right to decide what students wear. They believed dress codes limit students' rights to personal expression. Although the dress code remained in place, students were later allowed to wear white "protest shirts" that criticized the policy.

Your rights as a citizen, including freedom of expression, are protected by the Bill of Rights. These laws were added to the Constitution in 1791 as the first 10 amendments. They define and protect the rights of all American citizens.

Adding the Bill of Rights

As 18th-century Americans debated the Constitution, some pointed to the way the British had abused the colonists' civil rights before the revolution. They believed that the Constitution was missing ways to protect the rights of individuals from possible future abuse by the government. Some leaders agreed to ratify the new Constitution only if a "bill of rights" was added.

Protecting Citizens' Rights

Virginia already had a Declaration of Rights written in 1776 by George Mason, a member of the Virginia House of Delegates. Mason stated that people could form no government that took away their rights to life, liberty, and the pursuit of happiness and safety. These words are similar to what Thomas Jefferson wrote in the first part of the Declaration of Independence.

The Virginia Declaration of Rights also ensured other freedoms, such as:

* The right of people accused of a crime to know who their accusers are.
* The right to trial by a jury.
* The right of the press to speak freely.
* The right of the people to practice the religion of their choice.

People agreed that the success of the new government depended on whether the new Constitution would and could really protect citizens' rights.

Ratifying the Bill of Rights

On September 25, 1789, the First Congress of the United States proposed 12 amendments to the Constitution. These proposed additions answered most of the concerns people had about the original Constitution. By December 15, 1791, three-fourths of the states had ratified the 10 amendments now known as the Bill of Rights. These amendments are listed in the table opposite.

"He's big, all right, and he's definitely a wolf, but it'll be up to a jury to decide whether or not he's bad."

The Bill of Rights

First Amendment	Guarantees and protects freedom of religion, freedom of speech, freedom of the press, freedom of assembly, and the right to petition.
Second Amendment	Discusses the right to bear arms.
Third Amendment	Prohibits the government from forcing people to house and feed soldiers in their homes.
Fourth Amendment	Protects citizens from unreasonable searches and seizures.
Fifth Amendment	Guarantees that a person accused of a crime will not be denied the right to life, liberty, or property without due process of law.
Sixth Amendment	Guarantees the right of an accused person in criminal cases to trial by jury, representation by an attorney, and a speedy trial.
Seventh Amendment	Guarantees citizens the right to a trial by jury in civil cases.
Eighth Amendment	Protects accused persons against imprisonment or punishment that is excessive.
Ninth Amendment	Declares that people have rights beyond those mentioned in the Constitution.
Tenth Amendment	Declares that powers not specifically given to the federal government belong to the states or the people.

Did You Know?

Life Without a Bill of Rights

Many citizens in other countries around the world don't enjoy the rights guaranteed to Americans.

* In some Middle Eastern countries, women cannot participate in government, vote, or work outside the home.

* Freedom of speech and the press do not exist in some nondemocratic countries. The only news that people get comes from the government. The government may arrest and imprison people who speak out against its policies.
* Some countries require people to practice a certain religion.
* Some persecute individuals for following certain religions.

Inside the Bill of Rights

George Mason not only wrote the earlier Virginia Declaration of Rights, he also refused to ratify the Articles of the Constitution because he felt citizens' rights were not sufficiently defined and protected by the document. Many others agreed, and the first 10 amendments to the Constitution were added to address their concerns.

First Amendment

The First Amendment guarantees religious and political freedoms. The success of a democracy depends on the ability of the people to make informed decisions. To do so, citizens must be able to:

* Get reliable information about issues.
* Discuss ideas freely.
* Communicate ideas with their elected officials.

The First Amendment guarantees **five** specific rights that are vital to American life. It guarantees freedom of:

1. **Religion.**
2. **Speech.**
3. **The Press.**
4. **Assembly.**
5. **Petition.**

First Amendment Freedoms

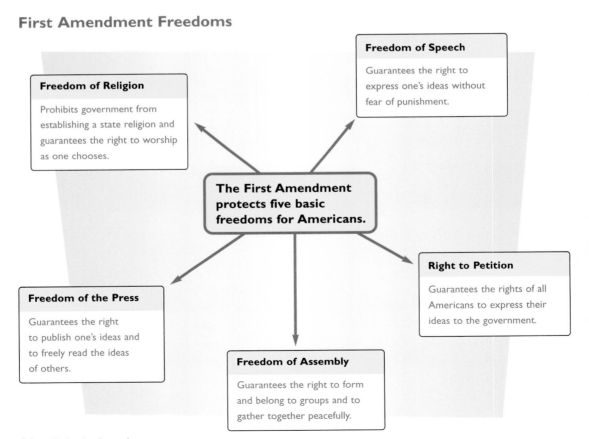

Freedom of Speech

Guarantees the right to express one's ideas without fear of punishment.

Freedom of Religion

Prohibits government from establishing a state religion and guarantees the right to worship as one chooses.

The First Amendment protects five basic freedoms for Americans.

Right to Petition

Guarantees the rights of all Americans to express their ideas to the government.

Freedom of the Press

Guarantees the right to publish one's ideas and to freely read the ideas of others.

Freedom of Assembly

Guarantees the right to form and belong to groups and to gather together peacefully.

The amendment was never intended to give citizens the right to do whatever they wanted. The rights of the community—the many—often outweigh the rights of a single individual. The Supreme Court interprets your First Amendment rights by also considering the rights of others.

Freedom of Religion

Many early colonists came to America from England, which had an official religion, the Church of England. Those who practiced another religion were often mistreated. The First Amendment prevents the government from establishing a state religion or from favoring one religion over another. This principle is often referred to as the "separation of church and state," although that phrase is not used in the Constitution.

The interpretation of this amendment is more complicated than it sounds. The Supreme Court is often asked to interpret whether certain activities violate this amendment. Some of the issues they have considered include:

* Can local governments require churches to pay taxes on church-owned property?
* Can public schools require students to pray? Can students participate in voluntary prayer in school?
* Can the government require people who don't believe in killing to serve in the military?
* Can public property be used to display religious symbols?

EXAMPLE: City governments have been sued because they allowed a nativity scene or menorah to be placed on the grounds of government buildings.

Supreme Court Case

Santa Fe Independent School District v. Doe (2000)

Before 1995, students at Santa Fe High School elected a student council chaplain. The chaplain delivered a prayer before each home football game. Some students and parents sued, saying the practice was illegal under the First Amendment because it promoted an official religious activity. The school argued that it was not trying to persuade students to participate in prayer. However, the Supreme Court ruled that, because the event was sponsored by a government-supported school and because the school's name was clearly visible, the school was promoting or encouraging prayer. By doing so, the Court decided, the school was potentially making students who were not participating in the prayers feel like outsiders. The Court ruled the prayers unconstitutional.

Freedom of Speech

The First Amendment guarantees that Americans can say what they believe to be true, in public or private, without fear of punishment. Open discussion helps improve our laws and systems. Over the years, the Supreme Court has faced **two** major issues with this aspect of the First Amendment:

1. **Expanding the Definition of Free Speech.** Since the First Amendment was written, the idea of "speech" has been interpreted as more than speaking your mind in words. The right to express yourself in art, music, or even the way you dress has been supported in Supreme Court decisions. The phrase "freedom of expression" is usually used to describe these rights. The First Amendment protects many types of self-expression.
   EXAMPLE: The Supreme Court ruled in 1989 and again in 1990 that the act of destroying the flag is a protected freedom of expression under the First Amendment.

2. **Limiting Free Speech.** However, the Supreme Court also recognizes some limitations to free speech. People may be stopped from expressing themselves when they:
   * Tell lies that may injure someone's reputation. This is called **slander**.
   * Create a false panic (for example, by yelling "Fire" in a crowded building).
   * Encourage others to riot or destroy property.
   * Commit **treason**—endanger the country by giving information to or helping an enemy.

Freedom of the Press

The First Amendment gives people the right to **publish** their ideas—make information known by word of mouth or in writing. Without a free press, wrongdoing by government officials couldn't be exposed. Newspapers and television could only report the official version of events.

The First Amendment also gives people the right to read what others have published. The government cannot ban books or other material, even if some people find them offensive—insulting or morally wrong. This right ensures that American people can get varied information and hear many different points of view. The press has the same limitations on free speech as the individual citizen. Deliberately publishing untrue statements about someone is called libel and is a crime.

▲
A television journalist in front of the White House.

School Uniforms

Some private schools require students to wear uniforms, and some public school districts require uniforms as well. In these schools, policymakers believe that uniforms provide many advantages for the students.

But not everyone agrees. Those opposed to uniforms argue that the First Amendment protects students' rights to wear what they want to school. What do you think?

Arguments for School Uniforms

Schools act *in loco parentis* (in the place of parents) in many instances. They have authority to say how students should dress.

Uniforms help students concentrate on their schoolwork rather than on their appearance and clothing. The way some students dress is a distraction.

Uniforms ensure that students come to school wearing appropriate clothing.

Uniforms help eliminate dress differences between rich and poor students.

No one will feel left out or uncomfortable because of clothing.

Arguments against School Uniforms

Students have the same freedoms of speech and expression as adults. Schools can't violate students' First Amendment rights.

One's dress can be an expression of oneself. So how one dresses is a form of communication, that is, *speech*.

Students need to learn to make appropriate choices. Requiring uniforms eliminates the lessons that come from making one's own choices, especially when they are inappropriate.

Students need to learn tolerance of differences, not be shielded from them.

Teasing of other students should not be tolerated under any circumstances.

Freedom of Assembly

The First Amendment guarantees that Americans can meet for demonstrations, parades, political rallies, or for any reason to discuss and share their opinions, as long as the assemblies are peaceful. The government may make laws about when and where meetings can be held, but they cannot ban them.

Other assembly rights protected by the First Amendment include your right to form or join organizations, such as political parties, social clubs, labor unions, and political action groups.

Freedom to Petition

Freedom to petition gives citizens the right to tell members of the government what they want. Petitioning allows you to be a part of solving problems and making laws to improve your community and country.

A **petition** is a formal request that an action be taken. Americans have the right to petition the government through their representatives. A petition can be a simple letter to a government official, commenting on a law, or a formal written request signed by thousands of citizens.

Second Amendment

The Second Amendment provides for the right to bear arms.

During the Revolution, small, local armies called **militias** helped fight the British. These militias also helped protect the peace and defend states and communities after the war. The members of a militia did such an important job that the right to bear, or carry, weapons is protected in the Second Amendment.

Today, many citizens debate what this amendment means. Private ownership of guns is legal. So is government regulation of guns and similar weapons. States require registration and background checks on owners and limit the types of weapons a person can own. Some cities have banned civilians from having certain kinds of weapons.

Third Amendment

The Third Amendment prohibits the government from forcing people to house and feed soldiers in their homes.

Before and during the Revolution, British laws forced American colonists to allow British soldiers to live in their houses. The colonists also had to feed the soldiers. The Third Amendment made it illegal for the government to take over private homes for use by the military.

Fourth Amendment

The Fourth Amendment protects citizens from unreasonable searches and seizures.

The Fourth Amendment protects the privacy of your home, your physical self, and your property. British common law recognized the right of people to defend their homes against unlawful entry, even by representatives of the king. "A man's house is his castle," wrote Sir Edward Coke, the great 16th-century English legal scholar. In the 18th century, William Pitt, the British statesman who often supported the colonists in Parliament, wrote, "The poorest man may in his cottage bid defiance to all the force of the crown. It may be frail—its roof may shake—the wind may blow through it—the storm may enter, the rain may enter—but the King of England cannot enter—all his force dares not cross the threshold. . . ."

Sometimes known as the Privacy Amendment, the Fourth Amendment prohibits authorities from:

* Entering and searching a person's home without reason.
* Unreasonably taking a person's property.
* Seizing or arresting a person without just cause.

The Fourth Amendment allows searches and seizures when there is **probable cause** —when reasonable people might assume that a crime has been committed. If law officers have reason to think that a suspect has committed a crime and that evidence might be found, they may request a **warrant** —a legal document issued by a judge. The judge may or may not grant it.

* A *search warrant* gives officers the right to search a particular location and to take items of personal property that might serve as evidence of a crime.
* An *arrest warrant* gives officers permission to take a person into custody.

Courts are often asked to rule on the question of probable cause—to define what is reasonable and what types of property can be searched or seized. Consider the examples in the table below.

Questions of Probable Cause	
Question	Example
Under what circumstances can a person's car be stopped and searched?	If a person is stopped for a traffic violation and appears to be trying to hide something, police may have probable cause to search the vehicle or person.
Under what circumstances can a student's locker or person be searched?	The courts have ruled that neither warrants nor probable cause are necessary if school officials have good reason to think that a search will turn up evidence that a student has broken the law or the rules of the school.
When is electronic surveillance legal? What rights should the government have to listen to cell phone calls or intercept e-mail?	When citizens feel threatened, they are often more willing to give up some of their rights in exchange for a feeling of security. For example, following terrorist attacks, some people are more willing to accept increased airport security, luggage searches, and monitoring of telephone conversations.

Fifth Amendment

The Fifth Amendment guarantees that a person accused of a crime will not be denied the right to life, liberty, or property without due process of law.

The Fifth Amendment addresses **five** major issues involving due process of law. It guarantees:

1. **Indictment by a Grand Jury.**
2. **Protection against Double Jeopardy.**
3. **Protection against Self-incrimination.**
4. **Due Process of Law.**
5. **Protection in Cases of Eminent Domain.**

Indictment by a Grand Jury

Before someone can be put on trial for a serious crime, the evidence must be presented to a **grand jury**—a group of citizens who decide whether the evidence suggests the person may have committed a crime. The Grand Jury can then issue an **indictment**—a formal accusation that leads to trial. This process protects people from being tried without evidence, and it also prevents the courts from being tied up in pointless trials.

Double Jeopardy

Double jeopardy means that you can't be tried again for a crime once you've been found not guilty of that crime. Even if more evidence is found after the trial, the government cannot try the person again.

Self-incrimination

Citizens can't be forced to testify against themselves in court. They also can't be forced to **incriminate** themselves—to say something that could be used to convict them of a crime or make others think they *might* have committed a crime. Refusing to answer a question in court is sometimes called "taking the Fifth," or using the Fifth Amendment to protect your rights.

Due Process

No person's life, liberty, or property can be taken away without due process—following procedures set up in the Constitution and

Primary Source

Miranda Warning

Before 1966, people who were arrested had no legal protection against police questioning methods, and some law enforcement officials used threats and physical abuse to obtain confessions that weren't completely voluntary. Often, people who were arrested weren't aware of their Fifth Amendment rights.

In 1966, the case of Miranda v. Arizona resulted in the introduction of certain procedures that police must follow before questioning someone in custody. The police must make sure the person understands his or her rights. Police now follow the procedures by reading the following statement. You've probably heard these Miranda rights on TV crime shows.

"You have the right to remain silent. Anything you say can and will be used against you in a court of law. You have the right to speak to an attorney, and to have an attorney present during any questioning. If you cannot afford an attorney, one will be provided for you at public expense."

other laws of the land. Due process also means that laws must be reasonable to an average person.

EXAMPLE: A law making it illegal to communicate by e-mail probably wouldn't meet this test.

Eminent Domain

The government has the power of **eminent domain**—the right to take private property for public use. However, the Fifth Amendment prohibits the government from taking a person's property without paying a fair price for it.

EXAMPLE: If a person owns a house and land that will be needed when the government builds a new highway, the government has the right to take the land even if the landowner objects. The Fifth Amendment ensures that the government must pay the landowner a fair market price for the land.

"Take my advise, pal, if you plan to fight white collar crime you'd do well to brush up on the intricacies of due process."

Sixth Amendment

The Sixth Amendment guarantees certain rights of an accused person.

The Sixth Amendment protects people accused of crimes in **four** ways. The accused person has the right to:

1. **Know the Nature of Charges.** People have the right to be told what charges have been brought against them. In other words, the accused must be told what crime he or she is accused of and who made the accusations. This provision assures that the accused can prepare an effective defense.

2. **Know the Witnesses.** The accused has the right to know who will act as witnesses and to challenge those witnesses in court, usually through his or her lawyer, to test their reliability and truthfulness. The accused may also use his own witnesses to testify in his defense.

3. **A Speedy Public Trial and Impartial Jury.** Anyone accused of a crime has the right to a speedy and public trial by an **impartial jury**—a group of people who are not prejudiced or biased toward the defendant or the case. Courts usually set a trial date as soon as the evidence and witnesses are ready, so that the accused isn't held in jail any longer than necessary.

4. **A Lawyer.** The accused has the right to be represented by an attorney. Sometimes, people can't afford to hire attorneys. In these cases, the government will pay for an attorney for the accused.

Seventh Amendment

The Seventh Amendment guarantees citizens the right to a trial by jury in civil cases.

Not all court cases deal with crimes. Sometimes, people or groups may disagree about property or money and ask a court to decide the issue. Participants may settle "out of court" and avoid a trial completely. Regardless, they are entitled to have the case heard by a jury, if they so desire.

Eighth Amendment

The Eighth Amendment protects accused persons against imprisonment or punishment that is excessive.

This breaks down into **two** elements:

1. Protection against excessive bail.
2. Protection against cruel and unusual punishment.

Excessive Bail

The Eighth Amendment gives the accused person a choice of either:

* Staying in jail.
* Posting a cash guarantee, called bail, to permit him or her to go free until the trial. If the person shows up, or appears, for the trial, the bail is returned. If not, the court keeps the money.

Courts must set bail high enough to discourage the accused person from running away and not showing up for the trial. However, the Eighth Amendment prohibits courts from setting bail so high that a person can't possibly afford it. Judges don't have to release a prisoner on bail if:

* They believe the accused may run away, regardless of bail.
* There is evidence the accused would be a danger to society.

Cruel and Unusual Punishment

In the 1700s, this amendment protected people from branding, and other physical punishments that had been used in the past. Today, it usually means that the penalty should fit the crime. For example, putting a person in jail for life for stealing a quart of milk would seem unreasonable to most people. On the other hand, if someone deliberately takes another person's life, most reasonable people would consider some time in prison to be a reasonable punishment.

Some people argue that the death penalty is, by its very nature, always "cruel and unusual." Do you?

EXAMPLE: Ohio state law prohibits execution by the electric chair, but allows execution by lethal injection.

Fighting for Victims' Rights

In 1993, 16-year-old Stephen Hollingshead, Jr., of Laurel, Montana, was killed by a drunk driver. Stephen's father, Stephen, Sr., started a memorial fund in his son's name. The fund has raised money to support anti-drug and anti-drinking programs and to sponsor a web site to help victims of drunk drivers understand their rights. Other citizens have started similar programs and spoken out for stronger victims'-rights laws.

Four amendments in the Bill of Rights protect the rights of those accused of crimes, but there are no constitutional amendments that address the rights of the victims. To address this issue, most states have amended their state constitutions to guarantee rights for victims. Additionally, a Victims' Rights Constitutional Amendment has been proposed in Congress. Opponents of the amendment, such as the American Civil Liberties Union, claim that some victims' rights threaten the rights of the accused.

Ninth Amendment

The Ninth Amendment declares that people have rights beyond those mentioned in the Constitution.

The writers knew that the Bill of Rights couldn't list every possible right, but they wanted people to know that additional rights existed, even if they weren't specifically mentioned. Therefore, they wrote the Ninth and Tenth Amendments to help deal with issues our country might face in the future.

EXAMPLE: Many of the rights we take for granted are not listed in the Constitution:

* The right to live where we want.
* The right to choose which school our children will attend.
* The right to work at a job we want.
* The right to marry and have children— or not.
* The right to travel freely.

These rights and others not specifically mentioned in the Bill of Rights are still protected by the Constitution.

Richmond Newspapers, Inc. v. Virginia (1980)

The Supreme Court is often asked to rule in cases involving rights not specifically mentioned in the Constitution. In a Virginia murder trial, the defense lawyer asked the court to keep the proceedings secret from the public. He argued that if testimony "got out," it would be difficult for his client to get a fair trial. The court agreed. Later, several citizens and reporters challenged that ruling.

The Supreme Court disagreed with the state court and ruled that a courtroom can't be closed to the public unless the rights of the accused to a fair trial will be damaged. The Court's ruling stated that, "The freedoms of speech, press, and assembly, expressly guaranteed by the First Amendment, share a common core purpose of assuring freedom of communication on matters relating to the functioning of government."

Tenth Amendment

The Tenth Amendment states that powers not specifically given to the federal government are given to the states or the people.

The Tenth Amendment stops the U.S. government from taking more power than the Constitution gives it. This amendment helps balance power between the national and state governments. It also keeps Congress and the president from becoming too powerful.

EXAMPLE: Federal law makes buyers wait five days for a background check before purchasing a gun. The federal government ordered local sheriffs and police chiefs to do the checks. Two sheriffs objected, saying that the federal government couldn't ask employees of a state to enforce federal law without giving them the money and people to do it. The court agreed.

▲
When the press is not allowed to photograph a trial, sketch artists document the trial.

The Universal Declaration of Human Rights

In 1948, the United Nations Commission on Human Rights adopted a Universal Declaration of Human Rights. The document includes the main civil and political rights recognized by democratic societies, including the rights mentioned in the United States' Bill of Rights.

The words below come from the Preamble to the Declaration.

The UN document also describes economic, social, and cultural rights, such as:

* The right to work.
* The right to an education.
* The right to participate in the cultural life of the community.
* The right to enjoy the arts.
* The right to share in the benefits of scientific advancements.

"... recognition of the inherent dignity and of the inalienable rights of all members of the human family is the foundation of freedom, justice, and peace in the world . . . .

"... disregard and contempt for human rights have resulted in barbarous acts which have outraged the conscience of mankind, and the advent of a world in which human beings shall enjoy freedom of speech and belief and freedom from fear and want has been proclaimed as the highest aspiration [desire] of the common people . . . ."

▲
A UN truck brings much-needed supplies to a refugee camp in Tanzania, in southeastern Africa.

The first 10 amendments to the U.S. Constitution, called the Bill of Rights, were added to the Constitution to guarantee certain basic rights for all citizens and to prevent the government from ever being able to take away those rights.

The First Amendment guarantees and protects five basic freedoms: freedom of religion, freedom of speech, freedom of the press, freedom of assembly, and freedom to petition the government.

The Second Amendment discusses the right to bear arms.

The Third Amendment prohibits the government from forcing people to house and feed soldiers in their homes.

The Fourth Amendment protects citizens from unreasonable searches and seizures.

The Fifth Amendment guarantees that a person accused of a crime will not be denied the right to life, liberty, or property without due process of law.

The Sixth Amendment guarantees the right of an accused person to trial by jury, representation by an attorney, and a speedy trial.

The Seventh Amendment guarantees citizens the right to a trial by jury in civil cases.

The Eighth Amendment protects accused persons against imprisonment or punishment that is excessive.

The Ninth and Tenth Amendments are included to protect rights and freedoms not specifically mentioned in the Constitution and to prevent the government from taking powers that belong to the states and the people.

Civics in America

double jeopardy—condition of being tried a second time for the same crime. *p. 61*

eminent domain—right of the government to take private property for public use. *p. 62*

grand jury—group of citizens who decide whether there is enough evidence against a person to bring him or her to trial. *p. 60*

impartial jury—group of citizens sworn to give a bias-free verdict in a trial, who have nothing to gain or lose as a result of the outcome of the case. *p. 62*

incriminate—make a person appear guilty of a crime. *p. 61*

indictment—formal laying of charges leading to a trial. *p. 60*

militia—army of citizens who are not professional soldiers and who may be called for service in times of emergency. The National Guard is a militia. *p. 58*

petition—make a formal request of an authority. *p. 58*

probable cause—grounds for a reasonable person to believe that a crime may have been committed. *p. 59*

publish—make information known to the public by word of mouth or in print. *p. 56*

slander—act of telling lies to damage someone's reputation; also the crime of so doing. (*Libel* is the crime of *writing or publishing* lies that harm someone.) *p. 56*

treason—crime of endangering the country by giving information to or helping an enemy. *p. 56*

warrant—legal document issued by a judge authorizing actions such as search, seizure, or arrest. *p. 59*

The Living Constitution

In this chapter, you will learn about:

- why we have constitutional amendments
- how and why the voting rights of Americans have changed
- how changes in society affect how our Constitution is interpreted

In 1776, Thomas Paine, a British-American political writer, criticized some voting requirements in the colonies with this riddle: "You require that a man have 60 dollars worth of property, or he shall not vote. . . . Here is a man who today owns a donkey, and the donkey is worth 60 dollars. Today the man is a voter and he goes to the polls and deposits his vote. Tomorrow the donkey dies. The next day the man comes to vote without his donkey, and he cannot vote at all. Now tell me which was the voter, the man or the donkey?"

Even with the Bill of Rights in place, our government continues to face new constitutional questions. Issues, such as civil rights and the voting rights discussed by Thomas Paine, have resulted in other constitutional amendments. Since the Bill of Rights, the Constitution has been amended 17 times.

The Constitution and Change

The Founders knew that no document they wrote could predict every issue that might come up in the future. They made the Constitution a living document when they created Article V. This article provides an orderly way to change or amend the Constitution.

Passing the Bill of Rights showed that the Constitution *could* be changed, but more additions and changes were needed as the years went by, including definitions of:

* **Who can vote?** When the Constitution was written, women, adults under the age of 21, and enslaved African Americans could not vote.
* **What is due process?** Although the Bill of Rights included terms such as "due process," not everyone agreed about what it and other terms meant.
* **How do states interpret rights?** States interpreted the Bill of Rights differently. Some states made laws that denied certain rights included in the Bill of Rights.

The table opposite lists the 17 Amendments that have been ratified, in addition to the Bill of Rights. You can read the complete text on pages 346–355.

Amendment	Year Ratified	What It Addressed
Eleventh	1795	Lawsuits against a state.
Twelfth	1804	Election of president and vice president.
Thirteenth	1865	Abolition of slavery.
Fourteenth	1868	Rights of citizenship, due process, and equal protection under law.
Fifteenth	1870	Voting rights of (male) citizens regardless of race, color, or whether they had been slaves.
Sixteenth	1913	Income tax.
Seventeenth	1913	Election of senators.
Eighteenth	1919	Prohibition of liquor.
Nineteenth	1920	Women's right to vote.
Twentieth	1933	Terms for president, vice president, and members of Congress.
Twenty-first	1933	Repeal of Eighteenth Amendment.
Twenty-second	1951	Two-term limit on president.
Twenty-third	1961	Presidential vote for District of Columbia residents.
Twenty-fourth	1964	Abolition of poll tax.
Twenty-fifth	1967	Presidential vacancy, disability, and inability.
Twenty-sixth	1971	Right to vote at age 18.
Twenty-seventh	1992	Changing pay for members of Congress.

Extending Civil Rights

In 1619, the first 20 Africans were sold to settlers in Virginia. Within 60 years, slavery was a growing practice. Many Americans, however, believed that slavery contradicted the country's ideals of liberty and religious values.

However, several Southern states, that relied on slavery to support their agricultural economy, had refused to join the confederation if any laws were made to stop slavery. So, to form a new nation, the founders did not address slavery in the Constitution or Bill of Rights.

Did You Know?

Slavery and the Fifth Amendment

Why didn't the Fifth Amendment make slavery illegal? The amendment guarantees that no person can "be deprived of life, liberty, or property, without due process of law." However, at the time of the Bill of Rights, slaves were seen as property, not as persons. Slave states argued that the Fifth Amendment made it illegal for the government to make laws that interfered with their right to own property—their slaves. Slavery did not become illegal under the Constitution until the Thirteenth and Fourteenth Amendments were ratified after the Civil War.

Slavery in a Growing America

Arguments over slavery didn't end with the ratification of the Constitution and the addition of the Bill of Rights.

The Northwest Ordinance

In 1787, Congress passed the Northwest Ordinance. This **ordinance**—regulation or law—described how the huge Northwest Territory that included the present states of Ohio, Indiana, Illinois, Michigan, and Wisconsin would be governed. The Ordinance banned slavery in the Northwest Territory but, to satisfy the slave states, required that escaped slaves who reached the Territory had to be returned to their owners.

The Missouri Compromise

Before 1819, there were 11 free states and 11 slave states, and this balance allowed the new nation to operate. Neither free states nor slave states had control. Then, in 1819, the Missouri Territory applied to join the Union. It would be a slave state.

Kentucky Congressman Henry Clay proposed the 1820 Missouri Compromise. His proposal would admit Missouri as a slave state and Maine as a free state—keeping the number of free and slave states equal and returning the balance of power. It was accepted.

The Dred Scott Decision

Dred Scott, a slave, accompanied his owner from Missouri to Illinois and the Wisconsin Territory, where slavery had been prohibited by Congress. When Scott's owner returned to Missouri, where slavery was still legal, Scott and his wife sued for their freedom. The Supreme Court ruled in 1857 that Congress had no power to limit slavery in the territories, and Scott must remain a slave. Chief Justice Roger B. Taney also declared that, as a slave, Scott was not a citizen and had no rights.

The Thirteenth and Fourteenth Amendments

Abraham Lincoln had made his feelings about slavery clear during his campaign for president. By 1861, when Lincoln took office, seven Southern states **seceded**—withdrew— from the Union and formed their own **Confederacy**—an alliance of states. Soon afterwards, the Civil War began.

In 1863, President Lincoln issued the **Emancipation Proclamation**, a document that freed slaves "within any state or . . . part of a state" still fighting the Union.

Primary Source

Frederick Douglass, Fourth of July Speech, 1852

Frederick Douglass was born a slave in Maryland but escaped to the North. In 1841, Douglass began attending abolitionist meetings and impressed abolitionist leaders with his powerful speeches. **Abolitionists** were people who worked to end slavery. Friends purchased Douglass's freedom in 1847.

In 1852, Douglass spoke at a Fourth of July celebration in Rochester, New York.

"I shall see this day . . . from a slave's point of view . . . I do not hesitate to declare, with all my soul, that the character and conduct of this nation never looked blacker to me than on this Fourth of July. . . . Go search where you will, roam through all the monarchies . . . of the Old World, travel through South America, search out every abuse and when you have found the last, lay your facts by the side of the every-day practices of this nation, and you will say with me that, for revolting barbarity [cruelty] and shameless hypocrisy [deceit], America reigns without a rival."

The Thirteenth Amendment (1865)

The Thirteenth Amendment made slavery illegal.

More than a proclamation was needed to make slavery illegal. In 1865, the Thirteenth Amendment was passed, outlawing slavery in the United States.

Even abolitionists weren't sure what effect the amendment would have after the Civil War had ended. Freeing the slaves was one thing. Recognizing them as equal citizens with full constitutional rights would take another amendment.

The Fourteenth Amendment (1868)

The Fourteenth Amendment gave citizenship and civil rights to all citizens, regardless of race or religion.

In 1868, the states ratified the Fourteenth Amendment, which was designed to protect the rights of freed slaves by defining them as citizens. It includes **three** important parts:

1. **Citizenship.** A citizen is anyone born in the United States or someone who is naturalized as a citizen.
2. **Due Process.** No state may take away the life, liberty, or property of any citizen without due process of law. The Supreme Court had ruled that the Bill of Rights applied only to the federal government. The Fourteenth Amendment said that no state could make a law that interfered with citizens' rights granted by the federal government.
3. **Equal Protection of the Laws.** Every state must give its citizens "equal protection of the laws."

Extending Voting Rights

The country's founders believed requirements for **suffrage**—the right to vote—should be left up to individual states. So, amendments were necessary to extend voting rights to groups of people who didn't have them.

The Fifteenth Amendment (1870)

The Fifteenth Amendment gave voting rights to all citizens, regardless of race, color, or having been slaves.

The Fifteenth Amendment said that race could not be a reason to deny citizens the right to vote. It was the first time that the Constitution addressed voting rights. With this amendment, there was now a limit on a state's ability to decide who could vote. States were free to make other requirements for voting, but race could not be one of them.

States could, and some did, make laws that said a man couldn't vote unless he could read. Or he couldn't vote unless he owned a certain amount of property. (At this time, no states let women vote in major elections.) Such laws had to apply equally in the state, regardless of color or race or whether or not people had been born slaves.

Amendments that Extend the Voice of the People in Government

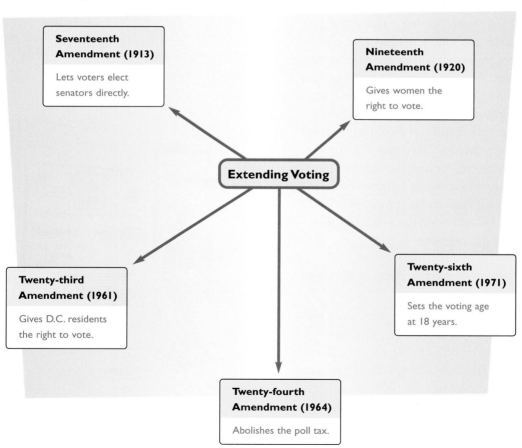

Seventeenth Amendment (1913)

Lets voters elect senators directly.

Nineteenth Amendment (1920)

Gives women the right to vote.

Extending Voting

Twenty-third Amendment (1961)

Gives D.C. residents the right to vote.

Twenty-sixth Amendment (1971)

Sets the voting age at 18 years.

Twenty-fourth Amendment (1964)

Abolishes the poll tax.

The Seventeenth Amendment (1913)

The Seventeenth Amendment allowed for the direct election of senators.

Under the Constitution, senators were not elected directly by the people, but were chosen by the legislatures in the different states. Each state got two senators. This plan recognized the importance of the power of the state legislatures. Our country's founders were showing the states that they would remain powerful in the new government, regardless of their size.

Reformers of the early 20th century challenged the Senate, saying it was like a rich man's club and totally useless. One representative proposed getting rid of it, saying the Senate was "an obstructive and useless body, a menace to the liberties of the people, and an obstacle to social growth."

His proposal did not pass, but change was clearly needed. Two years later, in 1913, the Seventeenth Amendment was ratified, and ever since, senators have been elected directly by the people. This amendment extended the voice of the people in government.

The Nineteenth Amendment (1920)

The Nineteenth Amendment gave voting rights to women.

After the colonies broke from England in 1776, men made all the laws. Even when women owned property on which they paid taxes, they had no say in government.

The Constitution did not say that women could not vote. But it did not say specifically that they could, either. As early as 1838, Kentucky allowed women to vote in school elections. In 1869, the Wyoming Territory granted women full suffrage, but by 1914 only 10 states did so.

Early **suffragists** worked to get women the right to vote. A few of the women who led the movement are profiled in the chart opposite.

In 1919, Congress finally proposed and passed the Nineteenth Amendment, granting voting rights to women. The amendment, ratified in 1920, stated that, *"The right of the citizens of the United States to vote shall not be denied or abridged by the United States or by any State on account of sex."*

Suffragist Leaders	
Elizabeth Cady Stanton (1815–1902), one of the first women to organize the women's suffrage movement, helped organize the first Women's Rights Convention in 1848.	**Lucy Stone (1818–1893)** was founder of the American Woman Suffrage Association and the first woman in Massachusetts to earn a college degree.
Susan B. Anthony (1820–1906) pioneered crusades for women's suffrage and served as president of the National Woman Suffrage Association from 1892 to 1900.	**Mary Church Terrell (1863–1954),** a daughter of former slaves, founded the National Association of Colored Women in 1896.
Sojourner Truth (1797–1883) was a freed slave and a speaker for abolition and women's rights.	**Jeannette Rankin (1880–1973)** was the first woman elected to Congress. Elected in 1917 and again in 1941, she worked for women's suffrage, welfare, and world peace.

Primary Source

The Seneca Falls Declaration (1848)

In 1848, Elizabeth Cady Stanton, one of the first women to organize the suffrage movement, wrote a Declaration of Rights that she presented to the more than 300 people who attended a convention. The Declaration was modeled after the Declaration of Independence, but added a key phrase.

"We hold these truths to be self-evident: that all men <u>and women</u> are created equal. . . ."

▲
Strong-minded women make a sensation at a New York Uptown polling place by trying to vote.

Woman Power

Although women could not vote in 1918, they could speak out for or against candidates for office. A proposal for a constitutional amendment to grant women the right to vote failed in the Senate by two votes. Women actively campaigned against four senators who were running for reelection in that year. All of them had voted against the amendment. All four lost their elections.

The Twenty-third Amendment (1961)

The Twenty-third Amendment gave citizens in the District of Columbia the right to vote in national elections.

The District of Columbia became the home of the nation's capitol in 1800, but it was not a state, so residents could not vote in federal elections.

In 1961, the Twenty-third Amendment gave citizens of the District of Columbia the right to vote in national elections for president and vice president. However, the District of Columbia has no senator, and its only representative has no vote in the House.

The Twenty-fourth Amendment (1964)

The Twenty-fourth Amendment eliminated poll taxes.

Beginning in 1889, 11 Southern states passed poll taxes. A **poll tax** was a tax that had to be paid before a person could vote. The poll tax was meant to discourage African Americans from voting, since most of them were poor. While most of these states got rid of it in the early part of the 20th century, by the 1960s, four states still used this form of **discrimination**.

The Civil Rights movement began in the '60s, and one of its achievements was the Twenty-fourth Amendment.

It states, *"The right of citizens of the United States to vote in any primary or other election . . . shall not be denied or abridged by the United States or any state by reason of failure to pay any poll tax or other tax."*

Nearly 100 years after they were given the vote in the Fifteenth Amendment, African Americans could finally enjoy their full rights as voters.

The Twenty-sixth Amendment (1971)

The Twenty-sixth Amendment lowered the voting age to 18.

In 1942, during the Second World War, a West Virginia representative proposed an amendment to lower the voting age from

21 to 18. There was little support until President Eisenhower proposed a similar amendment in 1954. Eisenhower remembered the brave young soldiers that he had led as a general during World War II.

The issue was not settled for another 15 years. Factors in the decision to lower the voting age to 18 included:

* **Baby-Boom Generation.** After World War II, many people married and had children. Our population increased by some 30 million people in the 1950s. The people in this "baby-boom" generation reached their teens during the 1960s and 1970s and pressured Congress for the right to let them vote at 18.

* **The Vietnam Conflict.** In the 1960s, many of the young American military people who were serving in Southeast Asia were too young to vote in national elections or to choose the lawmakers who sent them to war.

American Citizenship

The Seventh Generation Amendment

Around 1570, a Huron American Indian named Deganawidah united five northeast Indian nations in the Iroquois Confederacy. A great leader known by his people as the Peacemaker, he taught that people should live in such a way that they protect the "seven generations to follow us."

More than 200 years later, Walter Bresette, a Red Cliff Chippewa, proposed a Seventh Generation Amendment to the Constitution: *"The rights of citizens of the United States to use and enjoy air, water, wildlife, and other renewable resources determined by the Congress to be common property shall not be impaired, nor shall such use impair their availability for the use of future generations."*

Presidential candidate Ralph Nader, who ran on the Green Party ticket in the 1996 and 2000 elections, chose as his running mate a White Earth Chippewa, Winona LaDuke. LaDuke championed the amendment. Although these third-party candidates lost the elections, they brought public attention to their interest in the environment.

The amendment has yet to be proposed by Congress. But like many such ideas, with enough public support, it could become part of our Constitution.

Changing Interpretations in Changing Times

The ethnic and racial makeup of the population, as well as the attitudes of many Americans, have changed a great deal since 1776. The Constitution has been amended by the states and Congress and interpreted by the Supreme Court to reflect those changes.

The Constitution and Civil Rights

The Fourteenth Amendment guarantees equal protection of the laws to all citizens regardless of race, religion, or any other reason. What did equal protection of the laws really mean?

During the late 1800s, many states used policies of **segregation** to ignore the equal protection clause of the Fourteenth Amendment. They segregated people, meaning they separated one group from another on the basis of race:

* African-American children went to different schools from white children.
* Some hotels and restaurants banned African Americans, and railroads, streetcars, and buses had different sections for white and African American people.

In 1896, these segregation policies came before the Supreme Court in the case of *Plessy* v. *Ferguson*. Plessy, a man of mixed white and African-American heritage, sat in a seat reserved for whites on a train. He was asked to move to the African-American section and refused. The Supreme Court ruled that separation of the races was legal as long as the facilities for both races were equal. This "separate but equal" argument was used to continue segregation until 1954.

Civil Rights Timeline

Rosa Parks takes a seat in the white section of a Montgomery, Alabama, bus. She is arrested. In protest, Parks' supporters refuse to use the bus system for one day.

1960

1955

Martin Luther King, Jr., a local Baptist minister, turns the initial protests against the Montgomery bus company into a long boycott. Protests force the bus company to desegregate. These peaceful protests became a huge movement that spreads to other communities.

African-American students in Greensboro, North Carolina, insist on being served at a segregated lunch counter. Others hold similar demonstrations in department stores, supermarkets, libraries, and movie theaters.

Supreme Court Case

Brown vs. Board of Education (1954)

In 1954, 17 states and the District of Columbia allowed local school districts to prevent African-American children from going to public schools with white children. The National Association for the Advancement of Colored People (NAACP) brought several cases before the Supreme Court, challenging the "separate but equal" policy.

One of these cases centered on Linda Brown, a schoolgirl from Topeka, Kansas. Brown lived 7 blocks from a school for white children, but she was required to attend a school for African-American children 21 blocks from her home.

Thurgood Marshall, Brown's attorney and a future Supreme Court Justice, argued that separate schools had a harmful effect on black and white children. He presented evidence to prove that segregated schools could never really be equal.

The justices of the Supreme Court knew that their ruling would involve much more than picking Linda Brown's school. The judges were divided, but, in 1954, they ruled that school segregation was *un*constitutional. Other decisions followed, saying that states must begin desegregation "with all deliberate speed."

The Civil Rights Movement

The timeline below shows some of the significant events and people in the early civil rights movement.

President Kennedy is assassinated, and Lyndon B. Johnson becomes president.

Under President Johnson, the Civil Rights Act is passed.

1964

1963

Martin Luther King, Jr., leads civil rights supporters in a huge march in Washington, D.C., to protest racial discrimination and support civil-rights legislation. King gives his famous "I Have a Dream" speech.

Civil Rights Legislation

The Civil Rights Act of 1964 was an important step in ensuring equal rights for minorities. It:

* *Guaranteed* equal access to public accommodations, such as restaurants and hotels.
* *Disallowed* unfair voter registration requirements.
* *Challenged* employers and labor unions over discrimination in hiring and employment.
* *Demanded* that schools, unions, or other employers that received money from the federal government stop discrimination in their organizations.

The Open Housing Act of 1968 forbade anyone from refusing to sell or rent living space to any minority or to families with children.

Equality and Affirmative Action

Years of discrimination had prevented minorities and women from getting fair educational and job opportunities. Some people argued that the government should offset past discrimination with affirmative action.

Affirmative Action Policies

The federal government introduced **affirmative action** policies in the 1960s and 1970s to improve work and educational opportunities for women and members of minority groups:

* Employment or entrance tests that discriminated against women or minorities were forbidden in businesses or colleges and universities that received federal funding.
* Businesses that sold or wanted to sell services or goods to the federal government were required to show that they had affirmative action standards and plans.

   EXAMPLE: If a company wanted to apply for a government contract, company owners had to prove that their employee base reflected the general population in their area. For example, if the population in their area was 60 percent white, 30 percent African American, and 10 percent Hispanic, the company had to have 6 white employees, 3 African-American employees, and 1 Hispanic employee. Rules about the number or proportion of people admitted to an organization—school, company, or country—are called **quotas**.

The government used quotas in many of its activities. It set aside a certain number of contracts for companies owned or run by minorities.

Affirmative action goes to the core of the U.S. Constitution, putting individual rights and "group" rights in opposition to one another.

Reverse Discrimination

Because affirmative action policies treat groups within society differently, people have questioned whether they are constitutional. Some white males, for example, claim they are being discriminated against in what is called **reverse discrimination**. Courts have ruled on a number of challenges to affirmative action policies, as the chart below shows.

Expansion of Rights

As the population of the country continues to change, new groups have won recognition and rights:

* Senior-citizen groups work against being forced to retire at 65.

* Physically challenged or disabled people have gained freedom of access to buildings and other public places.
* Female athletes have fought for equal opportunities to participate in sports in school.
* Hispanic Americans in many schools have gained bilingual classrooms, where they are taught in Spanish until they have acquired English literacy skills.
* Many people have successfully challenged the practice called **racial profiling**—when police and other security forces go after people, making generalizations based on their skin color or ethnicity.

Affirmative Action in Action: Court Cases and Challenges	
The Weber Case	In 1979, Kaiser Aluminum Company set up training programs for African American workers based on seniority. A white worker was refused entrance into the program three times, although he had more seniority. The court ruled the programs legal because they were designed to make up for past injustices.
Johnson v. Transportation Agency of Santa Clara County	In 1987, a female employee of the Transportation Agency was promoted to a job that had always been held by a man. A man sued, saying that he had scored higher on an interview than the woman. The court ruled that no rights were violated.
California Proposition 209	In 1996, a majority of California voters approved Proposition 209. The law prohibits the state government and local governments from giving preferred treatment to any group, such as women or minorities, in state hiring or state college admissions, for example. The State Court of Appeals in California has upheld the law.

Affirmative Action and College Admissions

The number of African Americans, Hispanics, and Asian Americans attending college was given a boost with a Supreme Court decision in 1978. In Regents of the University of California v. Bakke, the Court ruled that colleges and universities could give special consideration to minority applicants. Some people argue that these affirmative action policies have prevented nonminority people with equal or higher qualifications from attending the schools of their choice. What do you think? What criteria do you think universities should use to select students?

Arguments for Affirmative Action

Minority group members have been discriminated against for most of U.S. history. To undo this wrong, we must take deliberate steps.

College admissions tests and tests for some jobs have been proved to be culturally biased. Able people have been shut out because they performed poorly on them. We need policies that don't rely solely on test scores for admission.

Discrimination and prejudice continue to exist in our society. If we eliminate affirmative action, minorities will again suffer discrimination.

We've made great strides in overcoming discrimination, we can't stop now.

Arguments against Affirmative Action

People should be treated as individuals, not as members of groups. It is just as wrong to consider people as group members for good reasons as for bad reasons.

We should work to improve the tests so that they measure the qualities needed. Admissions should be based on qualifications of applicants, not special treatment.

Affirmative action policies violate the civil rights of people not covered by them— white people and, often, men.

Minorities have had 40 years to "catch up," and that is long enough.

Unsuccessful Amendments

Although the Constitution has been amended only 27 times, many other amendments have been proposed but then voted down by the states.

✻ The Slavery Amendment of 1861. This amendment would have made it illegal for Congress to make any law interfering with slavery.

✻ The Equal Rights Amendment of 1972. This amendment stated that *"Equality of rights under the law shall not be denied or abridged by the United States or by any State on account of sex."*

Chapter 5 Wrap-up
THE LIVING CONSTITUTION

The Constitution is a document designed to change as the United States grows and develops. One of the major issues facing the growing nation during the 1800s was slavery. African Americans faced a long fight to get rights equal to those of other American citizens. The Thirteenth and Fourteenth Amendments gave freedom, citizenship, and civil rights to African Americans.

Other amendments extended voting rights to minorities (Fifteenth), women (Nineteenth), residents of the District of Columbia (Twenty-third), and people over the age of 18 (Twenty-sixth). The right of all citizens to elect senators was ensured in the Seventeenth Amendment, and the taxes that kept many African Americans from voting were prohibited in the Twenty-fourth Amendment.

Despite the amendments, discrimination continued in many parts of America. Segregation laws provided separate-but-equal facilities for African Americans and whites. These laws were eventually found to be unconstitutional by the Supreme Court. During the 1960s, the Civil Rights movement led to new legislation designed to protect and ensure equality for minorities. Today, new groups continue to ask the courts and Congress to extend rights and broaden the laws of the land.

abolitionist—person who worked to end slavery. *p. 73*

affirmative action—policies and efforts made to improve opportunities for minority groups. *p. 82*

Confederacy—alliance of Southern states that seceded from the Union and fought in the Civil War. *p. 73*

discrimination—act or process of treating people of one group differently because of race, religion, or any factor not based on individual merit. *p. 78*

Emancipation Proclamation—document issued by President Lincoln in 1863 that freed the slaves in the Confederacy. *p. 73*

ordinance—regulation or law. *p. 72*

poll tax—fee paid in order to vote. *p. 78*

quota—rule about the number or proportion of people admitted to an organization, school, company, or country. *p. 82*

racial profiling—making generalizations based on skin color or ethnicity in policing or security work. *p. 83*

reverse discrimination—discrimination against a majority group such as whites or males. *p. 83*

secede—formally withdraw from a group or organization, such as the Confederate states from the Union in 1861. *p. 73*

segregation—policy that forces the separation of one group of people from another, based on race, sex, religion, or other similar characteristic. *p. 80*

suffrage—right to vote. *p. 74*

suffragists—people who worked for women's right to vote. *p. 76*

CHAPTER 6

The Legislative Branch

In this chapter, you will learn about:

- the functions of Congress
- the members of Congress
- how Congress makes laws
- the powers given to Congress by the Constitution

When you get together with friends to go to a movie, do you ever spend time trying to decide which movie to see? How do you all come to a decision? It can be frustrating when your three friends each want to see a different movie. Multiply the difficulty of making this group decision by a factor of 280 million, and you have some idea of what it's like to be a member of the United States Congress.

Representing the wishes of the 280 million people in the United States is a very difficult job. The people who live in this huge country have very different needs, desires, and philosophies about what is best for the nation. Members of Congress have to listen to the people they represent, then work to pass federal laws that are best for the country.

Function of the Legislative Branch

"Man is not made for the State but the State for man and it derives its just powers only from the consent of the governed."—Thomas Jefferson

This quote from Thomas Jefferson is one of the many quotes found in the hallways of the U.S. Capitol—the meeting place for Congress. Just as Jefferson said, Congress gets its power from the people. These lawmakers are your national representatives.

The Congress of the United States was established by the Constitution as the legislative, or lawmaking, branch of the federal government. In 1789, with only 26 senators and 65 representatives, the first Congress met in Federal Hall in New York City.

Today, the 540 members and delegates of Congress meet in Washington, D.C. Members of Congress serve the people of the United States by writing federal laws that will bring the greatest good to the most people in the country.

Members of Congress

The U.S. Congress is **bicameral**—meaning it has two houses or chambers. The **two** houses of the U.S. Congress are:

1. **The Senate.**

2. **The House of Representatives.**

The two-chamber design is based on a central principle of American government—that government must be divided into units that share power to provide a system of checks and balances against possible abuses of power.

Duties, Terms, and Qualifications

The houses of Congress meet and carry out business separately. Senators and Representatives have different responsibilities, terms, leaders, and qualifications. But a proposed law—or **legislation**—is passed only when both houses agree to exactly the same law.

Comparing the House and Senate		
	House	**Senate**
Number of members	435 plus five delegates	100
Terms	2 years	6 years
Requirements	Must be at least 25 years old; a U.S. citizen for at least seven years; a resident of state represented.	Must be at least 30 years old; a U.S. citizen for at least nine years; a resident of state represented.
Leaders	Speaker of the House	Vice President
Duties	Represent congressional district	Represent state

You Decide

Term Limits

A member of Congress isn't limited in the number of times he or she can run for re-election. In 1997, one man, Strom Thurmond from South Carolina, became the longest-serving senator ever, with 43 years in office. He still served in the Senate at the age of 99!

In the 1980s and 1990s, many people began to call for a law that would set term limits, or prevent office-holders from serving more than a certain number of terms in a row.

What do you think? Should senators and representatives have term limits just like the president? Why or why not? If you agree with term limits, what limits would you set?

Arguments for Term Limits

With term limits, Congresspersons wouldn't have to continue to seek money for re-election from special interest groups. They would be more responsive to the citizens they represent while in office.

Challengers may be discouraged from running for office against someone already holding an office. Term limits would encourage more competition and more choice.

Politicians who serve too long in Washington lose touch with the people they represent. They're not able to represent the views of citizens.

Arguments against Term Limits

Politicians who know they can't run for office again have less interest in serving the wants and needs of the people they represent.

Politicians who have served in office have experience and can get more done in Congress. Term limits would result in many new lawmakers in office who will be less organized and less unified. The results would be inefficiency and chaos.

Term limits violate the constitutional right of people to express themselves by voting for whomever they want.

The Legislative Branch 89

House of Representatives

The House of Representatives is generally thought to be the house closest to the people. Our Founding Fathers believed short, two-year terms would ensure that House members understood and voiced the concerns of the citizens they represented.

Each of the 435 members of the House represents a **Congressional district**, or area within their state, that includes approximately 600,000 people. Each district gets to elect one representative. The total number of representatives for a state is determined by the state's population. The Constitution requires that the United States take a count, or census, of the population every 10 years to determine how to distribute the seats in the House.

Supreme Court Case

Wesberry v. Sanders (1964)

Article I, Section 2, of the U.S. Constitution describes how the members of the U.S. House of Representatives are to be elected. It says they must be "elected by the people," and it says that each state will get a certain number of representatives according to its population. The individual state governments—not the federal government—decide how to divide up state populations into groups called districts, each of which will get to elect one representative.

In 1964, the state of Georgia was divided into 10 districts. Wesberry was a citizen of the Fifth District. The Fifth District had about 820,000 people—more than twice the size of the average district population. One district, the Ninth, had only 272,154 people.

Wesberry complained that he didn't get equal representation in Congress because his Representative had to serve more people than other Georgia Representatives. He sued the state of Georgia, asking that the court order new districts with more equal populations. The U.S. Supreme Court agreed with Wesberry. The Court ruled that Georgia's districts discriminated against voters in the Fifth District. The Court's opinion stated that "as nearly as is practicable, one man's vote in a congressional election is to be worth as much as another's . . . . While it may not be possible to draw congressional districts with mathematical precision, that is no excuse for ignoring our Constitution's plain objective of making equal representation for equal numbers of people the fundamental goal for the House of Representatives. That is the high standard of justice and common sense which the Founders set for us."

EXAMPLE: As of 2000, California, the most populous state, had the most representatives—52. Alaska, the largest state geographically, had only 1 representative! Alaska, although it takes up the most territory, has one of the smallest populations of the 50 states.

In addition to the members elected by citizens of the 50 states, the House includes:

* A representative from the District of Columbia.
* A commissioner from Puerto Rico.
* Representatives from the three American territories—Guam, American Samoa, and the U.S. Virgin Islands.

These five members, called *delegates*, express the wishes of the people they represent. They may vote in some committees but only rarely in the full house, and they have no power to vote on laws.

Senate

Article I, Section 3, of the United States Constitution says that each state shall be represented by two senators—regardless of the state's population or size. Everyone in the state votes for both senators.

Senators are elected to serve terms of six years. Writers of the Constitution intended that these longer terms would give Senators some independence from the short-term pressures of popular opinion. James Madison reasoned that longer terms would provide stability. "If it not be a firm body," he concluded, "the other branch being more numerous, and coming immediately from the people, will overwhelm it."

Rules of Conduct

Both chambers have their own written rules for conducting business. They also have unwritten understandings about how to behave toward one another. Congressional proceedings are governed by:

* The Constitution, Article I.
* Parliamentary procedure.
* The *House Rules and Manual*.
* The *Senate Manual*.
* Precedents or past rulings of the presiding officer that fill in gaps in the written rules.
* Specific laws.

EXAMPLE: The Congressional Budget Act of 1974 sets guidelines for dealing with budget-related laws. The Trade Act of 1974 sets guidelines for laws related to trade agreements, like the North American Free Trade Agreement (NAFTA).

Because of its larger size, the House is more formal and has stricter rules than the Senate. For example, a member of the House is recognized to speak during a debate for a limited period of time, often five minutes or less. Senators may have unlimited debate unless three-fifths of all senators agree to a specific time limit.

House Ethics Rules

House and Senate members must follow certain guidelines for their behavior. These rules deal with issues such as campaign activities, interns, travel, and conflicts of interest. The following excerpt deals with gifts.

The House Gift Rule prohibits acceptance of any gift unless permitted by one of the exceptions stated in the rule. Gifts allowed by the exceptions include:

1. Any gift (other than cash or cash equivalent) valued at <u>less than</u> **$50**; however, the cumulative value of gifts that can be accepted from any one source in a calendar year is <u>less than</u> **$100**.
2. Gifts having a value of <u>less than</u> **$10** do not count against the annual limit.
3. Gifts from relatives, and gifts from other Members or employees.
4. Gifts based on personal friendship (but a gift <u>above</u> **$250** in value may not be accepted unless a written determination is obtained from the Standards Committee).
5. Anything paid for by federal, state, or local government.
6. Members and staff may never solicit a gift, or accept a gift that is linked to any action they have taken or are being asked to take.

The Role of Political Parties

Most members of Congress—and most voting citizens—belong to either the Democratic or Republican party. The particular party that has the largest number of members in a house is the **majority party**. The majority party usually has more power to pass laws and set priorities for a house. The party with the second greatest number of members in a house is the **minority party**.

Organization of Congress

Every two years, all of the members of the House of Representatives and one-third of the senators are elected. When these members meet, it is a new Congress—a new Congress begins every two years. Each Congress is made up of two sessions—one session each year.

EXAMPLE: The Congress elected in 2000 is known as the 107th Congress. Its first session was in 2001, and its second session was in 2002.

In any session of Congress, members consider hundreds of issues and laws. The organization of Congress is important to getting the work of Congress done.

Leadership

While each member of each house has one vote, not all members have the same degree of power. Each chamber has a group of members that act as the leaders. These leaders work to keep the House and Senate focused and in order as they study important national issues and make new laws.

Speaker of the House

The highest officer in the House of Representatives is called the **Speaker of the House**. The Speaker is elected by the members of the House to make sure that the House runs efficiently and smoothly. Usually, the Speaker is a member of the majority party because the members belonging to the majority party have the most votes.

The Speaker's duties are determined by the members of each new House. So the Speaker's power can change from Congress to Congress. More powerful Speakers have been able to:

* Assign legislation to committees for discussion and preparation before it goes to the House for a vote.
* Decide the legislative agenda for a session of the House.
* Decide who can speak on an issue and when.

Leader of the Senate

The Constitution specifies that the vice president of the United States is the presiding officer of the Senate. But the vice president has his own job in the Executive branch. If the vice president is unavailable, the **president pro tempore** (usually abbreviated to president pro tem) presides over the Senate.

Members of the Senate vote to select the president pro tem. In the Senate, the vice president and the president pro tem are mainly symbolic—that is, they have no real

Did You Know?

The Speaker Is Next in Line

The Speaker holds perhaps the most important position in Congress. The Constitution states that if both the President and the Vice President are unable to serve as president—because of death or sickness, for example—the Speaker of the House takes over as president until new presidential elections are held.

power to influence the legislation presented for study, discussion, and vote. The real leader of the Senate is the majority party senate leader.

Floor Leaders and Party Whips

In each chamber of Congress, members of the majority and minority parties have a floor leader and a whip.

Floor leaders act as spokespersons for their parties. They tell House and Senate members the priorities for their party— the kinds of laws and policies the party wants to pass. The floor leader works to persuade members of both parties to vote for specific laws.

The party **whips** assist the floor leaders, communicating with party members. The whips "whip" party members into shape, getting them to line up behind legislation important to their party.

Committees

More than 10,000 **bills**—new pieces of legislation—are introduced to Congress every two years. These bills address every type of issue that affects our nation—and these issues can get pretty complicated. Every member simply can't be an expert in every area.

So, Congress divides itself into committees focused on specific subject areas, such as education, agriculture, or science. These committees have **three** main roles:

1. **They research specific subjects,** holding hearings to get testimony from experts.
2. **They write legislation** related to their specific subject areas.
3. **They decide whether to send legislation to the chamber** for a vote.

Types of Committees

Four types of committees serve in Congress:

1. **Standing Committees.**
2. **Joint Committees.**
3. **Select Committees.**
4. **Conference Committees.**

Committee Membership

Each committee consists of:

* *The Members.* Political parties decide who will represent their party on each committee.
* *A Chairperson.* Chairpersons guide and set the priorities for their committees, so they have a great deal of power over the laws considered and passed by Congress.

American Citizenship

Michael J. Fox—Actor and Congressional Lobbyist

Congressional committees listen to the testimony of many people and groups. Some of these people are experts in their fields. Others have personal experience dealing with an issue. Actor Michael J. Fox was stricken with Parkinson's disease in 1991, at the age of 30. Parkinson's results in the death of certain brain cells. Over time, the patient loses control of his or her ability to move, becomes paralyzed, and dies.

Fox told Congress, "I didn't intend to become a professional witness. I'm not a politician, nor am I a doctor or a research scientist . . . . So what qualified me to be at this table? The answer is simple. I'm one of a million experts on Parkinson's disease in the U.S., battling its destructive nature as we wait for a cure. We need a rescue, and the country should know it."

Kinds of Congressional Committees

Category	Purpose	Example from the 107th Congress (2001–2002)
Standing Committees	Permanent groups set up in each chamber that are responsible for laws in specific areas. Most standing committees are divided into subcommittees, which study even more specialized issues within the committee's subject area.	* House Committee on Foreign Relations, which investigates all aspects of our relationship with foreign nations. * Senate Committee on Agriculture, Nutrition & Forestry, which is responsible for legislation concerning farms and rural communities.
Joint Committees	Permanent committees made up of members of both chambers. These committees investigate issues and make recommendations. They don't draft legislation.	The Joint Committee on Taxation studies the U.S. tax system and tries to find ways to simplify it. It sends its reports to the related standing committees in each chamber.
Select Committees	Committees (temporary or permanent) that are created to study an issue not addressed by a standing committee, or to investigate a particular event.	The Senate Committee on Aging is set up to study the ways to maximize the housing, health, and income of the elderly.
Conference Committees	Committees formed when the two houses can't agree on the details of a bill. When each chamber passes a different version of the same bill, a conference committee works out the differences and comes up with a single, final version. This final draft goes back to both chambers who then vote on the new version.	Each chamber passed a version of the "No Child Left Behind Act of 2001," designed to improve the school performance and opportunities of disadvantaged students. A conference committee met to create one new bill from the two versions. Both houses passed the new version, and the president signed it.

Congressional Staffs

Members of Congress as well as individual committees have groups of people that help them get the work of Congress done. Staff members help by:

* Providing research and education on specific issues.
* Summarizing legislation.
* Writing bills to be introduced to the chamber.

Powers of Congress

The Constitution gives Congress specific powers. Members of Congress rely on the Constitution to tell them the kinds of laws they can and can't pass.

Expressed and Implied Legislative Powers

The powers that authorize Congress to pass certain kinds of laws are listed in Article I, Section 8, of the Constitution, as well as in specific Amendments. The powers are either "expressed"—specifically listed in Article I—or "implied"—not specified, but necessary to carry out the intended action.

Expressed Powers

Expressed powers include:

* Deciding how to raise money by setting taxes and borrowing funds.
* Deciding how to spend this money for the benefit of the nation.

"Who's our representative?"

* Passing laws that regulate commerce—that is, trade—among the states and between the states and foreign nations.
* Declaring war.
* Coining—manufacturing—money.
* Regulating the process of becoming a citizen.
* Establishing a system of delivering mail.
* Creating the federal courts below the Supreme Court.
* Creating and maintaining the armed forces. (Congress creates them, but the President oversees them).

Implied Powers

Implied powers are the powers the Constitution gives to Congress that are not listed in detail. The Constitution gives Congress the power "to make all laws which shall be necessary and proper for carrying into execution the foregoing powers, and all other powers vested by this Constitution in the government of the United States or in any department or officer thereof."

This part of the Section 8 list is called the **Elastic Clause**. Elastic—like the waistband of your pants—can expand to give you more room if you need it. Similarly, the Elastic Clause in the Constitution expands the powers of Congress so that Congress can carry out its duties.

EXAMPLE: Congress has the specific power to collect taxes. Members of Congress can't literally go out and collect taxes. They have to create a system that does the collecting—the Internal Revenue Service—and they have to decide how much to collect.

Nonlegislative and Special Powers

In addition to writing laws, Congress has responsibilities mostly related to placing checks and balances on the power of the other two branches of the U.S. government. Some duties are committed to only one of the chambers, and some are committed to both.

Powers Shared by the Houses

Both houses have the power to:

* Investigate issues and events by calling witnesses and holding hearings.
* Propose amendments to the Constitution, which each house must pass by a vote of two-thirds of its members.

Unique Powers of the House of Representatives

The House of Representatives has the power to:

* Originate most bills that raise money for the government.
* Impeach, or formally accuse of wrong-doing, government officials—most importantly, the president.
* Choose the president if there is no majority in the Electoral College.

Unique Powers of the Senate

The Senate has the power to:

* Approve treaties by a two-thirds vote.
* Approve major presidential appointments.
* Conduct the trial when the House impeaches an official.

Limits on Power

The Constitution lists specific things that Congress can't do. Congress can't pass the following types of laws:

* **Ex Post Facto Laws**—laws that make an act illegal, then allow the government to punish those who committed the act *before* it was made illegal.
* **Bills of Attainder**—laws that provide for the punishment of specific people or a specific group of people—via jail or fine, for example—without a judicial trial.
* **Writ of Habeas Corpus**—an order that a prisoner be brought before a judge. If you're held in jail without being charged with a crime, this writ orders police to bring you before a court. The court then decides if the police have enough evidence of guilt to keep you in jail. If not, you're released. Congress can't take away the right to this writ except during periods of civil war or invasion.

The Constitution also prevents Congress from:

* Taxing exports.
* Giving titles of nobility. Nobility is the state of being recognized as special because of birth, such as that of knights or dukes.
* Treating individual states or groups of states differently to show favoritism.

Passing a Bill

The congressional lawmaking process is complicated. A bill must pass through a series of steps before it reaches a vote on the House and Senate floors. At any one of these steps, a bill can be delayed, defeated, or amended (changed). Most bills that are introduced do not survive this process and never become law.

How a Bill Becomes a Law

Most bills can be introduced in either the House or Senate. Regardless of where the bill is introduced, the process of approval is the same. The flow chart below shows what happens to a bill introduced in the House.

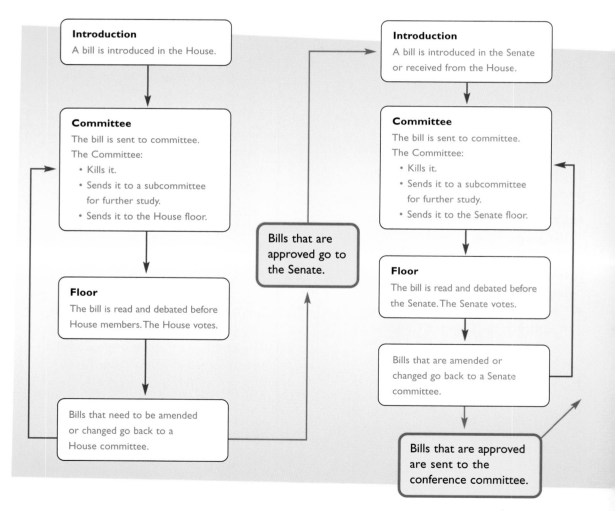

Introduction
A bill is introduced in the House.

Committee
The bill is sent to committee.
The Committee:
- Kills it.
- Sends it to a subcommittee for further study.
- Sends it to the House floor.

Floor
The bill is read and debated before House members. The House votes.

Bills that need to be amended or changed go back to a House committee.

Bills that are approved go to the Senate.

Introduction
A bill is introduced in the Senate or received from the House.

Committee
The bill is sent to committee.
The Committee:
- Kills it.
- Sends it to a subcommittee for further study.
- Sends it to the Senate floor.

Floor
The bill is read and debated before the Senate. The Senate votes.

Bills that are amended or changed go back to a Senate committee.

Bills that are approved are sent to the conference committee.

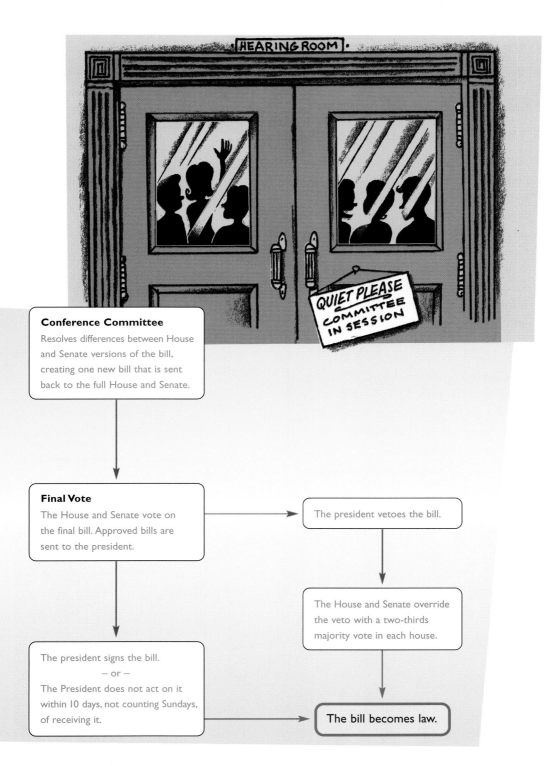

HEARING ROOM

QUIET PLEASE
COMMITTEE
IN SESSION

Conference Committee
Resolves differences between House and Senate versions of the bill, creating one new bill that is sent back to the full House and Senate.

Final Vote
The House and Senate vote on the final bill. Approved bills are sent to the president.

The president vetoes the bill.

The House and Senate override the veto with a two-thirds majority vote in each house.

The president signs the bill.
— or —
The President does not act on it within 10 days, not counting Sundays, of receiving it.

The bill becomes law.

The President as Legislator

At times, a proposal for legislation comes from the president or is announced formally by him—in a State of the Union speech, for example, or in a press conference. The U.S. Constitution in Article II, Section 3, states that the president "shall from time to time give to the Congress information of the State of the Union, and recommend to their Consideration such Measures as he shall judge necessary and expedient . . . ." The president cannot introduce a bill in Congress. The president can only recommend and persuade members of his party in Congress to introduce the legislation he desires.

Introducing a Bill

Bills can be written by anyone—a group of private lawyers or scientists or a teacher's association, for example. But only members of Congress can present bills to their chamber for formal consideration. Any member of Congress can introduce a bill. Once a bill is received by a chamber, the chamber refers it to a committee.

How Committees Work

After the committee receives a bill, the members usually study it. The committee members can decide to:

* Make no changes.
* Rewrite the bill.
* Simply ignore the bill, which "kills" the bill's chance of ever becoming law.

Senate Foreign Relations Committee holds hearings in 1968 on the conduct of the Vietnam War.

Often a committee refers the bill for study to a subcommittee. The subcommittee itself can then leave the bill as it is, rewrite it, or kill it. If a subcommittee recommends the bill, it sends the bill back to the committee with a report on its findings explaining why the legislation is good. Back with the full committee, the bill can be restudied, changed, or killed yet again.

If a bill makes it through the hurdles of committees and subcommittees, it is sent to the full chamber for approval.

The President's Role

When both chambers approve the same version, the bill goes to the president to be signed. When a bill goes to the president, he or she may choose to:

* Sign it into law.
* Veto—or reject—the bill.

Congress can override—or set aside—the President's veto and pass the bill anyway. In order to override a presidential veto, two-thirds of the members of each chamber must vote to pass it.

Chapter 6 Wrap-up
THE LEGISLATIVE BRANCH

The Congress of the United States is the legislative, or lawmaking, branch of the federal government. Congress consists of two chambers or houses—the House of Representatives and the Senate. In order for a bill to become a law, a majority of congressional members in both houses must approve it.

Members of the House serve two-year terms and represent geographical districts of about 600,000 people each in their states. The number of Representatives given to a state is determined by the state's population. Senators serve six-year terms and are elected to represent their entire state. Each state elects two senators.

Key leaders in Congress include the Speaker of the House, the vice president and president pro tempore (who preside over the Senate), floor leaders, and party whips. Much of the work of Congress is done in committees. Committees study and revise bills and decide whether to recommend them to the full House or Senate for debate and a vote.

Congress has specific legislative powers given by the Constitution, as well as implied powers. Some of these powers include raising and spending money, declaring war, making money, regulating trade, creating federal courts, and creating and maintaining the armed forces. Congress also has nonlegislative powers that are designed to maintain the system of checks and balances among the branches of government.

bicameral—composed of two legislative chambers. The U.S. Congress is bicameral. Its two parts are the House of Representatives and the Senate. *p. 88*

bill—proposed law presented for approval to a legislative body. *p. 94*

bill of attainder—legislative act making a person guilty of a crime without trial. Such acts are prohibited by the U.S. Constitution. *p. 97*

conference committee—group of House or Senate members who work to reconcile different versions of the same bill passed by the House and Senate. *p. 95*

Congressional district—area within a state representing about 600,000 people. Each member of the House of Representatives represents the people in one district. *p. 90*

Elastic Clause—part of Article I, Section 8, of the Constitution that gives Congress the power to make laws necessary for carrying out its duties. *p. 96*

***ex post facto* law**—law that affects an act done in the past, effectively allowing the government to punish a person for committing an act before the act was illegal. Such laws are prohibited by the U.S. Constitution. *p. 97*

floor leader—member of the House or Senate chosen by fellow party members to be in charge of some of the party's activities in the legislature. *p. 93*

joint committee—permanent group of House and Senate members who investigate issues related to legislation; they have no power to draft legislation. *p. 95*

legislation—proposed or enacted law or group of laws. *p. 88*

majority party—political party with the greatest number of members in a legislature. *p. 92*

minority party—political party with the second greatest number of members in a legislature. *p. 92*

president pro tempore—senator who presides over the U.S. Senate in the absence of the vice president. *p. 93*

select committee—group of House and Senate members formed to study an issue not addressed by a standing committee or to investigate a particular event. *p. 95*

Speaker of the House—member of the majority party elected to lead the U.S. House of Representatives. *p. 94*

standing committee—permanent group of House and Senate members responsible for laws in a specific subject area. *p. 95*

whip—member of a legislative body who helps the party leader by encouraging party members' loyalty and support. *p. 93*

writ of *habeas corpus*—written order that a prisoner be brought before a judge. It ensures that a person is not held in jail without being charged with a crime. Congress cannot take away the right to a writ except in times of invasion or civil war. *p. 97*

CHAPTER 7

The Executive Branch

In this chapter, you will learn about:

- **how to become president or vice president of the United States**
- **what powers the president has**
- **how the executive branch is organized**

Alben Barkley was vice president under former President Harry Truman. Barkley enjoyed telling a joke about a woman who had two sons. One of the sons became a sailor and went away to sea. The other became vice president. Neither was ever heard from again!

Is the vice president's job really that unimportant? What roles do the president and the vice president play in the government?

The president and vice president, with their advisors, lead a large and complicated organization called the "executive branch" that carries out the laws passed and explained by other branches of the government. Nearly three million people work in several hundred government departments and agencies of the executive branch. They help to arrange trade with other nations, improve the transportation of people and goods, protect our natural resources, and develop new technologies to help agriculture, energy, and public health.

The Executive Branch   103

Function of the Executive Branch

Article II of the Constitution begins with the words, "The executive power shall be vested in a President of the United States." As chief executive, the president **executes**— carries out—the laws of the land. He does not do it alone.

The executive branch of the government is made up of all the people, agencies, and organizations that help the president carry out the laws. These people are part of a permanent federal **bureaucracy**—a large and complex, hierarchical organization.

* Bureaucracies resemble a pyramid. In the federal bureaucracy, the president is at the top, senior managers and advisors are in the middle, and the millions of people who work in the many offices of the branch are at the base.
* People who work in a bureaucracy— **bureaucrats**—have specific duties.
* Bureaucracies have rules. People working in them follow regulations and procedures so they can provide the same service, the same way, everywhere.

EXAMPLE: The U.S. Postal Service is a part of the federal bureaucracy. The Postmaster General of the United States makes general regulations for all post offices and mail delivery. The Postmaster at your local post office is in charge of all the people who work in that post office and deliver your mail. Your mail carrier delivers mail to homes and businesses using the same rules and procedures as mail carriers all over the United States.

The president appoints the top-level managers in bureaucracies. They serve only for a period of time, usually the president's own term of office. All other workers in many government agencies and departments are regular employees. They are hired, not appointed, and they can continue in their jobs, regardless of who is president. This gives the government stability. Imagine what it would be like if three million people changed jobs every time a new president was elected.

Did You Know?

The Presidency

When George W. Bush became the 43rd president in 2001, only 42 different men had served as president. How could this be? Grover Cleveland was elected for two terms, but they were not in a row. He was the 22nd and 24th president.

Twenty-four presidents have been members of Congress. William Howard Taft was appointed to the Supreme Court nine years after he left the presidency.

Eight presidents have died in office. Only one president, Richard Nixon, has ever resigned. The youngest elected president was John F. Kennedy, who was 43 years old. The oldest was Ronald Reagan, who was elected at age 77.

The President and Vice President

The two highest-ranking positions in the U.S. government carry with them very different roles and responsibilities. The president is elected to be the chief executive of the country. His authority and responsibilities are vast. The vice president's role is likewise very important, but the demands of the office are not as great.

The President

The most important job in the executive branch is that of the president. Many Americans think the presidency is also the most important job in the country.

Qualifications

Could you become president? According to the Constitution, the person *elected* president must meet **three** formal qualifications:

1. **Citizenship.** The president must be a "natural born citizen" of the United States or, since the first few presidents weren't born as citizens, "a citizen of the United States at the time of the adoption of [the] Constitution."

2. **Age.** The president must be at least 35 years old. The youngest *elected* president was John F. Kennedy, who took office at the age of 43. Vice President Theodore Roosevelt took office at the age of 42 when President McKinley was assassinated in 1901.

3. **Residency.** The president must be a resident of the United States for at least 14 years, *any* 14 years of a person's life.

There are also *informal* qualifications that limit who can be elected. For example, it is unlikely that any political party would ever nominate for president someone who couldn't read or write.

Salary

On January 1, 2001, the job of President of the United States got a pay raise! Congress had voted to double the presidential salary from $200,000 per year to $400,000 per year, including a $50,000 expense allowance.

Benefits

In addition to salary, the president receives many other benefits. Some of these help to ensure his safety. The president receives:

* **Transportation** on the president's private jet—Air Force One.
* **Secret Service protection** for the president and his wife while he is in office, and for 14 years after they leave office. Agents also protect the president's children during his term of office and then until they reach the age of 16.
* **Free housing** in the White House.
* **Pension.** After retirement, a former president receives a **pension**—a retirement income or allowance. Every former president's wife also receives $20,000 per year.

Election

Do you think the person who gets the most overall votes in a presidential election automatically becomes president? That usually happens, but it isn't the law. The president is actually indirectly elected, by the **Electoral College**—a group of people chosen in each state and the District of Columbia, who then confirm their state's voters' choices for both the president and the vice president. Every state has a certain number of electoral votes based on the size of its population. Typically, all electoral votes from each state, except Maine and Nebraska, go to the candidates who get the most popular votes—even if those candidates win by only a few votes or lack a clear majority of votes. Electors almost always vote for the candidate they are pledged to their party to support, but nothing in the Constitution requires them to do so.

Many experts think the Electoral College system should be changed. Some people think that voters should directly elect the president and vice president.

▲
Electoral College delegate Illinois state senator Jim DeLeo casts his ballot in the 2000 presidential election.

Did You Know?

The Electoral College

The founders couldn't decide whether the president should be directly elected by the people or chosen by state legislatures or the legislative branch. They compromised and set up the Electoral College, whose members, called electors, were originally appointed by state legislatures. The electors voted for the persons they believed would be the best president and vice president. Their choices did not have to be the candidates who received the most overall votes from their state's or the country's voters. By the late 1820s, members of the Electoral College were appointed by their parties, and they promised to vote for their own party's candidates. The 12th Amendment mandated that electors vote separately for the president and vice president.

Term and Term Limit

The term of the presidency is four years. The founders thought that this was:

* Enough time for a president to gain experience, show his abilities, and make policies that would last.
* As long as a president should be in power without being re-elected by the voters.

Originally, there was no limit to the number of times a president could be re-elected. After Franklin D. Roosevelt was elected to a fourth term, the 22nd Amendment limited the presidency to two terms or ten years at most, if a president succeeded another president mid-term. From the time of the Revolution, Americans wanted to make sure that they would never have a ruler who became a monarch, or a ruler for life.

Primary Source

Presidents and Kings

In 1788, Alexander Hamilton wrote a letter to the people of New York. It is part of a series of documents called the *Federalist Papers*. In the letter, Hamilton describes the difference between the president and a king.

1. *The President "is to be elected for FOUR years; and is to be re-eligible as often as the people of the United States shall think him worthy of their confidence. In these circumstances there is a total dissimilitude* [difference] *between HIM and a king of Great Britain, who is an HEREDITARY monarch."* [Hereditary monarchs are born into royal families and inherit the job of king or queen, usually for life.]

2. *The President of the United States would be liable to be impeached* [charged with crimes], *tried, and, upon conviction of treason, bribery, or other high crimes or misdemeanors* [illegal acts], *removed from office; and would afterwards be liable to prosecution and punishment in the ordinary course of law. The person of the king of Great Britain is sacred . . . ; there is no constitutional* [court] *to which he* [answers].

The Federalist Papers, No. 69, March 14, 1788—"The Real Character of the Executive"

The Vice President

Some of the founders did not think the country needed a vice president. The Constitution gives executive power only to the president, but it does mention a vice presidential role. The job of vice president now has **two** main duties:

1. **Replace** the president if he dies or becomes disabled.
2. **Preside,** or officiate, over the Senate. The vice president does not vote in the Senate unless there is a tie vote.

People have said that the vice president is "a heartbeat away from the presidency." Eight presidents have died in office and one, Richard Nixon, resigned. Therefore, nine vice presidents have had to take over the job of president. Some vice presidents have later run for president.

Qualifications

The qualifications for vice president are the same as those for president.

Salary and Benefits

In January 2001, the salary of the vice president was raised to $186,300 per year. The vice president and his or her family are provided with a home in Washington, D.C., and also receive Secret Service protection and transportation benefits while in office.

Election and Term

Today, candidates for president and vice president run as a ticket, or together, as a team from the same political party. The vice presidential term is four years, the same as the president.

Presidential Succession

Presidential succession is the plan for what happens if the President dies or can't perform the duties of his office. If the president can't perform his duties, then the vice president takes over until the next election. If the president is temporarily ill or disabled:

* Formal notice is given to Congress.
* The vice president fills in for him.
* The president takes back his job when he recovers.

EXAMPLE: In 2002, just before he underwent a medical procedure that required anesthesia, President George W. Bush transferred power to his vice president, Dick Cheney. President Bush reclaimed the presidential powers after he awoke, nearly two hours later.

If a disaster took the life of *both* the president and vice president, then Congress would choose a successor. Currently, that chain of succession for Congress to follow would be in this order:

1. **The Speaker of the House of Representatives.**
2. **The President *pro tempore* of the Senate,** the person who leads the Senate when the vice president isn't there.
3. **The Secretary of State.**
4. **The rest of the Cabinet members,** in the order in which their cabinet posts were created. (See pages 117–119.)

Powers and Roles of the President

The Constitution gives the presidency the power to execute the law, but it lists only a very few specific powers. According to the Constitution, the president may:

* **Veto** or reject, bills passed by Congress.
* **Command** the military forces of the country.
* **Make** treaties.
* **Grant pardons**—legal forgiveness for crimes. A pardon prevents or ends punishment.
* **Enforce** the laws.
* **Appoint** certain officials.

The Constitution doesn't state that the president has the power, for example, to make a budget or give orders to department heads. The founders knew that they couldn't identify every power that future presidents might need to do their jobs, so they deliberately left open the opportunity for extra presidential authority. But they also set up ways to stop presidents from becoming too powerful.

Presidential Power	Factors
Executive powers—power to run the federal bureaucracy, to direct the actions of cabinet members, approve or disapprove department or agency regulations, and hire and fire key administrators.	The president is only one person. He can make decisions quickly and easily, with the input of advisors. Congress is made up of two groups with more than 500 individuals, too many to make day-to-day operational decisions efficiently.
Emergency powers—power to make decisions during times of war, rebellion, crisis, or threat of terrorism.	Only Congress has the power to declare war, but presidents have used the military to stop riots, act against pirates who threatened U.S. shipping, and order bombing raids after terrorist attacks.
Budgetary powers—power to create a budget for the federal bureaucracy that is presented to Congress for approval or disapproval.	At one time, individual departments of the executive branch had to ask Congress for the money they needed to carry out their work. Beginning in 1921, presidents have always prepared an annual budget for the entire federal bureaucracy.
Policy-making powers—Congress has voluntarily given to the executive branch powers to add details to the general laws passed by Congress. In this way, the president can set goals for the nation and decide how to carry them out.	As society becomes more complex, Congress has less time to consider fully laws governing everything from transportation to immigration, and welfare to education. Congress lets the executive branch work out the details to carry out the laws that it has passed.

Presidential Powers

Different presidents have had different ideas about what powers the presidency, or the office of the president, needs. Congress has not always agreed about what presidents have the power to do, but modern presidents have many more powers than George Washington, John Adams, or Thomas Jefferson did.

You Decide

Right of the President to Grant Pardons

According to the Constitution, the president has the power to grant pardons. Presidents can issue pardons only for crimes against the federal government, not those against state or local governments. **Amnesty** is a pardon given to a group of people who break the law.

Some people have questioned how presidents have used pardons. They have suggested that this right should be taken away.

Do you think the power to grant pardons and amnesty should be stopped altogether, given to Congress or the courts, or left with the president?

Arguments <u>for</u> Presidential Pardons

Pardons can undo past wrongs, correct injustices, and put an end to bitter disagreements so officials can focus on more important issues. For example, many citizens disagreed with America's role in Vietnam. Some broke the draft laws and did not perform their duty to fight for their country. However, by later giving amnesty to those who had opposed the war by resisting the draft, President Carter helped unify the country.

- -

The president usually only accepts or rejects recommendations for pardons made by his advisors. He rarely uses the power to protect his friends.

Arguments <u>against</u> Presidential Pardons

Presidents have pardoned people who were their friends, or who contributed to their election funds. Some presidents have been accused of trying to misuse pardons. President Clinton pardoned 177 people when he left office. Some critics thought this was a misuse of presidential power.

- -

The president should not be able to overrule the due process of law and the courts' sentences.

United States v. Nixon (1974)

The offices of the Democratic National Committee in the Watergate Building in Washington, D.C., were broken into and searched in 1972. A Senate committee ordered President Nixon to turn over tapes of conversations held in his office, which investigators believed contained evidence about the case. President Nixon used the executive privilege argument and refused. He claimed that the tapes contained private and confidential government information that would be dangerous to America if it was made public.

The Supreme Court, however, ruled that neither executive privilege nor separation of powers protected a president against a request for evidence from a judge. President Nixon had to give up the tapes to a federal court.

The tapes provided evidence against some of President Nixon's assistants who were accused of the break-in. When people heard the tapes, it was also clear that President Nixon himself knew about the break-in. He resigned and was later pardoned by President Gerald Ford before the case came to trial.

Executive Privilege

At times throughout the nation's history, presidents have claimed **executive privilege**. This means that they don't have to tell Congress everything they know (or turn over information) about matters they consider "top secret" or private. Presidents have claimed this privilege about military and diplomatic actions, arguing that national security and the safety of the country required them to keep some things secret.

EXAMPLE: In 1834, Andrew Jackson refused to give the Senate records of conversations he had with his Cabinet members. He said Congress had no constitutional right to be part of his private discussions with his advisors.

Executive privilege doesn't apply if a court requests evidence in an investigation or trial. Even a president must obey a court's request.

"I don't think you can blame the executive branch for this mistake. After all, you <u>are</u> the president."

Checks on Power

Presidents have tried to add new powers to the presidency. Congress or the Supreme Court, however, can stop the office of the president from becoming too powerful.

Congress can do this in **four** ways by:

1. **Approving or rejecting** programs or laws that the president recommends.

2. **Enacting a law** that the president has vetoed by a two-thirds vote of both houses.

3. **Setting guidelines** for how the president and the executive branch can implement policies.

4. **Creating or eliminating departments** that the executive branch runs.

Another way that Congress controls presidential authority is through approving the people the president appoints. The Senate must approve the following:

* *Heads of the Cabinet departments* such as education, labor, transportation, and the Attorney General.
* *Ambassadors*—people who represent the U.S. government in foreign countries.
* *Heads of government agencies,* such as the Environmental Protection Agency and NASA.
* *Federal judges and attorneys,* and U.S. marshals.
* *Officers in the military.*

The Supreme Court can check the actions of the president by:

* *Interpreting* the Constitution regarding powers and duties of all officials, including the president.
* *Overruling* any action by the president that the court decides is unconstitutional.

Presidential Roles

Unlike some jobs, the president's duties and responsibilities are not easy to describe.

Chief of State

The president speaks for the country, explains the goals and values of the people, and represents a symbol and ideal. When he acts in this role, the president represents all political parties and all Americans by:

* *Congratulating heroes* on their accomplishments and awarding medals for heroism or achievement.
* *Greeting important visitors* to the White House.
* *Making speeches* or informing the American people about important events.

Chief Executive

The president acts as the "boss" of the executive branch of government. In "executing the laws," the president decides how laws are carried out by:

* *Appointing high-level officials* to manage government departments.
* *Discussing national issues* with top advisors and officials and choosing the direction the government will take in addressing issues. Some presidents have been content to accept the recommendations of their advisors. Others have been very "hands on," making day-to-day decisions, especially in times of national crisis.

Chief Diplomat

The president is the most important representative of the United States to other countries. The Supreme Court has agreed that power over foreign policy belongs to the president and Congress. The president makes **foreign policy**—deciding how America will deal with other nations—and designs treaties, but only Congress can set aside money for specific foreign policies. The Senate has the power to approve treaties. Other duties of the president include:

* *Appointing* diplomats and ambassadors to other countries.
* *Entertaining and communicating* with foreign leaders.

▲
President George W. Bush and the Saudi Arabian Foreign Minister discuss security issues in November 2001.

Chief Policy Maker

Although Congress makes the laws, presidents influence legislation by:

* *Making recommendations to Congress.*
* *Persuading members of Congress* to support his policies.
* *Signing or vetoing* bills sent to him by Congress.
* *Reporting to Congress each January* in the State of the Union address, explaining how the U.S. is dealing with issues such as education, foreign policy, the economy, and the environment.

Commander-in-Chief

The president is Commander-in-Chief of the military forces of the United States— the Army, Navy, Air Force, Marines, and National Guard. Top military leaders, such as generals and admirals, take their orders from the president. Some duties of the role include:

* *Inspecting* military bases or navy shipyards.
* *Making major military decisions* in wartime.
* *Calling out troops* or the National Guard to stop riots, to keep the peace, to help deal with natural disasters such as forest fires, or to help protect the security of airports in this country.

Chief of Party

Since the beginning of the two-party system, the president has been the unofficial head of his party. He uses his power and popularity to help other members of his party achieve party goals or get elected by:

* *Choosing leading members* of his party to serve in high government positions or as advisors.
* *Traveling around the country* to campaign for party candidates in local and state elections.
* *Helping to raise money* for the party by speaking at fund-raising activities.

Chief Guardian of the Economy

Presidents watch over the country's economy and deal with issues such as unemployment, high prices, taxes, and the way business is done. Presidents don't control the economy, but they can influence consumers or businesses by:

* *Discussing with advisors* ways to encourage consumer spending, such as asking Congress to lower taxes.
* *Meeting with business and labor leaders* to help them solve problems that could lead to a strike or slowdown in production.
* *Encouraging Congress to give tax breaks* to certain businesses to be sure they survive difficult times.

Judicial Leader

Presidents can influence the interpretation of the Constitution. They do this through people they nominate to be Supreme Court Justices and other federal judges. Congress must approve their appointments.

Organization of the Executive Branch

The president heads a branch of the government with more than three million employees. The diagram shows how the Executive Branch is organized.

Executive
Departments

The Executive Office of the President

White House Office
Office of Management and the Budget
Council of Economic Advisors

National Security Council
Office of National Drug Control Policy
Office of Administration

Office of the United States Trade Representative
Council on Environment Quality

Office of Science and Technology Policy

Cabinet

The President
The Vice President

Major Independent Agencies and Commissions

There are more than 200 independent groups in the executive branch, including:

AMTRAK
Bureau of Alcohol, Tobacco, and Firearms
Bureau of Engraving and Printing
Bureau of the Census
Central Intelligence Agency (CIA)
Commission on Civil Rights
Drug Enforcement Administration
Environmental Protection Agency
Equal Employment Opportunity Commission
Federal Aviation Administration
Federal Bureau of Investigation (FBI)
Federal Communications Commission
Federal Energy Regulatory Commission
Federal Highway Administration
Federal Reserve System
Food and Drug Administration
General Accounting Office
Health Care Financing Administration

Immigration and Naturalization Services
Institute of Museum and Library Services
Internal Revenue Service
Medicare Payment Advisory Commission
National Aeronautics and Space
    Administration (NASA)
National Archives and Records Administration (NARA)
National Endowment for the Arts
National Institutes of Health
National Transportation Safety Board
Occupational Standards and Health
    Administration (OSHA)
Peace Corps
Small Business Administration
Social Security Administration
U.S. Customs Service
U.S. Fish and Wildlife Service
U.S. Postal Service

Executive Office of the President

The Executive Office is made up of people who advise the president on domestic—within the United States—and foreign policy.

White House Office

The White House Office includes the president's legal adviser, press secretary, appointments secretary, and office workers. The Chief of Staff directs the White House Office and works with Congress to help ensure that lawmakers consider the president's ideas.

National Security Council (NSC)

The NSC advises on domestic, foreign, and military policies that affect the nation's security. Members include the:

* President.
* Vice President.
* The president's National Security Advisor.
* Secretary of the Treasury
* Secretary of Defense.
* Secretary of State.
* Assistant to the President for National Security Affairs.
* Director of the Central Intelligence Agency (CIA).
* Chairman of the Joint Chiefs of Staff, the top military leader.

Council of Economic Advisors (CEA)

Members of the CEA advise the president on economic policy. The CEA predicts trends in the economy.

Office of Management and the Budget (OMB)

The OMB helps the president prepare and then manage the federal budget that Congress approves each year.

Other Executive Office groups advise the president on drug control, foreign trade, the environment, science and technology, and general administration issues.

Executive Departments

The 15 executive departments do the major work of running the government. Each department helps the president in one or more of his roles.

EXAMPLE: The Department of State handles diplomatic relations with other countries. It advises the president on foreign policy and then makes sure that the policy is carried out.

Leadership

Heads of the executive departments are appointed by the president, usually based on their experience and leadership ability. They must be approved by the Senate. Most are called Secretaries, such as the Secretary of State. The head of the Justice Department is called the Attorney General.

Cabinet

The president's **Cabinet** is an important group of policy advisors—experts who make suggestions about how to run the government and what actions to take. The Cabinet includes the heads of the executive departments and other advisors the president may choose.

In alphabetical order, the **fifteen** executive departments are:

1. **The Department of Agriculture (established in 1862)** helps farmers and farming groups by doing agricultural research, offering financial support to farms, inspecting food processing plants, and enforcing food safety standards.

2. **The Department of Commerce (1903)** promotes the growth of business in the nation by developing trade with nations around the world, providing businesses with technical and scientific information, and sharing information about the population through the Bureau of the Census.

3. **The Department of Defense, or DOD, (1789)** was originally called the War Department. It was reorganized in 1947 to manage the military forces needed to prevent war and protect the security of the United States. The DOD also develops new weapons and defense systems.

4. **Department of Education (1953,** as part of Health, Education, and Welfare**)** provides money and services to state and local agencies responsible for education, such as state universities, public high schools, and elementary schools, for Head Start (a program for young children in need), and for other educational programs.

5. **Department of Energy, or DOE, (1977)** was formed when foreign oil-producing countries limited the amount of oil sold to the United States during the 1970s.

American Citizenship

A Visit to the Nation's Capital

Many people have enjoyed a visit to Washington, D.C. They visit the Capitol Building to see where our laws are made. They tour the White House, the home of every president except George Washington. They climb the 555-foot Washington Monument for a fantastic view of the city. At the Smithsonian Institution, they see precious objects of history, from the flag that inspired the *Star Spangled Banner* to moon rocks returned to Earth by the astronauts of Apollo 11. A visit to Washington is a never-to-be-forgotten experience.

Its goals include managing the energy resources of the United States, developing new sources of energy, such as wind, solar, and nuclear power, and safeguarding the nation's nuclear power plants and weapons.

6. **Department of Health and Human Services (1979)** contains several familiar agencies. Medicare helps older citizens pay for medical care and hospitalization. The Food and Drug Administration tests and approves food products and new drugs. The Public Health Service offers medical services and advice to the poor, and provides vaccination shots and medical tests to the public.

7. **Department of Homeland Security (2002)** was set up in response to the terrorist attack of September 11, 2001. Its mission is to work to prevent terrorist attacks within the United States, reduce America's vulnerability to terrorism, and minimize the damage and recover from attacks that do occur. The U.S. Coast Guard and the Office of Immigration, among other government offices, were moved into it.

8. **Department of Housing and Urban Development, or HUD, (1965)** helps to ensure that less wealthy Americans have decent, safe places to live. It also provides inexpensive loans to low-income families and supports people trying to fix up houses in poor neighborhoods.

9. **Department of the Interior (1849)** manages the natural resources of the United States, including waterways, forests, minerals, fish, and wildlife. Several important agencies include The U.S. Fish and Wildlife Service, The Bureau of Mines, The National Park Service, and The Bureau of Indian Affairs, which addresses Native American issues and supervises reservations.

10. **The Department of Justice, or DOJ, (1870)** represents the United States in court, for example, in government investigations of unfair business practices. It also enforces federal laws and supervises federal prisons. Agencies within the DOJ include the Federal Bureau of Investigation (FBI), U.S. Marshal's Service, and Drug Enforcement Administration (DEA).

11. **The Department of Labor (1903)** works to create a safe working environment, to encourage opportunities for working people, and to develop good relations between employers and employees. One of its agencies, the Occupational Standards and Health Administration (OSHA), makes and enforces rules for safety in the workplace.

12. **The Department of State (1789)** was one of the original executive departments. Its role is to carry out the foreign policy of the United States. This is done through **diplomats**, who work with leaders of other nations and ambassadors who represent the United States in foreign countries. The Secretary of State often meets with foreign leaders to discuss issues and to help settle international disputes. The State Department also represents the United States in the United Nations.

13. **Department of Transportation, or DOT, (1966)** has as its mission ensuring fast, safe, efficient, and convenient transportation for people and goods. Its agencies include the Federal Aviation Administration, which safeguards air travel through regulations about how aircraft must be built and flown, how airports are run, and how pilots are trained; the Federal Railroad Administration; and the Federal Highway Administration, which helps build and improve many of the nation's roads and bridges.

14. **Department of the Treasury (1789)** is in charge of the nation's money. The Internal Revenue Service collects taxes. The U.S. Customs Service collects **duties** on goods entering the country, and works to prevent smuggling. The Bureau of Engraving and Printing makes the country's paper money and coins. The Secret Service, which protects the president, vice president, and visiting foreign leaders, is part of the Treasury Department.

15. **Department of Veterans Affairs, or VA, (1989)** is concerned with the health and welfare of the millions of men and women who have served in the country's military forces. It manages about 170 hospitals and 400 outpatient clinics for veterans.

Independent Agencies

As you saw on page 115, many independent agencies carry out the work of running the government. There are **three** types of independent agencies:

1. **Executive Agencies.** Executive agencies are created by Congress but are under the direct control of the president, who appoints their directors. Among the most important executive agencies are the:
   * National Aeronautics and Space Administration (NASA).
   * Environmental Protection Agency (EPA).
   * Civil Rights Commission.
   * Peace Corps.

2. **Independent Regulatory Commissions.** Congress gives regulatory commissions their powers, and these agencies are mostly not under of the president's direction and control. Regulatory **commissions** are appointed or official groups of **regulators**, who control aspects of government policy through rules and regulations. They set and enforce rules and rates for important parts of the nation's economy, such as:
   * Controlling the money supply.
   * **Licensing**, or providing permits for, interstate trucks and shipping.
   * Making rules about the use of nuclear materials.
   * Setting rates for gas, oil, and electricity.

3. **Government Corporations.** Congress has set up these organizations to provide important public services that might be too expensive for private companies to provide but that the nation needs. One of the most familiar government corporations is the U.S. Postal Service.

Did You Know?

U.S. Postal Service

In the year 2000, the U.S. Postal Service delivered nearly 208 billion pieces of mail to more than 136 million delivery addresses. The Postal Service employs more than 800,000 people.

The Federal Bureaucracy

Americans often complain about the size of the government bureaucracy, but few are willing to give up the services provided. In addition, the federal bureaucracy provides jobs to nearly three million people. Cutting the size of the bureaucracy would force many to find jobs in the **private sector**— the business world outside the government.

Civil Service System

Civil service refers to the people who work for the government. About 10 percent of all American bureaucrats live in the Washington area. The other 90 percent work in regional, state, and local offices around the country. In the early days of our country, these jobs were given to the friends of elected officials. Today's Civil Service System tries to avoid this by making sure that:

* Applicants for federal jobs take exams to see who is best qualified.
* Civil servants can't be fired because of their political opinions.
* Civil servants are promoted based on evaluations by their superiors instead of who their political friends are.

The system isn't perfect, but the government has tried to make the selection and promotion of government workers as fair as possible.

Chapter 7 Wrap-up
THE EXECUTIVE BRANCH

The executive branch of the government, led by the president and vice president, carries out the laws made by Congress. Because American society is so complex, there are hundreds of different offices, departments, and agencies involved in this process.

The Executive Office consists of the President's closest advisors. The president's Cabinet is made up of the Secretaries of 15 executive departments. Several hundred independent agencies—executive agencies, regulatory commissions, and government corporations—carry out the day-to-day jobs of keeping a nation as large and complex as the United States running smoothly.

ambassadors—person who represents the U.S. government in a foreign country. *p. 112*

amnesty—pardon given to a group of people who break the law. *p. 110*

bureaucracy—large, complex, hierarchical organization. *p. 104*

bureaucrats—people who work as part of a bureaucracy. *p. 104*

Cabinet—group of top advisors to the president. It includes the heads of the executive departments and other officers the president may choose. *p. 116*

civil service—all of the people working within the bureaucracy of the government. *p. 120*

commission—appointed or official group formed for a specific purpose. *p. 119*

diplomat—person who works with leaders of other nations to carry out U.S. foreign policy. *p. 118*

duties—taxes on goods entering the country. *p. 119*

Electoral College—group of people chosen from each state and the District of Columbia to elect the president and vice president. *p. 106*

execute—to carry out or enforce. *p. 104*

executive privilege—right of a president to keep information secret from Congress in order to protect the nation's security. *p. 111*

foreign policy—plan for how the United States will deal with foreign countries. *p. 113*

licensing—providing permits for an activity such as interstate transportation. *p. 119*

pardon—to give legal forgiveness for a crime and thus prevent or end punishment. *p. 109*

pension—retirement income or allowance paid by an employer. *p. 105*

presidential succession—plan for what happens if the president dies or can't perform the duties of the office. *p. 108*

private sector—business world outside the government. *p. 120*

regulator—person who controls something through rules and regulations. *p. 119*

CHAPTER 8

The Judicial Branch

In this chapter, you will learn about:

- how the federal court system works
- what **U.S. District Courts and Courts of Appeals** do
- how the **United States Supreme Court protects the Constitution**
- why the **Supreme Court has changed**

Charles Evans Hughes, Chief Justice from 1930 to 1941, stated that the Supreme Court is "distinctly American in concept and function." Few other courts in the world have the same authority, and no other court has had so much influence for so long. The French political observer Alexis de Tocqueville noted that "the representative system of government has been adopted in several states of Europe, but I am unaware that any nation of the globe has hitherto organized a judicial power in the same manner as the Americans . . . . A more imposing judicial power was never constituted by any people."

The federal judicial branch was established by the Constitution and Congress to protect the rights of all Americans. The federal Supreme Court, district courts, and appeals courts work together to ensure equal justice for all citizens. These courts protect the Constitution, and they apply the laws established by Congress. The U.S. federal courts impact all Americans.

The Constitution and the Federal Judicial Branch

The judicial power of the United States shall be vested in one supreme Court, and in such inferior Courts as the Congress may from time to time ordain and establish.—U.S. Constitution, Article III

With these words, the framers created the judicial branch of the federal government. These courts are often called "guardians of the Constitution" because they work to protect the rights and freedoms guaranteed by the Constitution. Federal courts decide on constitutionality, or whether laws or actions agree with the principles of the Constitution.

The federal court system consists of more than 100 courts across the country that *hear,* meaning "deal with," a wide variety of cases.

The courts do not make laws. That is the job of Congress. The courts also do not implement laws. That is the job of the president and the executive branch. The federal courts say what a law means and say how that law applies to the facts in a particular dispute. Collectively, the system of courts of law in the judicial branch is called the **judiciary**.

Protecting the Power of the Court

The framers of the Constitution were wise enough to know that the judicial branch had to be *independent* if it was to:

* Ensure fairness for all citizens.
* Make sure that the president and Congress couldn't influence decisions made by the courts.

The Constitution protects the judiciary from the influence of the other two branches of government in two ways:

1. **Federal judges are appointed for life** and can only be removed from office through **impeachment**—charging an official with a crime or corruption—and then conviction by Congress, a complex process.
2. **The salary of federal judges cannot be reduced** by a president or by Congress.

"Not guilty, Your Honor, and thank you for asking."

Checking the Power of the Court

The powers of the judiciary are balanced by checks from the executive and legislative branches.

* *The president nominates* people to become federal judges.
* *The Senate must confirm* anyone whom the president nominates to be a federal judge.
* *The House can impeach* judges and justices.
* *Congress creates federal courts* (other than the Supreme Court) and decides how many judges those courts need.
* *Congress decides* which types of cases the federal courts will hear.
* *Congress can amend* the Constitution, with the approval of the states, to reverse a judicial ruling.

Primary Source

Alexander Hamilton

Alexander Hamilton discussed the role of the judiciary and the balance of power in one of the famous papers he wrote.

"Whoever attentively considers the different departments of power must perceive that, in a government in which they are separated from each other, the judiciary, from the nature of its functions, will always be the least dangerous to the political rights of the Constitution; because it will be least in a capacity to annoy or injure them. The Executive not only dispenses the honors, but holds the sword of the community. The Legislature not only commands the purse, but prescribes the rules by which the duties and rights of every citizen are to be regulated. The judiciary, on the contrary, has no influence over either the sword or the purse; no direction either of the strength or of the wealth of the society; and can take no active resolution whatever. It may truly be said to have neither FORCE nor WILL, but merely judgment; and must ultimately depend upon the aid of the executive arm even for the efficacy [effectiveness] of its judgments."

The Federalist Papers, No. 78. From *McLean's Edition*, New York.

The Federal Court System

The Federal Court system follows some specific rules set up by Congress and the Constitution. These rules list the types of cases the courts can hear, or conduct, as well as how judges are chosen for the courts.

Jurisdiction

The **jurisdiction**—area of power or authority—of the federal courts is described by the Constitution, but not very clearly. Congress sets more specific guidelines for what federal courts may do.

All courts have rules about the types of cases they can hear. Traffic courts, for example, only hear cases about traffic violations. In the same way, the Constitution gives federal courts the power to hear cases that deal with:

* Laws and treaties written by the federal government.
* The meaning of the Constitution.
* Disputes involving ambassadors or other foreign officials.
* Maritime law (law on seas and oceans).
* Disputes in which the United States is suing or being sued.
* Disputes between two or more state governments.
* Disputes between citizens of different states.
* Disputes between United States citizens or states and foreign nations or citizens.

Definitions of Court Jurisdiction	
Court	**Example**
Courts of **original jurisdiction** can hear a dispute for the first time. These courts preside over and conduct trials.	Most federal trials are conducted by trial courts known as district courts. On very rare occasions, the Supreme Court conducts the trial—for instance, in disputes in which all the parties involved are states.
Courts of **appellate jurisdiction** review decisions made by lower courts and determine if the decisions are correct.	People who are unhappy with a district court's decision or with the conduct of a trial can ask a federal appeals court to review the decision. The Supreme Court is the highest appellate court in the country.
Courts of **exclusive jurisdiction** alone have the right to hear a particular type case.	Federal bankruptcy courts are the only courts that can hear cases concerning bankruptcy. State courts of any level may not hear such cases.
Concurrent jurisdiction refers to different courts that can both hear the same dispute at the same point in the process.	Federal and state courts have concurrent jurisdiction in a lot of cases. Federal and state courts can both hear disputes between citizens of different states.

Judges

Under Article III of the Constitution and under the power given to Congress by Article III to create lower courts, the president appoints and the Senate confirms the following federal judges:

* Justices of the Supreme Court.
* Judges in the courts of appeals.
* Judges in the district courts.
* Judges of the Court of International Trade.

These judges are appointed for life and can only be removed through the process of impeachment.

You do not need to meet any special qualifications to become a federal judge. However, people who are nominated are usually successful private-industry or government lawyers, state court judges, magistrate or bankruptcy judges, or law professors.

Each court in the federal system has a *chief judge* who hears cases and is responsible for the operation of the court. Usually—but not always—the chief judge is the judge who has served on the court the longest.

Did You Know?

Judicial Ethics

Federal judges must follow the Code of Conduct for United States Judges. This Code says that all judges should:

* Behave morally and ethically, and should protect the independence of the judiciary.
* Carry out the duties of the office without bias and with hard work.
* Not take part in activities outside their job that conflict with judicial duties.
* Not take part in political activity.

The Lower Courts

The Supreme Court is the only court specifically created by Article III. However, Article III gave Congress the authority to create *lower* federal courts to assist the Supreme Court. Today, these lower courts include:

* **District Courts**, which conduct trials of cases never heard previously.
* **Courts of Appeal**, which review or reconsider cases that have already been tried in other courts.

Additionally, Congress has created several special federal courts. The chart below shows the different types of federal courts.

U.S. District Courts

Congress created 13 district courts in 1789, when the country was much smaller and had fewer people. Today, we have 94 federal district courts spread out all across the United States to hear trials. Each has its own geographic territory. More than 600 judges work in our district courts.

The United States Federal Courts

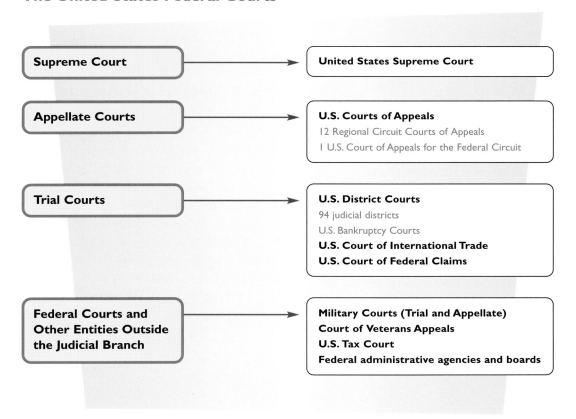

Supreme Court	**United States Supreme Court**
Appellate Courts	**U.S. Courts of Appeals** 12 Regional Circuit Courts of Appeals 1 U.S. Court of Appeals for the Federal Circuit
Trial Courts	**U.S. District Courts** 94 judicial districts U.S. Bankruptcy Courts **U.S. Court of International Trade** **U.S. Court of Federal Claims**
Federal Courts and Other Entities Outside the Judicial Branch	**Military Courts (Trial and Appellate)** **Court of Veterans Appeals** **U.S. Tax Court** **Federal administrative agencies and boards**

Trial Courts

United States district courts are **trial courts**, or courts that hear criminal and civil cases. District courts have authority to hear nearly all types of federal cases, within the limits set by Congress and the Constitution. Trials in district courts may be of **two** kinds:

1. **Bench Trials.** In these cases, only a judge hears and decides the case.
2. **Jury Trials.** Outcomes are decided by a jury of ordinary citizens.

Federal trial courts are not the only trial courts in the country. In fact, most legal cases are settled in the *state* court system.

Court Officials

District courts are busy places. In addition to the judges who run the court, many other officials play a role in the work of the court. **Three** types of these officials are: magistrates, U.S. attorneys, and marshals.

1. **Magistrates.** A **magistrate** is an officer of a district court who handles many of the duties of the district court judge. The magistrate helps the district court judge so that the judge can hear more trials. A full-time magistrate serves a term of eight years. Duties assigned to magistrates by district court judges are different from court to court. A magistrate might:
   * Issue warrants or orders for arrest.
   * Decide whether to hold a person for grand jury action.
   * Set bail.
2. **U.S. Attorneys.** U.S. attorneys are appointed by the president for each judicial district. The U.S. attorney works with a staff of attorneys to prosecute and defend cases for the federal government. **Prosecuting attorneys** bring charges and argue the cases against the accused for the government.
3. **Marshals.** Marshals have the job of keeping order in the court. They are U.S. federal officers within judicial districts who carry out court orders and perform duties similar to those of a sheriff.

U.S. Courts of Appeals

Congress created the U.S. Circuit Courts of Appeals in 1891 to help the Supreme Court. The Supreme Court had so many case appeals to consider that it needed help to deal with them all. The Courts of Appeals, therefore, were set up to be the first step in the appeals process. Congress hoped the Courts of Appeals could settle most of the cases, especially the less important ones. If the Courts of Appeals came to the proper decision, the Supreme Court wouldn't have to hear the case.

The Appeals Process

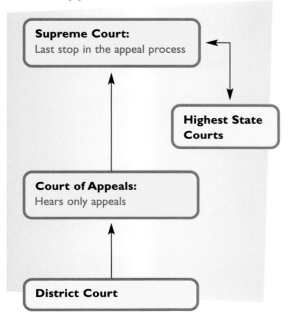

Supreme Court:
Last stop in the appeal process

Highest State Courts

Court of Appeals:
Hears only appeals

District Court

Organization

The 94 judicial districts are organized into 12 regional circuits. Each circuit has one United States Court of Appeals to hear cases appealed from district courts in that circuit. One judge from the Supreme Court is responsible for each court of appeals district.

Responsibilities

People who are dissatisfied with the result of an earlier trial can **appeal** the case, which means they ask the appeals court to review the way the lower court conducted the trial. Courts of appeals have no original jurisdiction, which means they never hear a case from the beginning (or *origin*) with all the evidence presented. No evidence is presented again. No testimony is reheard.

American Citizenship

The Jury System

As an American citizen, one day you will probably be called to serve on a jury. Citizens called for jury duty receive a notice to report to a federal or local court building for certain days. As court cases begin, judges and lawyers for each case interview the potential jurors. Their goal is to select jury members who don't have prejudice or bias in the case. If the lawyers and judge agree that a person can make a

decision about the case fairly and is suited to serve on the jury, the person is selected. Most juries have 12 members, and they may also have an alternate juror or two.

As a jury member in a criminal case, you decide, based only on the evidence presented, whether or not the guilt of the accused person has been proven "beyond a reasonable doubt." Jury duty is a responsibility and right that citizens should take very seriously.

A person making an appeal usually asks the appeals court to review the process by which the trial was conducted, or how the law itself was applied. A three-judge panel:

* *Reviews a transcript* of the prior court's proceedings.
* *Listens to arguments* from attorneys for both sides.
* *Decides* whether to uphold the trial judge's ruling, dismiss the case, or send the case back to the trial court so that it can be conducted properly.

If a particular case is considered very important (because, for example, it may apply to many other situations), all 12 judges in the appeals district will hear the case and make a ruling.

Special Federal Courts

The Constitution also let Congress set up **special courts**, which focus on specific types of controversies, such as disputes over the payment of taxes. The table below outlines the types of cases handled by several of these special courts.

Special Federal Courts
The Court of Appeals for the Armed Forces A civilian (nonmilitary) court that hears appeals of military courts-martial.
Local Courts of the District of Columbia Congress-created equivalent of a state court system in the District of Columbia.
U.S. Court of Appeals for Veterans' Claims Hears appeals over decisions given by the Department of Veterans' Affairs on veterans' benefits, such as pensions and medical care.
The Territorial Courts Provide a court system for American territories, including the Virgin Islands and Guam. These courts operate like district courts.
U.S. Court of Federal Claims Hears claims made against the United States for money damages.
U.S. Tax Court Hears appeals by people who believe that they were assessed the wrong amount of tax by the Internal Revenue Service.

The United States Supreme Court

The United States Supreme Court is the most powerful court in the country. It is the court of appeal whose decisions are final.

Responsibilities

Written above the main entrance of the Supreme Court Building in Washington, D.C., are the words, "Equal Justice Under Law," as a reminder of why the Court exists. The Court is charged with ensuring equal justice under the law for all Americans and is the guardian and interpreter of the Constitution.

As the country's highest court of appeal, the Supreme Court reviews cases appealed from:

* The Circuit Courts of Appeals.
* The highest state courts, when that court's decision is based at least in part on a federal constitutional or legal principle or a federal statute.

Judicial Review

The Supreme Court can choose the cases it will hear and exercises a power called **judicial review**. Judicial review is the power of the courts to decide whether acts of governments—national, state, or local—conflict with the Constitution. If the Court decides that a law is unconstitutional, the section of the law in dispute is considered *null and void*, no longer in force. This very important power of judicial review is implied in Article III of the Constitution, but it was not formally established until the historic case of Marbury v. Madison.

The Justices

The Supreme Court currently has nine justices. The first Supreme Court only had six justices, and Courts have had as many as ten justices (in the mid-1800s). Supreme Court justices serve life terms and do not have to retire at any specific age. Justices, like all federal officials, can be impeached and removed.

The position of Supreme Court justice is very important. So the process of nominating and approving a new judge is complicated enough to ensure that only the most respected candidates can become Supreme Court justices. The process follows **five** steps:

1. **When an opening on the Court occurs, the president asks advisors to suggest candidates,** such as other judges in the federal court system, state supreme court justices, senators, or governors.

2. **The president narrows down the list to a few potential nominees,** then interviews them. Presidents usually look for judges who share their own political beliefs.

3. **The president selects a candidate to nominate,** and his staff then asks the senators from the nominee's state to introduce the candidate to the Senate before the confirmation hearings. At this point, the nomination is formally announced.

Mandatory Sentences

Many states and the federal government, in an attempt to reduce the number of crimes committed, have established **mandatory sentences** for certain crimes. Mandatory sentences require specific punishments for specific crimes. These sentences are usually long because they are meant to discourage people from committing crimes. Some mandatory sentences only apply to repeat offenders, while others apply to first convictions.

Are mandatory sentences wise? You decide.

Arguments _for_ Mandatory Sentences

Some crimes are so terrible, anyone convicted of them should get the death penalty, or life in prison.

For repeat offenders, "three strikes, and you're out!" We're not going to put up with this. If you're convicted more than a certain number of times, you'll get at least x number of years in prison.

Judges are too lenient. For these kinds of situations, we don't need a judge to decide on the punishment. We, the people, as represented by our lawmakers, will decide.

Arguments _against_ Mandatory Sentences

For all the arguments _for_ mandatory sentences, there is really only one argument _against_: Situations are unique.

Should a 16-year-old-boy acting as a lookout for older friends involved in a criminal act get life in prison because one of _them_ shot a police officer?

We need judges to make sentencing decisions, because cases can involve circumstances that would make the mandated sentence a wrong one in most people's eyes.

4. **The Senate Judiciary Committee interviews the nominee** to determine his or her views on important political and Constitutional issues. When the interview is complete, the Senate Judiciary Committee makes a recommendation to the full Senate.

5. **The full Senate votes on the nominee,** usually supporting the recommendation of the Judiciary Committee.

Whenever a justice retires or leaves the Supreme Court, that departure creates an opening for a new justice. When that happens (and it is not a frequent event), the president is allowed to nominate a successor. Various interest groups may try to pressure the president to nominate someone who will support their views, or to discourage him from nominating someone opposed to their positions.

EXAMPLE: When Justice Thurgood Marshall retired, President George H.W. Bush was pressured to replace the retiring African-American justice with someone who was also African American to ensure that the Court would retain its racial mix.

The Supreme Court at Work

Every year, nearly 7,000 cases are appealed to the Supreme Court. The justices review all the appeals and choose which cases they will hear.

Selecting Cases

When any four justices feel a case is important enough for the Supreme Court to address (the **Rule of Four**), that case is added to the list of cases to be considered during that term, or session. The justices usually select only about 150 cases to hear in a year.

Hearing Arguments

Once the justices have decided to hear a case, the attorneys are notified and begin their preparations. The attorneys may be asked to do **two** things:

1. **Submit Briefs.** Attorneys on both sides of the case are asked to submit a **brief** outlining their positions. A brief is a document prepared by a lawyer to explain his or her legal position on the issue in question. Briefs often use decisions reached in previous Supreme Court cases to support a position. Interested groups may also submit **amicus curiae** —friend of the court—briefs.

2. **Make Oral Arguments.** If the justices choose to hear them, the lawyers for each side in the case (the petitioner and the respondent) are usually allowed 30 minutes each in which to present their oral arguments. The justices may, and often do, ask questions.

Did You Know?

Traditions of the Court

The "conference handshake" has been a tradition in the Supreme Court since the time of Chief Justice Fuller in the late 19th century. On those days when the justices *go to the Bench*, meaning appear in the courtroom, each justice shakes hands with all of the other justices. The handshakes are a reminder that the justices stand together in their purpose, in spite of possible differences of opinion among them.

Marbury v. Madison (1803)

Marbury v. Madison is one of the most important cases in Supreme Court and United States history. William Marbury had been nominated by President John Adams to become a federal judge. Marbury's nomination was confirmed by the Senate, and all the paperwork was completed on Adams's last day in office. The paperwork (Marbury's *commission*), however, was never delivered.

When Jefferson became president the next day, Marbury's commission was found on his desk. Jefferson told James Madison, the new Secretary of State, not to deliver the commission. Jefferson wanted to appoint someone from his own political party to the federal court system, instead of Marbury. When Marbury found out Madison was not going to deliver the commission, he sued Madison. In his suit, Marbury relied on part of the Judiciary Act of 1789. He asked the Court to issue a formal court order forcing Madison to deliver the commission.

The Supreme Court, headed by new Chief Justice John Marshall, found that William Marbury was legally entitled to get his commission. However, Marshall also ruled that the Court could not order Madison to deliver the commission because the Judiciary Act of 1789 was unconstitutional. It should not have allowed Marbury to bring his case to the Supreme Court without first going to a lower court.

The impact of this decision was significant. For the first time, the Supreme Court had ruled a piece of congressional legislation unconstitutional. Marshall stated that "it is emphatically the province and duty of the judicial department to say what law is." The Court had established the power of judicial review.

Making Decisions

Once oral arguments are made, the justices meet later in private to discuss the case. The Chief Justice runs these meetings and usually speaks first. Each justice, in order of seniority, which means length of service on the Court, gives his or her view of the case. If all views are the same, the decision is made. If not, discussion continues. When discussion is completed, a vote is taken. Votes that are 9-0 are said to be *unanimous*. All other votes are called *split votes*. The side with the majority of votes wins.

Writing Opinions

After the Court has reached a decision on a case, justices write **opinions**—written statements explaining the reasons for their decisions. **Three** types of opinions may be written by the justices:

1. **Majority Opinion**. A majority decision explains why the majority of the Court voted as it did on a particular case. The job of writing the opinion is assigned by either the Chief Justice or the justice with the most seniority on the side that won the decision, who can choose to write the opinion or to assign it to someone else.

2. **Concurring Opinion**. A concurring opinion is written by a justice who voted with the majority on the outcome of the case, but did so for a different reason than the majority. This opinion explains that justice's position.

3. **Dissenting Opinion**. A dissenting opinion may be written by any or all of the justices who voted with the minority (the losing side). These opinions explain the reasons for the justices' positions. Dissenting opinions often are used as a basis for challenging a Court ruling in future cases.

▲
Chief Justice John Marshall headed the Court in the 18th century, during its early, important decisions.

▲
Justice Thurgood Marshall was the foremost civil rights lawyer of the 20th century. As a Justice, he set a standard for determining what was "equal protection under the law."

The Court Through History

In 1789, John Jay began his service as the first Chief Justice of the Supreme Court. Since that time, the Court has defined its role and made critical decisions that have affected the life of every American.

Judicial Activism and Judicial Restraint

How does the Supreme Court define its role in the government? How do justices decide how to interpret the Constitution? Throughout history, justices have taken different positions on these questions. The different points of view boil down to **two** opposite interpretations of a justice's role:

1. **Judicial Activism**. Justices who believe the Court should take an active role in policy-making and Constitutional interpretation are called judicial activists.

They tend to interpret the Constitutional and federal laws broadly to achieve certain results. They are more likely to strike down state or federal laws and to ignore or overturn precedents—prior court decisions—in their rulings.

2. **Judicial Restraint**. Justices who tend toward judicial restraint believe that policy decisions should be left to Congress and the president, not to the Court. Justices with this viewpoint may refuse to review certain cases that they feel would force the Court to interfere with congressional and executive authority.

Landmark Decisions

Throughout its history, the Supreme Court has made many decisions that have changed our nation, laws, and government. Such Supreme Court decisions are considered landmark, or very significant, decisions.

The outcome of the presidential election of 2000 is in the hands of the Supreme Court, as it hears arguments about vote counting in Florida. Outside, police keep a watch on protesters. ▶

Landmark Rulings of the Supreme Court

Case	Ruling
Marbury v. Madison (1803)	Established that the Supreme Court has the final judgment on what is and is not constitutional.
Dred Scott v. Sanford (1857)	Ruled that Congress had no power to keep slavery out of new United States territories. Also ruled that African Americans and their descendants were not citizens. It took a Constitutional Amendment—The Fourteenth—to overturn this decision.
Plessy v. Ferguson (1896)	Ruled that *separate but equal* facilities for African-American citizens were constitutional. Effectively upheld segregation of the races.
Brown v. Board of Education of Topeka, Kansas (1954)	Reversed Plessy v. Ferguson. Outlawed segregation in public schools.
Engel v. Vitale (1962)	Ruled that states cannot require public school students to recite prayers.
Gideon v. Wainwright (1963)	Required states to provide an attorney for accused people who could not afford one.
Miranda v. Arizona (1966)	Ruled that people who are arrested must be informed of their right to an attorney, their right to remain silent, and the danger that they place themselves in if they talk.
Roe v. Wade (1973)	Established the federally protected right of a woman to decide for herself whether or not to have an abortion, with certain limitations.
United States v. Richard Nixon (1974)	Ruled that neither executive privilege nor separation of powers protects a president from judicial demands to supply evidence in a criminal trial.
Regents of the University of California v. Bakke (1978)	Allowed colleges and universities to consider a person's race as only one factor in deciding which students to admit. Prohibited racial quotas in admissions.
New Jersey v. T.L.O. (1985)	Allowed school officials to conduct searches of students without a warrant or probable cause as long as the search was reasonable.
Hazelwood School District v. Kuhlmeier (1988)	Allowed schools to censor student publications without violating students' First Amendment rights.

The federal judicial branch of government was established in Article III of the Constitution to protect the rights and freedoms guaranteed by the Constitution. Federal courts decide the constitutionality of federal laws and resolve other disputes over federal laws. Congress and the Constitution determine the jurisdiction or authority of these courts.

The judicial system includes the most powerful court in our country, the Supreme Court, as well as lower courts. The lower courts, including U.S. District Courts and U.S. Courts of Appeals, provide a system of trial courts and appeals courts. In the appeals process, cases can be transferred from a lower court to a higher court for a new hearing.

The United States Supreme Court is the guardian and interpreter of the Constitution. It is the final court of appeals in our country. The Court decides if acts of governments—national, state, or local—conflict with the Constitution.

Throughout history, justices have held different opinions about the role of the Supreme Court. Judicial activists believe the Court should take an active role in policy-making and Constitutional interpretation. Other justices take a position known as judicial restraint, based on the belief that policy decisions should be left to Congress and the president, not to the Court.

Civics in America

amicus curiae—party not involved in a particular case that is allowed by the court to submit a brief to advise the court's decision; means "friend of the court." *p. 133*

appeal—request made after a trial for review of the trial court's decision by a higher court (appeals court). *p. 129*

appellate jurisdiction—authority of a court to review the judgment of a lower court. *p. 125*

brief—document written to submit a legal argument to a court; usually sets out the facts of the case and a party's argument. *p. 133*

concurrent jurisdiction—authority shared by two courts when either court is able to hear a particular case. *p. 125*

concurring opinion—written statement prepared by a Supreme Court justice who voted with the majority, but for a different reason, explaining his or her position on the case. *p. 135*

courts of appeals—federal courts that review the process of how lower trial courts decided previous cases, or how the law itself was applied. They handle many cases that would otherwise overburden the Supreme Court. *p. 127*

dissenting opinion—written statement prepared by any Supreme Court justice who voted with the minority, explaining his or her position on the case. *p. 135*

district courts—federal courts that conduct trials of cases that have not previously been heard. *p. 127*

exclusive jurisdiction—authority held by a court to be the only court that can rule on a specific case. *p. 125*

impeachment—formal charge of an official with a crime or corruption. *p. 123*

judicial activism—manner in which a judge applies the law, based on the belief that the court can create new policy. *p. 136*

judicial restraint—manner in which a judge applies the law, based on the belief that the court should not create new policy. *p. 136*

judicial review—constitutional provision for courts to decide if acts of the government are constitutional. *p. 131*

judiciary—system of courts of law; judicial branch of government. *p. 123*

jurisdiction—area of power or authority; in the judiciary, it defines what particular cases or kinds of cases a court can hear. *p. 125*

magistrate—officer of a district court who handles many of the duties of the district court judge. *p. 128*

majority opinion—written statement prepared by a Supreme Court justice to explain how a majority of the Court voted on a case. *p. 135*

mandatory sentences—specific punishments required by law for certain crimes. *p. 132*

opinion—written statement explaining a Supreme Court decision. *p. 135*

original jurisdiction—authority of a court to hear a case argued for the first time. *p. 125*

prosecuting attorney—government's legal representative who brings charges in a case. *p. 128*

Rule of Four—Supreme Court practice for selecting cases; states that a case will be selected when any four justices agree to hear it. *p. 133*

special courts—federal courts, such as the U.S. Tax Court, established by Congress to deal with special issues. *p. 130*

trial courts—courts that hear civil and criminal cases. *p. 128*

State Government

In this chapter, you will learn about:

- how the **Constitution divides power between the federal government and the state governments**
- what services state governments provide
- how state governments are organized

While many other 20-year-olds were hanging out and trying to decide what to do with their lives, Jesse Laslovich of Anaconda, Montana, was elected to be a representative to the Montana Legislature. Jesse has always loved politics. After campaigning for a local candidate, Jesse decided to run for office himself. He was elected a state representative in 2001. Jesse's goals include becoming a state senator, governor, and, well, who knows?

States have all the powers that the U.S. Constitution doesn't specifically give to the federal government or doesn't prohibit the states from exercising. You are much more affected day to day by decisions of your state officials than by those of the federal government.

The head of each state's executive branch is the governor. Except for Nebraska, all state legislatures have both a house of representatives and a senate. Each state has a supreme court or high court and other lower courts that handle state and local matters.

The Federal System

The founders of the nation set up a system based on federalism, in which power is divided and balanced between the national and state governments.

Constitutional Basis

The United States Constitution **delegates**— or assigns—powers to the national government and to the states in several ways.

Division of Powers: National and State Governments

The national government has responsibilities to all citizens, in all states. So the founders gave the national or federal government specific **exclusive**—not shared—**powers** to:

* *Protect the states* from foreign invasion with military action.
* *Deal with foreign governments* in issues of trade or disputes.
* *Produce money* used throughout the United States.
* *Make laws about the movement of goods and people between states,* called interstate commerce.

Reserved Powers

The Constitution does not list the powers that states have. Instead, the Tenth Amendment says that any powers not delegated to the national government are **reserved powers**—set aside—for the states or the people.

The Constitution and the Amendments also specifically forbid states from making certain types of laws, such as:

* Treaties with foreign countries.
* Laws that deny people the right to practice their religion.

There are also several different kinds of **concurrent**—shared—**powers**. Both the states and the national government may:

* *Work together* on projects, such as building or improving roads and bridges.
* *Provide support* for poor people in the form of welfare services, such as food or health care that people get free or for a reduced cost.
* *Tax citizens* to get money needed to pay for services. Some of the taxes the national government collects are returned to the states in various ways.

Supremacy Clause

What would you do if your teacher asked you to follow a class rule that was the direct *opposite* of a school rule? A state government and the national government can both make laws that apply to the same citizens, so a law passed by one level of government could disagree with a law passed by the other level of government. Article VI of the U.S. Constitution—the **supremacy clause**—states that the U.S. Constitution and all laws and treaties made by the national government are the supreme, or highest, law of the land. If state and federal laws are in conflict with each other, the federal law rules.

State Constitutions

Each of the 50 states has its own constitution. Most are modeled after the U.S. Constitution, and most contain:

* A preamble, stating the ideals on which the government is founded.
* A bill or declaration of citizen's rights.
* A description of the powers and duties of the executive, legislative, and judicial branches.
* A description of how elections will be carried out, including qualifications for candidates and for voters, and rules to be followed in elections.
* A description of how the state will operate in such things as education, highways, law and order, and the collection of taxes.
* A procedure for amending it.

Overview of Typical State Government

Executive Branch	Legislative Branch	Judicial Branch
Governor and Lieutenant Governor	**State Legislature** House of Representatives Senate	**State Supreme Court**
State Executive Officials Secretary of State Treasurer Auditor Attorney General Superintendent of Public Instruction		**Appeals Court**
		General Trial Courts Courts of Common Pleas Superior Courts Circuit Court District Court County Court
State Departments, Agencies, Commissions, and Boards		**Lower Courts** Justice Courts Magistrates' Courts Municipal Courts Juvenile/Family Courts Small Claims Courts

Preambles of State Constitutions

The preambles of some state constitutions, such as that of South Dakota, are almost identical to the Preamble to the U.S. Constitution. Some are very brief, and others are quite long.

* *Utah:* Grateful to Almighty God for life and liberty, we, the people of Utah, in order to secure and perpetuate [continue] the principles of free government, do ordain and establish this Constitution.
* *Montana:* We the people of Montana, grateful to God for the quiet beauty of our state, the grandeur of our mountains, the vastness of our rolling plains, and desiring to improve the quality of life, equality of opportunity and to secure the blessings of liberty for this and future generations, do ordain and establish this constitution.

Cooperation among States

Article IV of the Constitution describes several ways that states must cooperate with other states and the national government.

Full Faith and Credit

States follow Article IV to respect the laws of other states, including:

* Decisions of the courts in other states.
* Actions such as marriage, divorce, or land deeds that are recorded in other states.
* Justice in other states. A person who commits a crime in one state cannot escape punishment by fleeing to another state. **Extradition** is the process of returning a fugitive to the state where the crime was committed.

Guarantee of Republican Form of Government

Every state's constitution must guarantee that voters can elect their state leaders.

Domestic Violence

The national government must assist any state that asks for help against anyone who tries to riot or rebel within a state.

EXAMPLE: If a riot breaks out in a city, the state legislature or governor can ask the federal government to help restore peace by calling out National Guard troops.

State Symbols

Each of the 50 states has adopted a state flag, state motto, and a number of symbols representing the history or interests of the state.

State mottos can range from one word to a sentence. Here are some examples:

* Alaska: North to the Future
* Missouri: Let the welfare of the people be the supreme law.
* New York: Excelsior (Ever upward)

Most states have official symbols that include a state flower, song, animal, bird, fruit, vegetable, tree, rock, and fossil. Hawaii's state sport is surfing, and Alaska's is dog mushing. Massachusetts has a state pie (Boston Cream). State beverages include orange juice (Florida), tomato juice (Ohio), and milk (Maryland). If you want something to go with your milk, three states have a state muffin! Minnesota's is blueberry, New York has claimed apple, and corn muffins are the official muffins in Massachusetts.

In many states, symbols are nominated and voted on by school children. What are your state symbols?

Services Provided by States

States provide many services to their citizens. These include:

* Holding elections.
* Providing education.
* Regulating businesses.
* Passing laws that govern people's actions.
* Providing and maintaining police forces, public buildings, and roads and highways.

Elections

Each state constitution provides citizens with a way to elect their government representatives. The state:

* Sets qualifications for state election candidates, as well as voting qualifications for citizens.
* Provides the **polls**—voting places—for citizens to cast their ballots for national, state, and local candidates.
* Arranges for people to count the ballots and report the election results.

Education

Each state establishes public schools for the education of the citizens. The state:

* Decides what types of schools will be established—universities, secondary schools, elementary schools, and special education programs.
* Provides funding for schools through taxes.
* Places regulations on schools, such as establishing statewide tests.

As with some other services, states allow local governments to create school systems, based on the state's constitution and laws.

Business

Some of the ways in which states regulate business include:

* **Certification**, or guaranteeing the qualifications of certain professions, such as doctors, teachers, or bus drivers.
* *Licensing* of contractors, tradespeople, and other service providers to ensure trustworthy and reliable business service.
* *Inspecting* businesses, such as hospitals, to protect public health and safety.

Laws Governing People's Actions

States pass and enforce laws dealing with marriage, divorce, and the ownership of property. They decide what actions are considered criminal and punishable by law, such as by setting speed limits on state highways. These laws protect the well-being of citizens.

Police

States maintain a state police force to insure safety on highways and in areas not policed by county or city police. Where state highways pass through cities and towns, state and local police cooperate in enforcing the laws.

Public Buildings

States use tax money to construct buildings, such as courthouses, public health clinics, or prisons, to carry out the work of government or provide services to citizens.

Highways

States maintain roads, highways, and bridges so all citizens have a safe and efficient road system.

The State Legislative Branch

The powers of the legislative branches in the national and state governments are similar.

Organization of State Legislatures

Different states have different names for their lawmaking branches:

* State Legislature.
* General Assembly.
* Legislative Assembly.
* General Court.

Except for Nebraska, every state legislature has two houses, like the U. S. Congress. The larger house, in terms of the number of legislators, is usually called the House of Representatives, and the smaller house is the Senate. The size of each house is set in the state constitution and differs widely from state to state.

EXAMPLE: Alaska, the largest state in area, has the smallest legislature—a 40-member House of Representatives and a 20-member Senate. New Hampshire, one of the smallest states, has the largest legislature. Called the General Court, there are between 375 and 400 members in the New Hampshire House of Representatives, and 24 senators.

Election

The legislature divides the state into legislative districts, each with an approximately equal population. Legislators represent and are elected by the people from a specific district.

Sessions

The legislature in many states meets each year for between one and six months. The governor may call a special session if something important must be decided.

Legislator Qualifications and Terms

Qualifications and terms for state legislators are described in each state's constitution.

Qualifications

Legislators must be U.S. citizens and have lived in the state and district they want to represent for a certain period of time. In most states, the minimum age is 25 for state senators and 21 for state representatives. Some states have a minimum age of 18.

Terms

In most states, members of the senate serve for four years and representatives for two years. About 20 states limit the number of times that legislators may be reelected. Some people feel these term limits should be eliminated. Others think the idea is so good that federal lawmakers should have term limits, too.

Responsibilities and Work

All legislatures have legislative and non-legislative powers.

Legislative Powers

State legislatures may pass any law that is not prohibited by the U.S. Constitution, by federal laws, or by any part of the state's constitution. Examples of state laws include these:

* Setting and collecting taxes on income and property.
* Establishing courts.
* Defining unlawful behavior and providing punishments.
* Controlling business activities.
  EXAMPLES: States license some businesses. Some require businesses to pay employees a minimum wage.
* Establishing and maintaining public schools.
* Protecting the health, morals, and welfare of citizens.
  EXAMPLE: States may require that children entering school have vaccinations to reduce the spread of diseases.

Nonlegislative Powers

Every state legislature is allowed to do more than make laws. They also have:

* *Executive powers.* When state governors appoint certain officials, they must get approval from one or both houses of the state legislature. In several states, the legislature appoints some state officials.
  EXAMPLE: In Tennessee and New Hampshire, the legislature chooses the secretary of state.

* **Judicial powers.** In every state except Oregon, the legislature has the power to impeach officers of the state's executive and judicial branches and to discipline its own members.
  EXAMPLE: Legislators may be censured—condemned or scolded—for inappropriate, but not illegal, actions, such as making racist remarks.

* **Constitutional powers.** State legislatures amend state constitutions.

Legislative Committees

Much of the work preparing and debating bills is actually done by **committees**— smaller groups appointed or elected to deal with specific issues—outside of the legislature, so valuable legislative session time isn't wasted.

Standing Committees

Standing, or permanent, committees discuss bills dealing with ongoing issues, such as:

* **Appropriations**—funding for government programs.
* Economic development.
* Commerce.
* Education.
* Natural resources.
* Transportation.

Interim Committees

Interim, or temporary, committees are appointed to discuss short-term issues.
EXAMPLE: Iowa has used interim committees to study e-commerce, parking near the capitol building, and distance learning.

▲
An Illinois legislative committee meeting.

Graduated Drivers' Licenses

States set the age at which a person can get a driver's license. In some states, drivers used to be able to get a driver's license at the age of 16. Now, many states are using a graduated licensing process, which creates an intermediate or provisional license. Teens cannot be fully licensed until the age of 18.

As a citizen, do you think the states should have graduated licensing requirements for drivers under age 18?

Arguments for Graduated Licenses

In 2000, more than 6,000 people who were 15–20 years old died in motor vehicle crashes. The crash rate for 16-year-old drivers is 15 times that of 20- to 24-year-old drivers.

States with graduated licensing requirements have reduced teen crashes and injuries by 5–16 percent.

Car insurance costs for drivers under 25 are sky-high. With provisional licensing, there would be fewer accidents in this age group, so rates would drop.

Arguments against Graduated Licenses

Many younger people are good drivers and are never involved in accidents. It's not fair to make them all wait.

Many young people under age 18 work after school and at night. They need to be able to drive to and from their places of employment.

Seventeen-year-olds can't drive their dates to evening movies or concerts because provisional drivers can't carry passengers at night.

Citizen Legislative Action

Although we don't live in a direct democracy, such as ancient Athens, citizens in many states can still take direct action to bring a bill before their elected legislature or affect the legislative process.

* Citizens can propose a new law through the **initiative** process—starting a bill on their own. They ask other voters to sign a petition to show their agreement.
* If the required number of voters signs the petition, it becomes a **proposition**, or proposed law. It then either passes

through the legislative process or appears on the next ballot for voters to decide.

* In many states, propositions on some issues must be decided by the voters as a **referendum**.

* Citizens can influence the legislature through **recall**—removing an official from office by getting the required number of signatures on a recall petition.

The State Executive Branch

Just as in the U.S. government, the executive branch of a state government enforces and carries out laws made by the legislative branch.

The Governor

The governor is the top executive officer of the state, whose powers are defined in the state constitution. The powers and roles of governors are similar to those of the president, but on a smaller scale.

Selecting the Governor

Generally, each major political party in a state nominates a candidate to run for governor, sometimes after holding party primary elections. The governor is elected by the voters in the state.

Qualifications

The qualifications for governor are defined in each state's constitution. The candidate must have been a resident of the state for a number of years. The minimum age in most states is 25 or 30.

EXAMPLE: In Nevada, candidates for governor must have lived in the state for two years. In New Jersey, they must have lived in the state for seven years.

Term

In all but two states, governors are elected for a four-year term. New Hampshire and Vermont have two-year terms. More than half of the states don't allow the governor to serve for more than two terms. Virginia allows only one term.

Powers and Duties of the Governor

The governor, like the president, must fulfill many roles.

Chief of State

The governor often acts as the spokesperson for the state's goals and values. Some duties are ceremonial, such as awarding medals for heroism. The governor also meets with governors of other states to solve common problems.

Head of the Executive Branch

The governor manages the managers and agencies of the executive branch. He or she makes sure that laws are enforced and policies are carried out. Some duties include:

* *Appointing* advisors and agency officials. A governor's appointment powers are different from those of the president. EXAMPLES: In many state elections, several top officials, such as the secretaries of state and education and the state treasurer, are elected, not appointed as in the federal government. In many states, the governor cannot appoint more than a certain number of members of one political party.

* *Preparing* the state budget that goes to the legislature for approval. The budget influences the state's spending.

* *Commanding* the state police and National Guard to, for example, stop riots or help citizens during natural disasters.

Did You Know?

Facts about Governors

* Seventeen governors from nine states have gone on to become president. These include Thomas Jefferson (Virginia), Franklin D. Roosevelt (New York), Jimmy Carter (Georgia), Bill Clinton (Arkansas), and George W. Bush (Texas).

* As of 2001, there had been only two governors of African-American descent. Pinckney Benton Stewart Pinchback served as governor of Louisiana for one month (1872–1873) after the elected governor was impeached. Governor L. Douglas Wilder of Virginia was the only African-American governor elected to office (1990–1994).

* As of 2001, 20 women had served as governors. As early as 1924, women served as governors when their husbands, who were governors, died in office or were impeached. The first woman elected without succeeding her husband was Connecticut Governor Ella Grasso, in 1975.

* According to the *Book of the States 2000–2001*, New York's governor had the highest salary ($179,000). The governors of Arkansas and Nebraska earned less than $70,000 per year.

Legislative Role

The governor has the power to sign or veto laws made by the legislature and to influence the legislature by:

* *Convincing legislators* to support recommended legislation.
* *Rallying support* among voters so that they pressure their legislators to vote for or against a proposed law.
* *Reporting on the state of the state* in a speech to the legislature each year on successes and problems in the state, and suggesting actions that should be taken.

Judicial Role

Many of a governor's judicial powers are **clemency** powers—power to exercise mercy toward those convicted of crimes—including:

* The power to pardon—to release a person from punishment for a crime.
* The power to **commute**—reduce—a sentence imposed by a court. For example, a death sentence may be commuted to life in prison.
* The power to **reprieve**—postpone—an execution so that appeals can be heard.
* The power to **parole**—to release a prisoner before the end of his or her sentence.

In many states, the governor shares these powers with other agencies, such as a state Board of Pardons and Paroles. Decisions are made jointly.

Other Executive Officials

The governor needs help to run the state. He or she shares control with officials who act as advisors or as heads of various state departments. In most states, the following major offices are filled by popular vote or are appointed by the governor or legislature.

The Lieutenant Governor

The lieutenant governor's position is much like that of the vice president: He or she presides over the state senate and succeeds to governorship if the governor can't perform the duties of the office. The governor and lieutenant governor generally run for office as a team. Several states do not have this office.

The Secretary of State

The secretary of state supervises elections and is in charge of state records, such as those regarding business licenses, births, deaths, and marriages. If a state doesn't have the position of lieutenant governor, the secretary of state may act in that role.

Attorney General

The attorney general handles legal issues for the state, such as:

* Representing the state in court cases.
* Advising state and local officials on the constitutionality of their actions.
* Assisting local courts in prosecuting criminals.

State Treasurer

The state treasurer controls all state funds. The treasurer's office directs the collection of taxes and pays the state's bills.

State Auditor

An auditor examines financial records to make sure they are correct. State auditors make sure that no public funds are spent without authorization by a state official.

Superintendent of Public Instruction

States provide public schools and universities for their citizens. The superintendent of public instruction, or commissioner, follows the policies of the state board of education and distributes state funds to local school districts, such as yours.

American Citizenship

Youth in Government

You can go to school to learn to be a lawyer, plumber, or artist, but how do you learn to be a better citizen, lawmaker, or governor? Since the 1930s, the YMCA in many states has run a program called Youth in Government. In Minnesota, for example, more than 1,000 students take part each year in a program that teaches them how government operates. Participants perform the duties of government officials and work in local clubs to:

* Practice **parliamentary procedure**—the rules under which legislatures and other groups run their meetings.
* Discuss current social and economic issues.
* Campaign for office.
* Hold party meetings and elections.
* Write legislative bills.

In the spring, students travel to the state capitol where they enact their own state government. Students take over the state offices, legislature, and courts. Some are "elected" to executive positions such as governor and secretary of state. Others sit in chambers of the state legislature as they present the bills they've written. Still others are members of the state supreme court.

As a result of the program, students:

* Develop an understanding of the inner workings of a democratic government.
* Develop responsibility and problem-solving abilities.
* Recognize that they can make a difference in the world.

State Executive Agencies

The task of running a state government requires many different departments, agencies, boards, and commissions, whose directors are appointed by the governor or by the legislature. Each is responsible for one service area. Important state agencies include:

* State Board of Education.
* Department of Human Services.
* Commerce Department.
* Department of Natural Resources.
* Transportation Department.

"I thought football players, not judges, held huddles!"

The State Judicial Branch

Every citizen must obey at least two sets of laws—federal laws and state laws. A state's constitution and laws are interpreted by state courts.

Responsibilities and Work

The state courts handle different types of cases, depending on the type of dispute being judged.

Criminal Cases

Criminal cases are those in which someone has broken a law or acted in a way that harms other citizens or society in general. They may be either:

* **Felonies**—serious or violent crimes or those involving valued property. Felonies are punished with large fines, lengthy jail terms, or both.
* **Misdemeanors**—lesser crimes, punishable by small fines, short jail terms, or community service.
  EXAMPLE: Murder and armed robbery are felonies. Taking a fruit drink without paying for it is a misdemeanor. Both are crimes!

Civil Cases

Civil cases are disagreements involving individuals or businesses. They may also be disputes between businesses or individuals and the government.
EXAMPLE: A car owner might claim that a mechanic didn't use the quality of auto parts that the owner paid for. He wants his money back. The court has to decide who is legally right.

Organization of State Courts

State courts deal with everything from petty theft to cases involving the death penalty. Each type of court handles cases of a particular type or seriousness. Not all states are the same, but many state court systems include the following:

The State Court

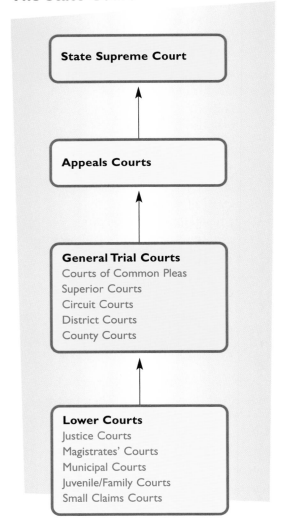

State Supreme Court

↑

Appeals Courts

↑

General Trial Courts
Courts of Common Pleas
Superior Courts
Circuit Courts
District Courts
County Courts

↑

Lower Courts
Justice Courts
Magistrates' Courts
Municipal Courts
Juvenile/Family Courts
Small Claims Courts

Lower Courts

Lower courts handle misdemeanors and civil cases that don't involve much money. They are assigned depending on the size of the community they serve. These generally include **three** types of courts:

1. **Justice Courts.** In many rural areas, justices of the peace (JPs) act as judges for misdemeanors, such as public mischief, traffic tickets, or disturbing the peace. They also rule on minor civil cases involving small amounts of money. These judicial officials can assign small fines and short jail terms.

2. **Magistrates' Courts.** Magistrates handle the same kind of cases as JPs, but do so in larger cities and towns. Magistrates' courts are sometimes called police courts.

3. **Municipal Courts.** Larger cities have municipal courts that hear cases involving more serious misdemeanors and civil cases in which damages involve larger amounts of money. Municipal courts are divided into smaller courts:

   * *Traffic Court.* Cases involving driving violations.
   * *Family Court.* Cases involving disputes between members of a family, such as child custody.
   * *Juvenile Court.* Cases involving crimes committed by minors.
   * *Small Claims Court.* Civil cases involving claims for amounts less than approximately $5,000.

Municipal courts are presided over by judges who hear cases without a jury. They get the facts of the case from the people involved and order a fair and legal settlement.

General Trial Courts

Important criminal and civil cases are heard in **general trial courts**, sometimes called superior courts or courts of common pleas. In most cases, a judge presides, and the case is heard before a jury. In many states, trial judges are elected by the people of the county or district they serve for terms of between two and eight years.

In some states, there are also county and district courts, which hear cases arising from actions within a county or district. States with large areas or smaller populations may have circuit courts, in which judges travel from county to county to hold hearings and preside over trials.

Appeals Courts

Sometimes people challenge the results of a trial because they feel that something unfair or unconstitutional has taken place. They may appeal their case—request a review—to a higher court. Most states have appellate courts that hear such cases. One purpose for these courts of appeal is to reduce the number of cases that go to the state supreme court.

Courts of appeal don't hold trials. They hear oral arguments from lawyers representing both sides and study briefs, or written arguments that might refer to previous court decisions on similar issues. Appellate courts decide whether the previous (and lower level) courts correctly interpreted the law in making their decisions.

Appellate court judges are elected in some states and appointed by the governor, the state supreme court, or state legislature in others, for terms of from two to ten years, or longer.

State Supreme Court

The highest court in each state is usually, but not always, called the supreme court. Its judges are elected in most states, but appointed by the governor in others, for terms of 10 to 12 years, or longer. The state supreme court hears appeals from either the appeals courts or general trial courts. Like appeals courts, it is concerned with whether the state constitution and laws were correctly interpreted by the lower courts in making their decisions. The decision of the state supreme court is final unless the case involves federal law. Then it may be appealed to the U.S. Supreme Court.

Overcrowded Courts

All citizens have the right to ask a judge to reconsider a case, perhaps for a new trial. In recent years, so many people have used this freedom that the courts are dangerously overcrowded with work. Some courts are a year behind in hearing cases. The right to appeal has resulted in the taking away of another right—the right of citizens to a speedy trial. Many people have called for improvements in how criminal and civil cases are settled in state courts.

Supreme Court Case

Clark v. Kmart Corp. (2001)

Not all cases heard by state supreme courts involve important issues or constitutional rights. In one case, the Michigan Supreme Court was asked to rule on an appeal by a woman who sued a popular chain store. She claimed to have slipped and fallen on loose grapes that were on the floor of the store. The woman accused the store of negligence, which means carelessness or inattention, in 1994. A lower court jury heard the evidence and awarded the woman $50,000 in damages. The store appealed, claiming that the grapes hadn't been on the floor long enough for store employees to know about them and clean the floor. The appeals court overturned the lower court decision and found in favor of the store. Eventually, the state supreme court overturned the appeals court, ruling that the original jury had enough evidence about the suspect grapes to find the store negligent.

The grapes had no comment on the case because, as you know, only bananas have the right to a peel.

Chapter 9 Wrap-up
STATE GOVERNMENT

Powers of states, which are described in state constitutions, include all powers not given to the federal government or prohibited to state governments by the U.S. Constitution and federal laws.

States provide services for their citizens that include managing state and federal elections, providing public education and health services, building and maintaining safe roads and bridges, and aiding businesses and the needy.

Like the federal government, state governments have three branches—legislative, executive, and judicial. The legislative branch in all but one state is composed of a house of representatives and a senate that make the laws. The state executive branch is led by the governor and a number of elected officials who oversee other executive agencies and departments. Their job is to enforce the laws and manage the day-to-day operations of the state. The judicial branch is divided into lower courts serving rural areas, towns, and cities; general trial courts; courts of appeals; and the state supreme court.

WORDS TO KNOW

appropriations—funding for government programs. *p. 147*

censured—condemned or scolded. *p. 147*

certification—guarantee of a person's qualifications for a job. *p. 145*

civil cases—disagreements involving individuals or businesses. *p. 153*

clemency—exercise of mercy toward those convicted of crimes. *p. 151*

committee—working group of legislators established to solve a problem or series of issues. Standing committees deal with ongoing issues. Interim committees deal with one-time problems. *p. 147*

commute—to reduce a sentence imposed by the court. *p. 151*

concurrent powers—lawmaking areas shared by the states and the federal government *p. 141*

criminal cases—cases in which someone has broken a law or acted in a way that harms other citizens or society in general. *p. 153*

delegate—to assign. *p. 141*

exclusive powers—powers assigned only to the national government. *p. 141*

extradition—process of returning a fugitive to the state where a crime was committed. *p. 143*

felony—major crime punishable by a large fine or a long jail term. *p. 153*

general trial courts—sometimes called superior courts or courts of common pleas; courts that hear important state criminal and civil cases. *p. 155*

initiative—process in which a voter or group initiates—proposes—a law. *p. 148*

lower courts—state courts, such as justice, magistrate's, and municipal courts that handle misdemeanors and civil cases that don't involve much money. *p. 154*

misdemeanor—minor crime punishable by small fine or short jail term. *p. 153*

parliamentary procedure—formal set of rules under which legislatures hold meetings. *p. 152*

parole—to release a prisoner before the end of his or her sentence. *p. 151*

polls—places where citizens go to vote. *p. 144*

proposition—proposed law. *p. 148*

recall—to remove or call for the removal of a public official from office. *p. 149*

referendum—proposition taken directly to the voters. *p. 149*

reprieve—to postpone a sentence. *p. 151*

reserved powers—powers set aside for the states. *p. 141*

supremacy clause—article in the U.S. Constitution making federal laws the highest law of the land. *p. 141*

Local Government

In this chapter, you will learn about:

- the services provided by local governments
- the authority of local governments
- how city, county, town, township, and special district governments work
- challenges faced by local governments

By 8:45 A.M., the morning of Tuesday, September 11, 2001, New Yorkers were either already at work or rushing to get there. From out of the blue, an American Airlines jumbo jet, filled with passengers, crashed into the North Tower of the World Trade Center. At 9:03 A.M., a second jet crashed into the South Tower. By 10:30 A.M., both of the 110-story towers of the World Trade Center had collapsed, killing thousands of people. More than 300 firefighters, emergency workers, and police officers died as heroes as they worked to save people trapped in the buildings.

The city government and its fire and police departments provided all possible help at the disaster site, later known as Ground Zero. The entire nation applauded Mayor Rudolph Giuliani's leadership, and Time magazine chose him as their "Person of the Year." People across the country who had taken local government for granted now regarded their city's workers as heroes.

What Local Governments Provide

Local governments serve the common good through the services they provide. What would your community be like if your local government didn't provide police and fire protection, safe water, garbage removal, or schools?

Most local governments operate at several different levels, including:

* City governments.
* County governments.
* Town, township, and village governments.
* Special districts.

All provide a wide range of important services to citizens in their areas.

Local Services

Local governments, whether they're large or small, provide many of the same basic services. These generally fall into **six** broad categories:

1. **Education.** Local governments spend the most money on education. Counties, cities, and school districts provide all public education through the end of high school.
2. **Public Safety.** Local governments provide emergency services and police and fire protection. They also hire people called inspectors to make sure that safety rules are followed in buildings and businesses.

3. **Health and Welfare.** Local governments work with state and federal officials to offer help to people in need. These services include health care, child care, and job training
4. **Environment and Housing.** Local governments provide low-cost housing, public parks, garbage collection, and sewage treatment.
5. **Land Use.** Local **zoning** rules divide a community into areas. Community planners specify how these areas will be used—some for homes and some for businesses.
6. **Utilities.** Government utility services include water, gas, and electricity.

Local Taxes

All of these local services, as you've probably guessed, cost money. Usually, communities don't have enough money to provide all the services people want. Local governments have to make difficult decisions about how to spend the money they have.

Where do local governments get most of the money they need to do their work?

* *Taxes.* Property taxes, which are taxes on land and buildings, provide more than 30 percent of local government money. Some communities also have a local sales tax.
* *Federal and State Governments.* Federal and state governments often give money to local governments. These **grants** are usually given to help support services that are state or national priorities.

Local Government Income

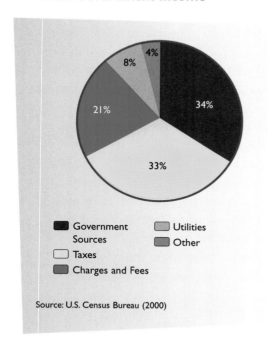

Government Sources 34%
Taxes 33%
Charges and Fees 21%
Utilities 8%
Other 4%

Legend:
- Government Sources
- Taxes
- Charges and Fees
- Utilities
- Other

Source: U.S. Census Bureau (2000)

Local Government Spending

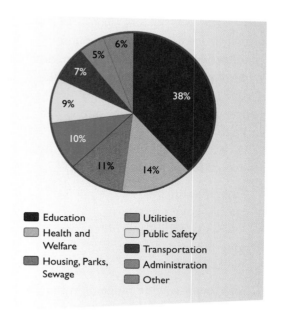

Education 38%
Public Safety 14%
Utilities 11%
Health and Welfare 10%
Housing, Parks, Sewage 9%
Transportation 7%
Administration 5%
Other 6%

Legend:
- Education
- Health and Welfare
- Housing, Parks, Sewage
- Utilities
- Public Safety
- Transportation
- Administration
- Other

* ***Other Income.*** Communities can also make money through special fees and charges. Building inspection fees, parking meters, and government-owned utilities are just a few sources of local income.

The Authority of Local Governments

When America was young, new settlements and communities were created as the nation expanded. When these communities grew, people began to establish local governments to provide necessary services.

The U.S. Constitution makes no mention of local governments. State governments determine the authority or powers of local governments within their boundaries. Today, different states give different powers to their local governments.

Supreme Court Case

New Jersey v. T.L.O. (1985)

The Fourth Amendment to the Constitution is sometimes known as the Privacy Amendment. It says, in part, that authorities cannot unreasonably search or take a person's property.

In 1980, local government employees—in this case, school officials in a town in New Jersey—searched the purse of a 14-year-old student known as T.L.O. (Because T.L.O. was a minor, her real name could not be made public in court.) She had been caught smoking cigarettes in the school bathroom. She was taken to the principal's office, where she denied the charge. However, thinking there was probable cause, an assistant principal searched T.L.O.'s purse and found not only cigarettes, but also what the school authorities believed was evidence that T.L.O. was dealing drugs. The school authorities suspended her.

A legal battle followed. T.L.O.'s family hired a lawyer and sued the school. In court, the judge ruled in T.L.O.'s favor, declaring that the assistant principal had conducted an unreasonable search in violation of the Fourth Amendment.

But the battle did not end there. The school appealed the ruling. In 1985, the Supreme Court decided that T.L.O.'s constitutional rights had not been violated and overruled the lower court's decision. According to the Supreme Court, students are protected by the Fourth Amendment in that authorities cannot search all students. But searches without a warrant are permissible as long as school authorities have a suspicion that a particular individual has broken a law. In their decision, the justices made the following statement: "Against the child's interest in privacy must be set the substantial interest of teachers and administrators in maintaining discipline in the classroom and on school grounds."

Dillon's Rule

Judge John F. Dillon was the chief justice of the Iowa Supreme Court in the mid-1800s. Dillon strongly distrusted local government because many local government officials of his day were dishonest. Government corruption led to changes and reforms in local government.

In 1868 in Iowa, Judge Dillon responded to the increasing corruption by ruling that all local governments in Iowa must be authorized by the state, and that the state has total control over them. This became known as **Dillon's Rule**. It meant that local governments could do only those things that the state *said* they could do.

During the late 1800s, cities grew and began to provide more services, such as full-time police and fire protection, school systems, sewer systems, libraries, and city parks.

↓

Taxes increased, and so did government debt.

↓

Cities had more money to spend and the power to spend it.

↓

The money and power in politics attracted political parties and party "bosses" who took control of local governments.

↓

Corruption and inefficiency became major problems.

Did You Know?

The Tweed Ring

During the late 1800s, the growth of local governments led to political corruption. The best-known gang of corrupt local officials was New York City's Tweed Ring, named for Boss William Tweed.

By encouraging contractors to overcharge the city and illegally give some of their profits to politicians, the Tweed Ring spent $13 million to construct a courthouse originally estimated to cost $250,000. A well-known reformer claimed that the building "was conceived in sin, and its dome, if ever finished, will be glazed all over with iniquity."

The state of New York sued Tweed in the Supreme Court of New York for more than $6 million. Tweed fled in 1875, but the next year, he was identified in Spain and arrested. Returned to jail in New York, he died before the suit was tried.

Home Rule

In 1871, Michigan judge Thomas Cooley objected to Dillon's Rule. Cooley stated that cities should be able to govern themselves. This led to a **home rule** movement by local governments that wanted greater independence from the state.

Home rule powers are generally granted by a state government to the local governments by one of **two** methods:

1. **Charter Form.** Local government writes a charter to be approved by the state. This charter outlines the principles, functions, and organization of a local government. It serves as the government's "constitution" and defines the rights and powers of the local government.

2. **Optional Form.** The state government provides specific choices of structures for local government, such as the council-manager form or the mayor-council form.

Home rule doesn't give a local government absolute authority. Since counties and other units of local government are created by state government, they will always be affected by state law.

Today, Dillon's Rule exists in only a few states. In some states, a mixture of home-rule and Dillon's Rule is observed. **EXAMPLE:** Virginia is generally seen as a Dillon's Rule state. However, over the years, the state legislature has granted local government broader powers.

City Governments

The government officials of early America's small towns and cities spent most of their time managing the growth of business and dealing with problems such as livestock running through the streets. In most places, city governments remained relatively small until the mid-nineteenth century.

The earliest American city governments had a mayor and **council**—a group of people who made laws and carried out the business of running the city. Reform movements of the 1800s led to new forms of government. Today, most city governments are based on one of **three** organizational plans:

1. **The Mayor-Council Plan.**
2. **The Council-Manager Plan.**
3. **The Commission Plan.**

"No, I don't want to be President. Can't you see I'm grooming myself to be a mayor or an alderman?"

Mayor Rudolph Giuliani

On December 27, 2001, New York City's mayor Rudolph Giuliani bid an emotional farewell to the city he had served for eight years. He spoke to an audience gathered in St. Paul's Chapel, which is located very close to Ground Zero, the former site of the World Trade Center. Giuliani was a strong leader during a time of terrible tragedy. In his farewell speech, he talked about it and about his city.

"I really believe we shouldn't think about this site out there, right behind us, right here, as a site for economic development. We should think about a soaring, monumental, beautiful memorial that just draws millions of people here that just want to see it. . . . We have to be able to create something here that enshrines this forever and that allows people to build on it and grow from it. And it's not going to happen if we just think about it in a very narrow way. . . . Although I have to leave you as the mayor soon, I resume the much more honorable title of citizen. And the people of the city should understand that all of the sources of my strength absolutely endure because you have it, and you have that strength and you've displayed it. . . . This place has to become a place in which, when anybody comes here, immediately they're going to feel the great power and strength and emotion of what it means to be an American."

Mayor-Council Plan

The **mayor-council plan** is the most widely used city government plan and consists of a:

* *Mayor.* The elected head of the executive branch of the city government, the equivalent of a president's or governor's role.
* *Council.* The legislative body (like Congress) elected to make laws and policies. The council typically has from five to nine members. Larger cities may have larger councils. For example, Chicago has 50 council members, called **aldermen**.

Some cities have a **strong-mayor plan** with an elected mayor who has power to veto city council action, hire or fire agency heads, and prepare and carry out budgets. Other cities have a **weak-mayor plan**. Under this plan, the mayor's power is limited. In some, the council chooses the mayor from its own members, chooses city officials, makes laws, and determines the budget. In others, like Chicago, the mayor is elected, but the state charter gives the council power to block him. Chicago's mayors have gotten around this by using the workings of the political party, the "machine," to build strong alliances with council members.

Council-Manager Plan

In response to corrupt political parties and bosses, reformers tried to lessen the role of party politics in local government. Reformers developed a **council-manager plan** with a:

* ***Council.*** The council is chosen through an election, in which candidates are not associated with any political parties. The council makes laws and hires the city manager.
* ***City Manager.*** The **manager** is a professional, nonpolitical director hired by council members. The manager can hire or fire local government employees and is responsible to the council.

The council-manager system effectively deals with many of the abuses in city government. But no form of local government is perfect. This model also has weaknesses:

* It provides no strong executive leader.
* It doesn't provide a system of checks and balances for the powers of the council.

Commission Plan

A hurricane in Galveston, Texas, in 1990, led to another plan for city government reform. The weak-mayor government of Galveston could not effectively organize the rebuilding of the city. As a result, the citizens of Galveston changed their charter to replace the mayor and city council with a **commission plan**. In this type of plan:

* Each member of the commission—a group of people authorized or elected to perform certain governmental duties—is responsible for heading a particular city department, such as housing or public safety.
* The commission is responsible for passing laws and controlling spending.
* The mayor represents the government, but has no real power.

While this plan worked well in the rebuilding of Galveston, it did not provide for a strong leader. In recent years, Galveston and many other cities have decided not to use the commission plan.

▲
New York Mayor Rudy Giuliani (right) tours Ground Zero of the World Trade Center with Secretary of Defense Donald Rumsfeld, November 2001.

County Governments

States are divided into areas, usually called counties. In Louisiana, these are called parishes. In Alaska, they are called boroughs. A **county** is another division of local government, the largest within a state.

In some places, county and city boundaries overlap. And in some places, the state government has merged the city and county. San Francisco, for example, is a city and a county. The city of New York consists of five counties or boroughs: Brooklyn (also known as Kings County), Queens, the Bronx, Manhattan, and Staten Island (also known as Richmond County).

How They Developed

The county developed in England from the *shire*, a unit of local government. Each shire was ruled by a shire-reeve, or sheriff, appointed by the king. The king appointed justices to help the sheriff take care of county business. Eventually, power passed from the king's officials to county councils elected by local residents.

English colonists established the county form of government when they came to America. Colonies were divided into counties to help carry out laws in rural areas.

In the past, counties performed duties as ordered by the state, such as:

* **Property assessment**—determining the value of buildings and land for tax purposes.
* Record-keeping for property and county information.
* Maintenance of rural roads.
* Administration of election and judicial functions.
* Assistance for the needy.

Today, counties offer other types of services and programs, as well, including child welfare, consumer protection, economic development, employment training, planning and zoning, and water quality.

How They Work

The county government is located in the county courthouse in a town called the county seat, which is a sort of county "capital." Generally, county government takes one of **three** forms:

1. **Commission.**
2. **Commission-Administrator.**
3. **Council-Executive.**

Commission

This type of county government plan usually consists of a board, or small group, of supervisors or commissioners. Board members have both executive and legislative powers. They set up programs and policies, and they pass local laws. The board members are elected by the voters of the county.

Commission-Administrator

Under this form, the county board of commissioners appoints an administrator to carry out its plans and policies. That individual may have a broad range of powers, including the authority to hire and fire department heads, and to make a budget.

New England Towns

In the New England colonies, a different form of rural government developed. Many settlers came to this country to farm, and villages soon developed as churches, schools, and other services were set up to serve the settlers. Towns were made up of the village and the farmlands around it.

In these towns, as in the model developed by the Pilgrims for the Mayflower Compact, all adult male citizens had a voice in government. The town meeting was the basis of local self-government. All townsmen had to vote in agreement before any new law or policy was passed.

Today, in the New England states of Connecticut, Maine, Massachusetts, New Hampshire, Rhode Island, and Vermont, town governments combine the function of city and county government in one unit. Each town carries on the tradition of the annual town meeting—an example of direct democracy in action. Once a year, each citizen of the town can attend the meeting at the town hall and vote on a variety of important issues affecting each of them. They also vote for local officials. The townspeople act directly in making their own laws.

Council-Executive

This form of county government has a strong executive. A county executive is the chief administrative officer who has the power to veto laws passed by the county board, and to hire and fire department heads.

Most counties still operate under the commission form, but many have moved to either the county administrator or the elected executive type.

Other Officials

Various other county officials help the board do its work.

* *County or district attorney*—lawyer for the government.
* *Sheriff*—elected official who enforces the law.
* *Superintendent of schools*—supervisor of the school system.
* *Treasurer*—official who collects taxes.
* *Auditor*—official who reviews the cash accounts of other county officers.
* *Property assessors*—officials who determine the value of property to decide the amount of taxes due from property owners.

Town, Township, and Village Governments

As counties grew, town, township, and village governments were established to provide necessary services to people living in smaller communities.

Towns and Villages

A town or village is established when the state gives power to the local government. Villages and towns today are usually governed by a board of elected officers. These officers may include a mayor or supervisor, and a council or board of **trustees**—people elected or appointed to direct the funds and policy of the government. Other officials may include a clerk, or record keeper, a justice, a health officer, and police officers.

Townships

In most northeastern and midwestern American states, counties are divided into **townships**. Townships were first established to help set up schools and to repair roads in areas far from the center of county government. Today, many duties of the township have been taken over by city and county governments.

Primary Source

Mission of Anderson Township, Cincinnati, Ohio

Board of Township Trustees
Township government in Anderson exists primarily to provide basic public services to its residents in a professional, courteous, timely, and cost-effective manner. To assure the resources necessary to provide such services, it will diligently protect its tax base and maintain its political integrity by encouraging economic development . . . and favorable state legislation. Beyond the basic services of fire and rescue, law enforcement, road maintenance, and planning and zoning, township government will work to heighten the sense of community by encouraging citizen participation and by facilitating enhancements to the quality of community life, insofar as allowed by current or future Ohio Revised Code provisions and attainable resources. Examples of current enhancements include the Anderson Trails network for walking and biking, Greenspace acquisition, passive and active recreational opportunities, senior services, historical preservation, recycling, beautification, and civic education.

Townships provide many services the county would otherwise provide, including road maintenance, fire and rescue, and law enforcement. The structure of township government varies from place to place, but township officials usually include trustees, a supervisor, a clerk, and a treasurer.

You Decide

Should a Town Put Limits on Its Growth?

In 1972, citizens of Petaluma, California, began a new trend in town planning by limiting the future growth of their town. Petaluma decided to allow no more than 500 building permits per year for new homes. Residents of Petaluma were worried about the rapid growth of their town and wanted to protect their traditional, small-town quality of life. Towns in other parts of the country have followed Petaluma's example. In each town, some residents supported the limits. Others argued against the limits. Here are some of their arguments.

Do you think a town should have the right to limit the rate of its growth? Why or why not? What would happen in your own town if a limit were placed on the rate of growth? Would you be in favor of such a limit? Give specific reasons for your answer.

Arguments <u>for</u> Limiting Growth

Limiting the size of the town protects the small-town quality of life and avoids problems like traffic congestion and pollution.

Limiting growth preserves green space that would otherwise be paved over for new housing developments.

Limiting growth avoids a boom in the local housing market and keeps home prices at an affordable level.

Lower home prices usually mean lower property taxes for residents.

Arguments <u>against</u> Limiting Growth

Growth, new businesses, and new housing developments improve the local economy.

Growth would result in a real estate boom and rising home prices that would benefit town residents who sell their homes.

An increase in population, higher home prices, and new businesses all result in higher tax revenues that can pay for important services in town.

Growth would allow more people to move into a town in which they would like to live.

Special Districts

Believe it or not, the most common kind of local government in the United States is known as the **special district**. Some special districts are called boards, authorities, or corporations.

What They Do

Special districts are units of local, special-purpose government set up to operate within specific limits. They are created to provide specific services to citizens that existing local governments do not provide, such as:

* Water districts.
* Fire districts.
* Park districts.
* Library districts.
* Insect control districts.
* Metropolitan transit districts (for public transportation).

Special districts may be created by general law, special act, local ordinance, or by rule of the governor and cabinet.

Did You Know?

The First Special District

Benjamin Franklin established the first special district in Philadelphia in 1736, the Union Fire Company of Philadelphia, which was a volunteer fire department. People living in certain neighborhoods paid a fee for fire-protection services. Soon, many volunteer fire departments formed throughout the city. Franklin boasted that his city had the best fire service in the world.

How They Work

Many special districts are governed by an elected board of directors. The directors of some districts are appointed. Districts raise money to pay for their services by:

* Charging fees.
* Receiving funding from the state, city, or county.

The boundaries of some special districts are large enough to include several **municipalities** or urban governments. Some districts even cut across state lines. **EXAMPLE:** The Port of New York Authority was created by the states of New York and New Jersey to operate the harbor facilities on both sides of New York Harbor.

Issues in Local Government

By now you may be wondering how all of these governments relate to one another and work together to provide services to citizens. What challenges do they face?

Finances

What happens if there's not enough tax money to pay for the services that citizens need? Local governments may have to cut services to the community.

In 1978, the California state legislature passed Proposition 13. The new law was the result of complaints from taxpayers. Many California homeowners were upset about high property taxes. The value of homes in the area had risen dramatically in just a few years, and the taxes went up in response. Proposition 13 reduced taxes back to 1976 levels, and limited how much the government could raise the taxes in future. Property owners across the state saved billions of dollars in taxes.

However, although lower taxes made many Californians happy, lower tax *revenues* meant less money for the state to spend and, therefore, fewer services for citizens. The budgets for California's county governments were reduced, and spending cutbacks followed in education, law enforcement, and public services.

Fragmentation

By the 1920s, people were moving in larger numbers from the cities into the suburbs. This resulted in more and more local government bodies sharing authority within a single **metropolitan area**—a city and its surrounding suburbs.

EXAMPLE: The number of local governments in suburban St. Louis County, Missouri, increased from 21 in 1930, to 41 in 1940, to 83 in 1950.

All of these suburban governments faced a challenge. How could they work together to provide services and policies? Some metropolitan areas take a regional approach to tackle their problems. These governments tend to:

* *Combine.* The city government adds on or incorporates the suburbs. The entire area is governed as a whole by the city government.
* *Cooperate.* The city government handles problems affecting the entire metropolitan area, and the individual governments within the area deal with local issues.

Cooperation

Even though their priorities may not always be the same, federal, state, and local governments can work together to solve problems effectively. Groups such as the National League of Cities and the

National Association of Counties coordinate policies and share information across levels of government.

EXAMPLE: Federal, state, and local governments work together to solve crimes. The Federal Bureau of Investigation (FBI) trains local law enforcement officers. And local police depend on the FBI for information on known criminals who may have committed crimes in other cities and states.

It is not always clear which government body within an area is responsible for providing or funding a particular service. Sometimes the different government units share the responsibility. As government layers overlap, groups must cooperate to solve problems.

Chapter 10 Wrap-up
LOCAL GOVERNMENT

Local governments throughout the United States include cities, counties, towns, townships, villages, and special districts. Local governments provide important services related to education, public safety, health and welfare, land use, utilities, and housing. Money for these services comes from taxes, federal and state governments, and local income.

The U.S. Constitution doesn't mention local governments, so states determine how much power local governments have. Some states put strong limits on local governments. Other states allow home rule, giving local governments greater authority and independence.

Most city governments are organized by one of three plans: mayor-council plan, council-manager plan, or commission plan. County governments are usually organized by one of three plans: commission, commission-administrator, or council-executive. Smaller divisions of local government include townships, villages, and towns.

Special districts are formed for specific functions. They are run by boards and raise money to pay for their services through fees and government funding.

Local governments face many challenges. Often, the authority and responsibilities of various levels of local government overlap, so local governments must cooperate to solve problems.

alderman—city council member; legislator in a local government. *p. 164*

commission plan—form of city government in which commission members take responsibility for specific departments; commission members have both executive and legislative powers. *p. 165*

council—group of people elected or appointed to serve as legislators or administrators. *p. 163*

council-manager plan—form of city government that includes an elected council and an appointed manager. *p. 165*

county—largest division for local government within a state. The county seat is the location of county government. *p. 166*

Dillon's Rule—1868 ruling by Iowa judge John F. Dillon that local governments must be authorized by the state and have no powers except those specifically granted by state law. *p. 162*

grant—money given for a specific purpose. *p. 159*

home rule—power of a local government to direct its own affairs with some degree of independence from the state. *p. 163*

manager—person who controls or directs; nonpolitical person hired by city council to manage city business. *p. 165*

mayor—head of government for a city, town, or municipality. *p. 164*

mayor-council plan—form of city government that includes a mayor and council. *p. 164*

metropolitan area—city and its suburbs. *p. 171*

municipality—city, town, or village with a local government; usually an urban area. *p. 170*

property assessment—calculation of the value of buildings and land for tax purposes. *p. 166*

special district—local government unit, often called a board, authority, or corporation, created to provide a specific service. *p. 170*

strong-mayor plan—form of local government in which an elected mayor has executive powers. *p. 164*

township—in most northeast and midwest American states, an area within a county that has a unit of local government. *p. 168*

trustees—people elected or appointed to direct the funds and policy of a government body or of a corporation or institution. *p. 168*

weak-mayor plan—form of local government in which a mayor is responsible to a council and given limited powers. *p. 164*

zoning—dividing an area by law for different purposes; areas may be zoned for homes, business, and the like. *p. 159*

How Our Political System Works: Parties, Politics, and Participation

In this chapter, you will learn about:

- why we have political parties
- election campaigns
- how voting and elections work

John Adams feared the "division of the republic into two great parties, each arranged under its leader, and concerting measures [arranged agreements] in opposition to each other." James Madison referred to political parties as a "mortal disease." According to Alexander Hamilton, political parties were an "avenue to tyranny," and encouraged such undesirable qualities as "ambition, avarice, and personal animosity." George Washington thought political parties caused "frightful despotism."

Why did the Founding Fathers distrust political parties?

The writers of the Constitution avoided any discussion of political parties when they wrote their plan for a new government. Yet the ink on the Constitution was barely dry when America's two-party system of government began to take shape. Still today, many people still distrust political parties. Nonetheless, parties play an important role in the American political process.

Political Parties

Have you ever supported a candidate for student government in a school election? Or maybe you cheered for a candidate in the last presidential election. If so, you have been part of a political process.

American citizens can vote for their elected representatives. And elected representatives can vote for or support proposed new laws. But one citizen or one representative can cast only one vote. **Political parties** are organized groups who choose, support, vote for, and promote party-approved candidates for public office, based on shared beliefs. Party members (and the candidates they elect) are people with similar views. They join forces to get more political power. Members of parties pool their voting numbers and organizational strength to:

* Back candidates to help them win elections.
* Organize support for specific new laws and issues.

I STRONGLY SUPPORT CAMPAIGN REFORM!

AND I SUPPORT IT TOO, BUT DOUBLE WHAT HE SAYS!!

If the parties are successful, their chosen candidates are elected. As government representatives, those elected leaders gain power and can directly determine **public policy**—the principles that form the basis for our laws. The party has plans and ideas that it tries to turn into government actions and laws.

Members of a political party share certain beliefs about what the government should do, and the members of the party decide as a group:

* Which issues are most important.
* How to deal with those issues for the public good.
* Which candidates and lawmakers should represent their views.
* How elected lawmakers should support the party's shared vision and what laws should be proposed and passed.

If a party can get enough members elected to office, it can control policy on local, state, and national levels.

Voters support a party because they agree with its basic ideas and positions on particular issues. Members and supporters of the same party may not agree on every party policy, but they compromise on minor differences for the good of the group. By participating in political parties, citizens can become an active and stronger part of the political process.

Functions of Political Parties

Political parties carry out their activities at local, state, and national levels. They use their organization, numbers, and shared resources to shape government and government policy. Political parties do **seven** different things. They:

1. **Choose and Support Candidates.** Parties recruit and support candidates for all elected political offices.
2. **Work to Win Elections.** Parties organize voter registration drives, recruit volunteers to work at the polls, and work to encourage citizens to vote, especially for that party.
3. **Act as Watchdogs.** Political parties provide a system of checks and balances. Each party watches other parties. They report wrongdoing and oppose other parties' policies and decisions.
4. **Set Policy.** Each party develops a **political platform**—the party's formal declaration of its principles and policies on important public issues. Party members elected to office work together to get these policies carried out in government.
5. **Communicate Information.** Parties educate and try to influence citizens on policies and issues.
6. **Lobby.** Parties help keep government officials informed of voters' opinions.
7. **Provide Leadership.** Parties work to elect their members to office and to gain support for policies among elected officials.

"I think it was an election year."

Political Parties in America

In his farewell address to the nation after two terms as America's first president, George Washington urged Americans to prevent political parties from causing conflict and weakening national unity. Later, Thomas Jefferson, in his inaugural address, spoke of the divisions between the two political parties, the Republicans and the Federalists, that had emerged in his era:

"Every difference of opinion is not a difference of principle. We have called by different names brethren of the same principle. We are all Republicans—we are all Federalists."

History of Political Parties

President George Washington had hoped to build a strong, unified nation in which there would be no need for political parties. But Washington's vision proved to be unrealistic. In the earliest years of our nation's history, major differences of political opinion made unity difficult to achieve.

Development of Major Political Parties

Federalists

Alexander Hamilton, George Washington's Secretary of the Treasury, was the leader of the Federalists. The party supported a strong national government. The party lost power in the early 1800s.

Democratic Republicans

Thomas Jefferson supported the power of the states and opposed a strong national government. He led the Democratic Republicans. From 1816 to 1828, voters regularly elected Democratic Republicans to the presidency and to Congress.

Whig Party

In 1828, some members of the Democratic Republicans left that group and formed the Whig Party (first called the National Republicans). During the 1850s, the Whig Party fell apart because of sharp disagreements over the issue of slavery.

Democrats

After Andrew Jackson was elected in 1828, the group who supported him took on the name Democrats. (Earlier, they had been known as Democratic Republicans.) They held their first national presidential nominating convention in 1832, and are the world's oldest continuing political party.

Republicans

The Republican Party emerged during the 1850s as an antislavery party. It took the label of Grand Old Party, or GOP. In 1860, Abraham Lincoln was elected the first Republican president.

"Yes, son, we're Republicans."

Comparing Party Platforms

2000 Democratic Platform Education Reforms	2000 Republican Platform Education Reforms
By the end of the next presidential term, we should have a fully qualified, well trained teacher in every classroom, in every school, in every part of this country—and every teacher should pass a rigorous test to get there.	Raise academic standards through increased local control and accountability to parents, shrinking a multitude of federal programs into five flexible grants in exchange for real, measured progress in student achievement.
By the end of the next presidential term, every failing school in America should be turned around—or shut down and reopened under new public leadership.	Assist states in closing the achievement gap and empower needy families to escape persistently failing schools by allowing federal dollars to follow their children to the school of their choice.
By the end of the next presidential term, we should ensure that no high school student graduates unless he or she has mastered the basics of reading and math.	Ensure that all children learn to read by facilitating state reading initiatives that focus on scientifically based reading research, including phonics.
By the end of the next presidential term, parents across the nation ought to be able to choose the best public school for their children.	Help states ensure school safety by letting children in dangerous schools transfer to schools that are safe for learning and by forcefully prosecuting youths who carry or use guns and the adults who provide them.
By the end of the next presidential term, high-quality, affordable preschool should be fully available to every family, for every child, in every community.	

Importance of Third Parties

Although the Republican and Democratic parties dominate politics in America today, many third parties have challenged them. Third parties—like the Green Party, the Reform Party, and the Libertarian Party—have been formed to support a specific issue or candidate for office and to challenge the major parties.

No third-party candidate has ever been elected president, but these political parties have shaped politics in America by:

* *Influencing the outcome of elections.* A third-party candidate can draw votes away from one major party, giving an advantage to the competing party. **EXAMPLE:** In 1912, Theodore Roosevelt's Bull Moose Progressive Party split off from the Republican Party. Roosevelt attracted some (mostly) Republican votes, allowing Democrat Woodrow Wilson to defeat Republican William Taft.

* *Raising important issues.* Many minor parties have been formed to support specific issues. **EXAMPLE:** H. Ross Perot, an Independent candidate in the 1992 election, based his campaign on the budget deficit issue. The Green Party, led by Ralph Nader, focused on environmental and consumer issues in the 2000 presidential election.

* *Getting candidates elected to office.* In 1998, former pro wrestler Jesse Ventura, a Reform Party candidate, was elected governor of Minnesota.

Party Organization

Each level within a political party organization—local, state, and national—works closely with the other levels. However, each level is independent. No level of the party has real control over any other level.

Local and State Levels

At the local level, party members work to get party candidates elected. The voting districts, or **precincts**, are the building blocks of party organization. Each precinct has a party leader or chairperson who organizes volunteers. These volunteers do the real work of the campaign. They make phone calls, mail brochures, and do door-to-door visits to persuade voters to vote for their candidates.

At the state level, party leaders write a state party platform. They also nominate candidates for office, raise money, hold state conventions, and help with election campaigns.

National Level

At the national level, the party organization holds a large meeting—or **political convention**—in presidential election years to choose a party presidential candidate. In addition to choosing candidates, convention delegates also write the party's platform for the election. The party then organizes election campaigns and helps candidates with advice from campaign consultants, by fundraising, and other by activities.

Party Structure

National chairpersons and national committee   (National)

State committees and state conventions   (State)

Congressional district committees   (State)

City and county committees   (Local)

Precinct organizations   (Local)

Party members and volunteers   (Local)

Texas delegates on the floor of the Republican National Convention, August 2000. ▶

Political Parties Today

America's two-party system of government is always changing. The role of political parties in elections changes to fit the current situation. In recent years, **three** main changes have been seen:

1. *Party Loyalty Is Weaker.* Voters today are less likely to vote for only one political party. More and more citizens now vote a **split ticket**, voting for who they think are the best candidates, regardless of the candidates' parties.

   EXAMPLE: A citizen might vote for a Republican for president and a Democrat for Congress.

2. *There Are More Independent Voters.* The number of voters who consider themselves "independent"—not loyal to either major party—increased from less than 20 percent of voters in the 1940s to more than 30 percent in the 1990s. Independent voters sometimes support third-party candidates.

3. *More Elections Are Nonpartisan.* In a **nonpartisan** election, candidates run without any official association with a political party. The **ballots**—lists of candidates' names that voters mark when they vote—do not include any party names.

Election Campaigns

An **election campaign** consists of all of the pre-election activities used to secure votes in an election. The campaign begins with the selection of candidates.

Choosing Candidates

The process used to **nominate**—or propose a candidate for office—can be simple or complicated. The higher the office, the more complicated the process. A person can become a candidate for political office in several ways:

* *Self-nomination.* A person can simply declare that she or he is running for office in many local campaigns.
* *Caucus.* Some states use a **caucus**, or meeting of party members, to select candidates and decide on policies. Most caucuses are open to the public.
* *Write-in.* Voters can write any name, their own or someone else's, as a candidate on a ballot in any election.
* *Nominating petition.* In many places, someone who wants to be a candidate must obtain a certain number of voter signatures on a petition to get nominated.
* *Convention.* For some offices, candidates are chosen by vote of party members or delegates at a party convention.

Primary Elections

In a direct **primary election**, voters decide which of the candidates within a party will represent that party in the general election. Primary elections were first ordered in Iowa in 1903 to allow more of the ordinary party members, not just those with influence or money, to become the party's candidates.

In some states, entering a primary as a candidate is fairly easy. In New Hampshire, for example, anyone can be listed on the primary ballot just by paying a $1,000 filing fee! Most states use one of **two** types of primaries:

1. **Closed Primary.** Voters must be registered as party members to vote in that party's primary.
2. **Open Primary.** Citizens can vote in either party's primary without stating their party affiliation.

Nominating Convention

At one time, presidential candidates were actually chosen at the Democratic or Republican national party conventions. Party leaders made all of the decisions. Today, the primary process usually makes the party's choice for a presidential candidate clear before the convention takes place. The convention delegates vote to make the party's choice of candidate official. Delegates also:

* **Approve** the candidate for vice president, who is usually chosen by the nominee for president.
* **Write** and approve the party platform.
* **Carry out** other party business.

Running the Campaign

After a candidate is nominated for office by his or her party, the campaign to win the actual election begins. The general election campaign needs careful planning and organization.

Planning and Organizing

A successful campaign requires a large team of volunteers and hired staff—all working to inform the public and persuade people to vote for their candidate. Key campaign workers include:

* **Campaign manager.** The manager directs and coordinates the campaign.
* **Finance manager.** This person coordinates fundraising for the campaign.
* **Pollsters.** These experts conduct public opinion surveys on important issues. Survey results help the candidate to understand the feelings and concerns of voters.
* **Press secretary.** The press secretary releases news about the candidate and the campaign to the media. The press secretary makes sure that the candidate is in the news and helps shape the candidate's public image.
* **Volunteers.** Volunteer staff workers carry out important, behind-the-scenes campaign activities. They make telephone calls to the voters, pass out print promotion (sometimes called campaign literature), and organize campaign events.

Media and Messages

Candidates use a variety of tools to try to influence the news media and the public. A wide range of communication tools are used to influence voters' ideas and opinions. Some of the methods used to influence and persuade voters to vote for them are:

* Direct mail campaigns.
* Bumper stickers, buttons, and posters.
* Fliers or small brochures.
* Speeches, political rallies, and personal appearances.
* Press conferences.
* **Debates**—public discussions of the issues—with the opposing candidate(s).
* Television, radio, newspapers, magazines, and the Internet.

Media consultants determine the strategy for their candidate's television, radio, and print advertisements. Political ads can be either, or a mix, of **two** approaches:

1. **Positive.** Focusing on the candidate's qualifications, family, experience, or ideas on various issues.

2. **Negative.** Attacking an opponent's character, ability, or believability on issues. More and more ads today use this approach, although many voters would like to see the practice stopped.

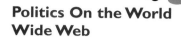

Did You Know?

Politics On the World Wide Web

In recent years, the Internet has become an important (and fairly inexpensive) tool in political campaigns. In 1998, Reform Party candidate Jesse Ventura was elected governor of Minnesota by using the Internet to defeat his established Democratic and Republican opponents. Ventura built, expanded, and promoted his campaign over the Internet. Political parties and individual candidates now have web sites. Millions of Americans log on to the Internet to get campaign and election information.

Campaign Financing

Candidates need a lot of money to run successful political campaigns, especially at the national level.

EXAMPLE: The Dole and Clinton presidential campaigns spent a combined total of $232 million in the 1996 presidential election.

Politicians receive donations from many sources, mostly private but also public. The **Federal Election Commission** (FEC) is responsible for ensuring that all contributions are made and received according to the law.

Private Sources

Four important sources of private funding include donations from:

1. **Individual Citizens.** Federal law allows individuals to contribute up to $1,000 per election to a federal candidate. Individuals can also contribute up to a maximum amount per year to a political party.

2. **Political Action Committees (PACs).** These special interest groups raise money for political causes. You will learn about them in Chapter 12.

3. **Democratic and Republican National and State Committees.**

4. **The Candidate.** Many candidates use some of their own money to pay for campaigns.

Public Funds

Citizens can give $3 from their income taxes to a presidential campaign fund. To be eligible to receive grants from these funds, candidates must do **two** things:

1. Agree to limit their spending to the amount of the grant.

2. Agree not to accept private contributions for the campaign. As a result, few candidates ever accept these funds.

Campaign Finance Reform

Current campaign financing laws are designed to make sure that the public knows where politicians get their money and how much money they get. The theory behind these laws is that voters need to know which special interest groups may be influencing politicians in an election.

You've already learned about how politicians can legally raise money for their federal elections. However, corporations, labor unions, and other interest groups have made large contributions over and above the legal limits. This happened because the law allowed these groups to give "soft" money for *general* voter activity—for example, contributing to a party's efforts to register voters.

Some groups and politicians are trying to make these contributions illegal and remove the role of "soft" money from campaigns. Others think that the soft money system is fair and should not be changed.

Do you think that campaign finance reform is necessary? Why or why not? If money were no longer an issue in an election, what do you think would be the most important factors in determining a winner?

Arguments for Campaign Finance Reform

Money plays too large a role in the political process and corrupts the democratic process.

Groups who contribute large sums of money to a political campaign are, in effect, buying the influence of the candidate. Groups who give more money to campaigns have more influence with politicians than average voters.

The current system gives an unfair advantage to the candidate whose campaign can raise the most money.

Arguments against Campaign Finance Reform

All groups have a right to express their political opinions in a democracy.

New limits on campaign spending might prevent a candidate from successfully competing against an opponent whose campaign is better-funded.

Spending limits might make it harder for a challenger to defeat an incumbent, who already has the advantage.

Voting and Elections

In the lack of judgment, great harm arises, but one vote cast can set right a house.
—Aeschylus, ancient Greek author

Citizens help create their governments by the choices they make at the polls. They need to know the candidates and the issues. As an informed voter, you can influence the world around you.

Requirements for Voting

Voting requirements vary slightly from state to state, but as a general rule, you can vote in the United States if you are:

* An American citizen.
* At least 18 years old.
* A resident of the state in which you vote.

People convicted of felonies and people being treated for mental disabilities are not allowed to vote.

Additionally, you must be registered to vote. **Registration** is the process of signing up to vote in the district or area where you live.

Voter Turnout

In the United States, slightly more than half of all eligible voters actually vote in a presidential election.

People choose not to vote for a variety of reasons. Some feel the government is not effective and doesn't represent their point of view. Others don't trust the candidates or are turned off by negative campaigns and by fighting between the parties.

Reasons Registered Voters Give for Not Voting

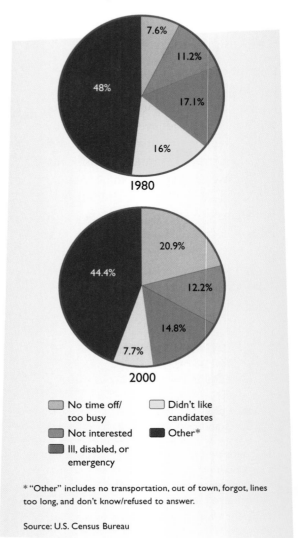

1980

2000

☐ No time off/ too busy
☐ Not interested
☐ Ill, disabled, or emergency
☐ Didn't like candidates
☐ Other*

* "Other" includes no transportation, out of town, forgot, lines too long, and don't know/refused to answer.

Source: U.S. Census Bureau

Even if you agree with some of these reasons, remember that voting is an important responsibility. Your vote tells people in government what you think and feel. Voting is the most powerful tool you have for influencing your government.

You Can Participate in Politics

What can you do to be a part of the election process? Here are **four** ideas:

1. **Work for Voter Registration.** Contact your local voter registration office and ask what you can do to help get people registered to vote.

2. **Get Directly Involved.** Become a student member of your local school board, neighborhood committee, or community council. Work to establish a student position if there is none.

3. **Work to Support or Defeat a Particular Local Issue.** Write letters to editors of local newspapers or talk to neighbors.

4. **Campaign for a Candidate Who Is Running for Office.** Call or visit your candidate's staff to find out how you can help. Run errands for the staff; conduct a letter-writing campaign; telephone residents urging them to vote for your candidate; hand out fliers; or write an article about the candidate for your school or local newspaper.

Elections

Every four years, Americans vote for their president. Federal congressional and presidential elections always take place on the Tuesday after the first Monday in November.

Casting and Counting Votes

Citizens can vote in one of **two** ways:

1. **Secret Ballot.** On Election Day, most voters go to a **polling place**. The voter goes into a voting booth and casts his or her vote in secret. Some ballots have to be marked (next to candidates' names). Others are marked with a hole-punch device. Some polls use mechanical voting machines, which ask voters to pull levers to record their votes.

2. **Absentee Ballot.** Voters who are ill, disabled, out of town, or in the military at election time can vote using an **absentee ballot**. Absentee ballots sent by mail must be received by the close of the polls on Election Day in most states.

As soon as each poll closes on Election Day, the process of counting the votes begins. Although problems in the counting process can occur, such as in Florida during the 2000 presidential election, the system almost always works well.

If the results of an election are very close, a state may require a **recount** of the votes. A candidate or a voter may also file a petition to request a recount. Rarely, a recount leads to an order for a **runoff election**—a new election between the candidates to settle any confusion in a close outcome from the first round of voting.

Supreme Court Case

Bush v. Gore (2000)

Weeks after Election Day in 2000, supporters of George W. Bush and Al Gore were still arguing for the presidency. To win, either candidate needed 270 electoral votes. The nation focused its attention on Florida, where Bush and Gore each received about 49 percent of the vote. Both candidates needed Florida's 25 electoral votes to win.

After weeks of court battles and disagreements during vote recounts (mostly about how to interpret any ballots that had been improperly punched), the Florida Supreme Court ordered certain counties to recount their ballots. The Bush group protested the decision, and the case went to the U.S. Supreme Court.

That Court's decision made Bush the country's new president.

In their decision, the majority justices stated that the recount process had been unconstitutional because the Florida Supreme Court had not set up statewide guidelines for how to "read" unclearly punched ballots. As a result, the Court said, there was no way to make sure the recounts were done fairly. For example, the Court ruling stated: "A monitor in Miami-Dade County testified at trial that he observed that three members of the county canvassing board applied different standards in defining a legal vote."

The Court went on to say that "This [the recount process] is not a process with sufficient guarantees of equal treatment . . . The recount process, in its features here described, is inconsistent with the minimum procedures necessary to protect the fundamental right of each voter in the special instance of a statewide recount."

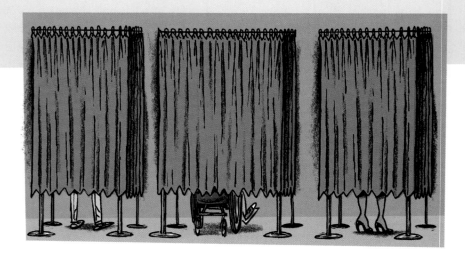

The Electoral College

You already know that final ballots in a presidential election (the ones that actually elect the president) are cast by members of the Electoral College—representatives from each state, known as electors.

Article II of the Constitution established the Electoral College, but the Twelfth Amendment changed the electoral voting process. The chart below shows how the Electoral College works today.

How the Electoral College Works Today

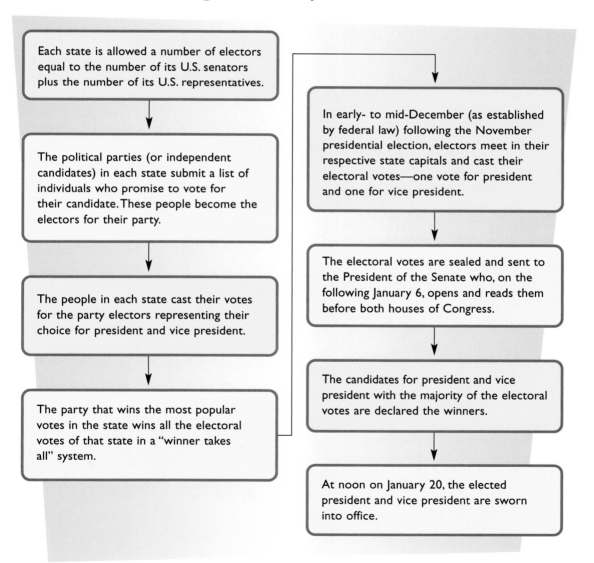

Each state is allowed a number of electors equal to the number of its U.S. senators plus the number of its U.S. representatives.

The political parties (or independent candidates) in each state submit a list of individuals who promise to vote for their candidate. These people become the electors for their party.

The people in each state cast their votes for the party electors representing their choice for president and vice president.

The party that wins the most popular votes in the state wins all the electoral votes of that state in a "winner takes all" system.

In early- to mid-December (as established by federal law) following the November presidential election, electors meet in their respective state capitals and cast their electoral votes—one vote for president and one for vice president.

The electoral votes are sealed and sent to the President of the Senate who, on the following January 6, opens and reads them before both houses of Congress.

The candidates for president and vice president with the majority of the electoral votes are declared the winners.

At noon on January 20, the elected president and vice president are sworn into office.

What's on a Ballot?

National elections are held along with state and local elections. When you look at a ballot, you will see candidates' names for such offices as:

* President and Vice President.
* Senator.
* Congressional Representative.
* Governor.
* State House member.
* State Senator.
* Mayor.
* Alderman.
* Judge.
* Board member.

We vote for president and vice president every four years, but we have elections every two years, because the term of office of members of Congress is only two years.

In addition to candidates' names, a ballot may contain questions for the voters to decide, such as:

* Whether to issue bonds to raise money for the schools.
* Whether the town should purchase a parcel of land for a new park.
* Whether the state's power to raise taxes should be limited.

Some questions on the ballot are "binding," which means the governing body must do what the voters say. Others are not binding, but help elected officials understand what the voters want.

Going to the Polls

Polling places are in public buildings, like schools, libraries, government buildings, and in private places the public can easily get to, such as shopping malls, the lobbies of office buildings, and the like. When you register to vote, you will get a card that shows the district in which you are registered. Your local government office can tell you where the polling place is for your district.

As you approach the polling place, you'll see an American flag flying. Often there may be people handing out literature or "sample ballots" that urge you to vote for certain candidates or for or against the issues on the ballot. Local laws will prevent these people from getting too near the polling place.

It is perfectly all right to bring notes or newspaper articles to help you remember how you want to vote.

Inside, you will join a line of people waiting to vote. As you get to the front, you'll see citizens serving as election judges sitting at a table. One will ask you to register. You sign in, and the judge matches your signature with one in a big book that was obtained when you registered.

You may see people in the room who are neither voters nor election judges. These people are observers. Political parties send observers to be sure everything is done fairly. So do interested organizations, such as the League of Women Voters. Often there is also a policeman there to protect the voting process.

After you've registered, a judge will hand you a ballot, and you may have to wait until a voting booth is free.

Inside the voting booth, you will mark the ballot. There will be instructions on how to do it. Also, you may ask an election judge for assistance, if you are unsure. There are three kinds of ballots:

* Paper ballots you mark with a pen or pencil.
* Cards that you insert into a slot in a book with the candidates' names and issues. You punch holes next to the items you vote for with a special punch, and your vote is recorded on the card.

* Voting machines in which you pull down levers beside the names you want to vote for. When you are certain you have voted s you intended, you pull a large lever to record your vote.

Your vote is confidential. No one in the polling place may ask you how you voted. No one can pressure you to vote a certain way. This is one of our most important freedoms. And remember, your vote counts!

Chapter 11 Wrap-up
HOW OUR POLITICAL SYSTEM WORKS

Political parties are groups of citizens organized to promote and support specific ideas for government and candidates for public office. Parties choose and support candidates, organize and run elections, set policy, communicate information to and from the public, and provide leadership.

Today, the Republican and Democratic parties dominate politics in America. Several third parties exist to challenge them, supporting specific causes or candidates for office.

The various levels of a political party—local, state, and national—all work to get party candidates elected to office. Party members help write plans or platforms, nominate candidates, raise money, and work on election campaigns.

Campaigns begin with the nomination of a candidate for office, sometimes after a primary campaign. Political campaigns include all of the activities undertaken to secure votes and win an election—organizing rallies, fundraisers, debates, candidate speeches, and press conferences, and advertising in the media.

Voting is an important right and responsibility, and there are specific rules for making sure that voters and their ballots are treated fairly.

WORDS TO KNOW

absentee ballot—ballot submitted for an election by a voter who is not able to be present at the polls. *p. 187*

ballot—list of candidates' names that a voter marks when casting a vote. Secret ballots are cast privately. *p. 181*

caucus—meeting of party members for the purpose of choosing a candidate or setting policy. *p. 181*

debate—orderly discussion of issues between two parties; for example, a discussion of issues between two candidates for president. *p. 183*

election campaign—organized series of actions and events designed to get a person elected to office. *p. 181*

Federal Election Commission (FEC)—government organization responsible for seeing that all financial contributions to political parties and candidates are made and received according to the law. *p. 184*

nominate—to propose someone as a candidate for office. *p. 181*

nonpartisan—not associated with a political party. *p. 181*

political convention—meeting of the delegates of a political party for the purpose of writing a platform and choosing candidates for office. *p. 179*

political party—group of citizens organized to promote and support specific ideas for government and candidates for public office. *p. 175*

political platform—formal declaration of the principles and policies of a political party. *p. 176*

polling place—place where votes are cast. *p. 187*

precinct—for election purposes, a division of a county, town, or city. *p. 179*

primary election—election in which voters decide which of the candidates within a party will represent the party in the general election. In a closed primary, only voters registered as party members may vote for candidates of their party. In an open primary, voters may vote for the candidates of either party (but not both parties) without stating their party affiliation. *p. 182*

public policy—principles that form the basis for our laws. *p. 175*

recount—formal process of counting votes again. *p. 187*

registration—process of signing up to vote. *p. 186*

runoff election—new election held to decide a close outcome in the first round of voting. *p. 187*

split ticket—ballot cast by a person who votes for candidates from more than one party. *p. 181*

Public Opinion and Interest Groups

In this chapter, you will learn about:

- **how public opinion is shaped and measured**
- **how propaganda is used to influence public opinion**
- **what special interest groups are and how they influence government**

Do you think the Internet should be censored? Do students take too many tests in school? Is there too much violence on TV for little kids to see? When large numbers of people answer questions about current issues like these, the result is called public opinion.

Lawmakers and other groups use polls and other tools to find out what opinions voters hold. In this way, public opinion shapes how elected officials act.

Public opinion, however, can also be shaped and changed. Governments and other organizations try to influence public opinion, using a variety of techniques, to get voters to understand and support their policies or vote for them in elections.

Citizens can do more than answer polls to make their opinions known. They can join special interest groups—organizations that actively work to inform and influence the public and lawmakers about issues. Some people think that these groups have too much influence on the government. Others believe that they are an important part of the democratic process.

Propaganda and Public Opinion

You have your own personal opinions about ideas, things, and people around you. **Public opinion** refers to the feelings, thoughts, and positions that many Americans have on political or social issues, such as:

* Should college athletes get paid?
* Is the president doing a good job?
* Should people be able to copy music from the Internet for free?

Factors Influencing Public Opinion

Several factors shape what you and other citizens think and believe. These factors may include:

* *Your family.* Young children learn the values and opinions of their families, even when those values are not directly taught. They hear adult discussions about news items, people, and ideas.
* *The schools.* One of the tasks of schools is **enculturation**—passing on the beliefs and values of the culture.
  EXAMPLE: Schools often have written or understood codes of conduct that ask students to show respect toward other people. Respecting other people is a cultural value that schools encourage.
* *Your religion.* The values of a person's church or religious beliefs often influence her or his opinions.

* *Molders of public opinion.* Many people, and maybe you, are influenced by famous people.
* *The mass media.* What people hear on radio, see on television, or read about in newspapers, magazines, or on the Internet influences their opinions.

Propaganda

Frequently, the government and other institutions and individuals try to get people to believe certain ideas. **Propaganda**—the communication of information to spread certain ideas, beliefs, or practices and shape public opinion—is one way to do this. Propaganda can be deceptive or dishonest. This form of communication and opinion making often disregards truth and is misleading.

Common Propaganda Techniques

Some propaganda techniques are intended to interfere with your ability to listen closely and think things through clearly.

"No, I _don't_ want to know what my approval rating is."

Types of Propaganda

Propaganda Technique	How It Works	Example
Name-Calling	Insulting or describing someone negatively.	When a lawmaker urges budget cuts, those who oppose the budget cuts may say she is *stingy, cheap,* or *penny-pinching* to try to make her look wrong-minded.
Glittering Generalities	Linking what someone says with something most people consider good or positive; the opposite of name-calling. **Generalities** are broad, sweeping statements.	People who want citizens to support a military effort use terms such as *patriotism, defending democracy,* or *protecting rights.* Because the generalities are positive, anyone who questions the effort might appear to be unpatriotic or anti-democratic.
Euphemisms	Using indirect or different words to make something sound less unpleasant.	Enemy civilians accidentally killed during bombing raids are called "collateral damage."
Transfer	Connecting two ideas that aren't really related, either to encourage or to criticize an idea.	After Sept. 11, a number of companies used ads that featured patriotic, red-white-and-blue images, suggesting that loyal Americans should buy their products.
Testimonial	Using someone famous to promote an idea, even though he or she may be no more qualified to make a judgment about an idea than the average person.	A famous actress endorses a line of cosmetics or a perfume. Famous athletes are seen on the front of a cereal box. TV and movie stars endorse political candidates.
Plain Folks	Using "folksy" images and speech to make candidates or ideas appear good for ordinary people; the opposite of testimonials.	Campaign TV clips have shown President Clinton eating hamburgers and President Reagan chopping wood on his ranch. These images made both men appear to be "regular guys."
Bandwagon	Creating a sense of excitement to make people want to join in because "everyone else is doing it."	Political conventions feature happy people wearing colorful hats, waving flags, and cheering to upbeat music. The excitement makes people want to join in and not be left out.

more **Types of Propaganda**		
Propaganda Technique	**How It Works**	**Example**
Card Stacking	Offering only those facts that support one side of an issue. Propagandists rarely present arguments both _for_ and _against_ an issue; listeners need to recognize that they might be hearing only one side from each group.	When some environmentalists protest logging or mining, they provide scientific evidence about the damaging effects on the earth and people. Pro-logging and mining groups might focus their evidence just on protecting jobs and the economy. Both sides have arguments that should be considered, but each side presents only facts to support its own position.
Fear	Suggesting that something terrible will happen if people don't believe or behave in a recommended way.	In 1964, President Lyndon Johnson's campaign suggested that if his opponent, Barry Goldwater, became president, he might start a nuclear war.
Exaggeration	Making predictions or statements without enough facts to support them.	You may have friends who exaggerate. You may even have told your own parents that you should be able to do something because "_everybody's_ parents let them do it." Everybody?

Shaping Public Opinion

Of course, shaping of opinion is not always unfair or dishonest. Public opinion helps check government power. James Madison once said, "Public opinion sets bounds to every government and is the real sovereign in every free one."

Public officials listen to public opinion, but they shape it, too. Public opinion is also shaped by the mass media and special interest groups.

Public Officials

Public opinion is shaped by government officials, such as:

* **Legislators.** Elected representatives attempt to shape public opinion so voters will support them and their policies. EXAMPLE: Before an important vote is taken in Congress, a senator may send out a mailing to citizens to explain why passage of the bill will (or won't) be a good thing for them. He or she may also point out why opponents' arguments are wrong or weak.

* **The executive.** Modern presidents and governors and their advisors can use the reach of **mass media**—media that reach large numbers of people, like television and newspapers—to explain their ideas or ask the public for support on issues. The voter support they gather this way, sometimes called **grassroots support**, can influence legislators. Presidents with high **approval ratings**—the measure of how much public support they have—can get their (and their party's) policies and ideas supported more easily by lawmakers. An unpopular president who lacks broad public support can drive voters away from a party.

Mass Media

Mass media—television, newspapers, radios, magazines, books, film, audiotapes, CDs, DVDs, and the Internet—have power to shape public opinion.

* Newspapers or TV stations can choose to broadcast or publish information that supports a politician or issue—or ignore it.
* Media and media personalities frequently criticize politicians and government policy.
* Media outlets decide on the issues they choose to present and the way they present them.
* The more time the media spend on an issue, the more important it seems to the public.

Did You Know?

Politicians and the Media

The media have been a shaper of public opinion for many decades.

* In the 1930s and 1940s, President Franklin Roosevelt used "fireside chats"—radio programs during which he spoke to the public about his policies.
* In the late 1960s, TV coverage of the Vietnam War increased the number of antiwar protests.
* *Washington Post* journalists Bob Woodward and Carl Bernstein uncovered evidence of White House involvement in political dirty tricks that eventually brought about President Nixon's resignation over the Watergate episode.
* Televised coverage of President Clinton's impeachment proceedings made the public aware of presidential character issues.
* On September 11, 2001, the country watched a hijacked airliner crash into the World Trade Center's second tower as the first tower burned. The image forged public opinion in support of a war on terrorism.

Media Conglomerates

During the 19th and much of the 20th centuries, America had many different and separate media outlets—magazines, newspapers, and later, radio and TV stations. Many different people and companies owned and operated these media businesses. The media provided many different viewpoints, so citizens got fairly balanced views of government and other news.

In the past 20 years, smaller media companies have been bought by larger ones, forming media **conglomerates**—large business corporations made up of a number of different companies that operate in widely diversified fields. These media giants own many radio and TV stations, newspapers, and even satellites.

EXAMPLE: The 2001 merger of AOL-Time Warner combined more than 75 media businesses, including TV networks and cable TV operations, book and magazine publishers, recording companies, and Internet services, with combined sales of $165 billion.

Some people fear that conglomerates with control over what news and opinions are offered in the media have too much influence on public opinion.

Media Spin

Governments, large businesses, and many other institutions today have public relations advisors who help them manage communications with the media. Some of these specialists create **spin**—ways of talking about the organization's role in an issue or event that make it the "good guy." The catchy phrases that make up "sound bites" can also limit the public's understanding of complex issues.

Investigative Reporting

Politics has never been a job for people who are easily hurt by criticism. Candidates and elected officials are considered fair targets for journalists and reporters. Nothing in the candidate's life is free from examination. Reporters sometimes find information about embarrassing or questionable behavior by public officials. Here are some of the arguments for and against such reporting.

Should there be a limit to what kinds of information about politicians that journalists share with the public? What should be the media focus during a campaign?

Arguments **for** Investigative Reporting of Candidates	Arguments **against** Reporting of Candidates
Voters deserve to know as much about a candidate as possible.	Few people have led a perfect life. If you dig deep enough, you can find something almost any person might be ashamed of or regret.
Investigative reporters have turned up instances of officials lying to the public. If they lied before, they may lie again, and voters deserve to know that.	The risk of having their life exposed to the public is driving away good, qualified candidates. Just because people run for office doesn't mean that the public has a right to know all the details of their personal lives.
Investigative reporting has discovered instances of officials breaking laws. Citizens shouldn't have to worry about whether they are electing someone who might later be convicted of a crime.	**Muckraking**—digging up dirt on a candidate—distracts voters from the true issues.

Special Interest Groups

Special interest groups are public or private groups that try to influence public opinion and, ultimately, the government in support of their own members' interest.

Special interest groups range from small, informal groups that gather to protest local political decisions at a town meeting to large organized associations, such as the American College of Surgeons or the National Association of Intercollegiate Athletics. The larger the group, the more influence it can usually exert on the public and on lawmakers.

Measuring Public Opinion

Public **opinion polls**—surveys of the views of a sample of the population—have increased in number and importance in the last several decades. Polls can be taken to determine:

* How strongly people feel about an issue.
* What people really want and need.
* How public opinion is changing.
* How much the public is divided or unified in their feelings about an issue.

Many different organizations conduct polls of public opinion.

* *Candidates and politicians* use polls to discover how well the public accepts them.
* *News organizations* use polls to report on campaigns and the performance of public officials.
* *Organizations interested in influencing public policy* or legislation use polls to inform themselves and to persuade others.

Polls and Election Results

During the 2000 presidential election campaign, polls by groups like CNN and Gallop measured public opinions according to:

* Region of the country.
* State.
* Eligible voters.
* Registered voters.
* Likely voters.
* Ethnic and racial groups.

Different polls predicted different results. Why were there such differences?

Opinion Polls

The results of a poll depend on many factors.

* *Who conducts the poll?* If a candidate's supporters take a poll, they may influence the answers they get. The results of polls taken by neutral organizations are much more likely to be accurate.
* *What is the sample size?* The number of people polled must be large enough to represent the general population.
* *Who is polled?* Voters of all races, religions, age groups, interests, and economic statuses must be included for a poll to be representative of the real voting population.

  EXAMPLE: Results of a poll depend on which "voters" are surveyed. There are many more people who are eligible to vote than people who *do* vote. In some elections, only 30–40 percent of eligible voters actually vote. To be accurate in predicting winning candidates, poll results must reflect the views of people who actually vote.
* How were the questions asked? Are the questions phrased clearly? Must people choose between a few alternatives, or can they answer in their own words?
* How was the poll conducted? Was it in person or by mail? Were people stopped while rushing to work, or did they have time to think about their answers?

The results of polls are used by politicians and other groups to make decisions about policy and strategy.

Interest Groups

Although one person can certainly make a difference by voting, public officials are more likely to pay attention when *many* people express the same opinion. Interest groups are organizations whose members share common concerns and who try to influence others to agree with them.

Why Interest Groups Form

Interest groups aim to bring their concerns to the attention of the public and legislators and to influence public policy.

Another word used to describe special interest groups is a **lobby**—a group that tries to get legislators to vote a certain way.

Early Special Interest Groups

Because America was founded on democratic principles, groups of people with special interests have always had the power to influence government. James Madison discussed **factions**—groups of citizens with conflicting interests—in the *Federalist Papers*.

The First Amendment secured the rights of citizens to assemble, to speak freely, to publish their ideas, and to petition the government.

Interest groups have used these rights:

* Suffragists lobbied for women's right to vote.
* Prohibitionists got a constitutional amendment passed that banned alcohol. (It was later repealed by the 21st Amendment.)
* Labor unions secured laws dealing with hours and working conditions.

Primary Source

James Madison and Factions

In *The Federalist Papers*, No. 10, November 1787, Madison wrote:

"There are two methods of curing the mischiefs of faction: the one, by removing its causes; the other, by controlling its effects.

"There are again two methods of removing the causes of faction: the one by destroying the liberty which is essential to its existence; the other, by giving to every citizen the same opinions, the same passions, and the same interests.

". . . the first remedy [is] worse than the disease. Liberty is to faction what air is to fire; it could not be less folly to abolish liberty because it nourishes faction, than it would be to [destroy] air, which is essential to animal life, because it [supports] fire. . . .

"The second [method] is impractical as the first would be unwise. As long as the reason of man continues fallible, and he is at liberty to exercise it, different opinions will be formed. . . ."

Interest Groups Today

Type of Group	Examples

Economic	Organizations representing businesses and workers:
	1. Businesses:
	  * National Association of Manufacturers.
	  * National Small Business Association.
	2. Labor unions/workers:
	  * American Federation of Labor and Congress of Industrial Organizations (AFL-CIO).
	  * American Farm Bureau.
	3. Trade associations that represent entire industries:
	  * American Public Power Association.
	  * Tobacco Institute.
	4. Associations dealing with general economic issues:
	  * United States Chamber of Commerce.
	  * National Small Business Association.

Political or Ideological	Organizations that work toward legislation for the common good, as they see it:
	1. Consumer advocacy groups:
	  * Consumer Federation of America.
	  * Public Interest Research Group (PIRG).
	2. Environmental organizations:
	  * Sierra Club.
	  * National Wildlife Federation.
	3. Voter-education groups:
	  * Emily's List.
	  * League of Women Voters.
	4. Groups that promote the improvement of government:
	  * Common Cause.
	  * Americans for Democratic Action.

Professional	Organizations that represent a particular profession:
	  * American Bar Association (ABA—attorneys).
	  * American Medical Association (AMA—doctors).

more **Interest Groups Today**	
Type of Group	**Examples**

Governmental	Organizations of public officials:
	   * National Conference of Mayors.
	   * National Governors Association.

Civil Rights	Organizations that promote issues related to:
	1. Race:
	   * National Association for the Advancement of Colored People (NAACP).
	2. Gender:
	   * National Organization of Women (NOW).
	3. Age:
	   * American Association of Retired Persons (AARP).

Single-Issue	Organizations that promote a single cause, such as:
	1. Discouraging impaired driving:
	   * Mothers Against Drunk Driving (MADD).
	   * Students Against Destructive Decisions (SADD).
	2. Gun ownership:
	   * National Rifle Association (NRA).
	   * National Coalition to Ban Handguns.

▲
Sierra Club members remove tires and other debris from the San Francisco Bay at low tide.

How Interest Groups Work

Whether large or small, interest groups work to influence government and public opinion.

Methods and Actions

Most interest groups use **four** similar methods to accomplish their goals. They pursue their objectives by:

1. **Forming.** Special interest groups form when a number of people with common concerns agree to work together.
   * *Small groups* formed around community issues, such as a school closing or the plans for a new ball park, often begin informally as neighbors come to recognize they share a viewpoint and want to work together for the results they prefer.
   * *Large groups* that try to influence national policy are formed when people find they have a common interest, such as the environmentalists who formed the Sierra Club, or are members of a professional organization, such as the American Medical Association. Large groups often conduct recruiting campaigns to gain members.
2. **Organizing.** Small groups tend to be manned by volunteers and their organization is loose. A large group will have a complex organization. It will adopt by-laws to guide its operation. Officers will be elected. Membership dues may be charged. The group may hire professionals to run the day-to-day operation of the organization, recruiting members and raising funds.

3. **Operating.** The group decides how to promote its ideas, either by individual efforts or whole-group actions. Individual actions may include:
   * Writing letters to newspapers.
   * Participating in public demonstrations for or against some action.
   * Letter-writing campaigns to political officials.
   * Fundraising activities.

   Group actions may include:
   * Hiring lobbyists.
   * Starting "grassroots campaigns."
   * Forming Political Action Committees (PACs).
4. **Influencing and Electing.** Special interest groups ultimately want to get candidates elected who support the group's position. In this way, they can influence what laws are passed or defeated.

Most Influential Interest Groups

The National Rifle Association, with more than 3 million members, spent nearly $18 million on political action during the 1999–2000 election campaign. The American Medical Association spent $5 million. A relatively small group, Emily's List, was actually the largest political spender. In the same campaign, it spent more than $21 million.

Emily's List was founded in 1985 by 25 women who wanted to see more women elected to government office. The name is an acronym for "Early Money Is Like Yeast" or EMILY. The name suggests that money helps candidates grow stronger, as yeast helps bread dough rise. This group provides its members with information about candidates and encourages them to write checks directly to the candidates they choose. Although Emily's List has fewer members than the NRA (about 68,000 members in 2001), those members have been extremely successful in increasing the number of women in elected offices.

Lobbyists

Lobbyists are paid or unpaid professionals used by interest groups to try to influence the way legislators vote. The word *lobbyist* comes from people who wait in the lobbies of government buildings to talk to legislators as they go to and from work. Successful lobbyists:

* Know a lot about the political process and the people they are lobbying.
* Are very familiar with the goals of the group they represent.
* Are truthful in their dealings.
* Show legislators how supporting the group's position can benefit them.

Lobbying efforts are mainly directed at state and federal decision makers, such as:

* Members of congressional committees that consider legislation.
* Administrative agencies that write or enforce regulations.
* Officials of executive departments.
  EXAMPLE: The huge Chicago welfare agency that places and oversees neglected, abandoned, and abused children in foster care hires lobbyists to help the state legislators of Illinois understand the situations it faces. When the state budget is being discussed, these lobbyists help protect the funds earmarked for the agency's operation.

Supporters of lobbyists say that legislators don't have time to gather information about the issues on which they are voting. Lobbyists can provide them with that information, making them better informed when they vote. Critics say that interest groups with large memberships and money to hire lobbyists have too much influence.

Grassroots Campaigns

Special interest groups sometimes launch grassroots campaigns, going directly to the public to gain support for their issues by:

* Urging their members and other citizens to write to their representatives or senators about issues coming up for a vote.
* Sending informational mailings to nonmembers, explaining the issues from the group's point of view.

Political Action Committees

Political action committees (PACs) are groups that raise money and distribute campaign funds to candidates for political office. PACs help elect candidates who will support their issues. Well financed PACs bring their views to the public and politicians by:

* Testifying at public hearings.
* Providing officials with research information.
* Trying to influence the media to present the PAC's point of view.
* Suggesting and supporting legislation.
* Hiring lobbyists.
* Endorsing candidates.
* Working on election campaigns.

Interest Groups and Public Policy

Despite the fears of some of America's founders, as well as some people today, interest groups serve the public good.

Contributions of Interest Groups

Interest groups help make governments work more effectively in **four** broad ways:

1. **They Make Issues Known.** Busy legislators or the public may be unfamiliar with all of the issues unless those issues are pointed out to them. Interest group activity, especially when it receives national coverage, increases the chances that legislators and citizens will pay attention.

2. **They Help Group Members.** Special interest groups share information among their members to strengthen the group and improve the economic and social well-being of the members.
   EXAMPLE: The Mexican-American Legal Defense and Education Fund (MALDEF) represents a group that has historically faced legal discrimination. The group protects its members' rights and educational opportunities. This leads to better lives and jobs for Mexican Americans.

3. **They Support Candidates.** Special interest groups support political candidates who favor their views. Interest groups contribute money to candidates' election campaigns. They also encourage members and other people to vote for candidates who will support the group's issues.

4. They Use the Courts. If lawmakers do not respond to their concerns, special interest groups can ask the courts for help by:

* Filing suit against the government, individuals, or other groups.
* Supporting a defendant by paying for his attorneys.
* Testifying or acting as an *amicus curiae*—a friend of the court. These people present information so that the court is better informed about the technicalities of a case.

  EXAMPLE: The NAACP played a major role in the civil rights cases that eventually led to civil rights legislation in the 1960s and 1970s.

▲

Interest groups like SADD sometimes stage simulated accidents to show students the effects of drunk driving.

American Citizenship

Students Against Destructive Decisions (SADD)

In 1981, two students at Wayland High School in Wayland, Massachusetts, were killed in separate car crashes. Teacher Robert Anastas and his students at the high school worked together to found SADD. Originally, the organization addressed the issues of underage drinking and impaired driving among students. Today, the organization has broadened its interest to any "destructive decisions" made by young people, such as drug and alcohol use and other health- or life-endangering decisions. SADD encourages students and their parents to sign the Contract for Life, which begins:

"I recognize that there are many potentially destructive decisions I face every day and commit to you that I will do everything in my power to avoid making decisions that will jeopardize my health, my safety and overall well-being, or your trust in me. I understand the dangers associated with the use of alcohol and drugs and the destructive behaviors often associated with impairment."

Supreme Court Case

Reno v. ACLU (1997)

In 1996, Congress passed the Communications Decency Act (CDA) to protect young people from inappropriate material on the Internet. A number of special interest groups, including the American Civil Liberties Union (ACLU), immediately filed suit, claiming that people using the Internet were entitled to the same First Amendment rights to free speech as those using newspapers or other communications media.

In 1997, the Supreme Court agreed that the CDA was unconstitutional. Justice John Paul Stevens wrote:

"As a matter of constitutional tradition, in the absence of evidence to the contrary, we presume that governmental regulation of the content of speech is more likely to interfere with the free exchange of ideas than to encourage it. The interest in encouraging freedom of expression in a democratic society outweighs any theoretical but unproven benefit of censorship."

You should understand that the courts did not approve (or disapprove) of the online material, or of exposing children to it. The Supreme Court *did* say that, unless laws contain a clear and more generally agreed-upon definition of what is "harmful," "offensive," or "indecent," such laws are unconstitutional.

Controlling Interest Groups

Critics fear that large interest groups:

* Have too much wealth, power, and political influence.
* Can corrupt individual politicians.
* Improperly impact voter choice and the democratic political process.

Some lawmakers want to reform campaign finance laws to restrict how interest groups can make donations to:

* **Candidates** through **hard money** donations. These are direct donations to individual politicians' election campaigns. There are limits on the amount a single person or group can give to an individual candidate.
* **Parties or issues** through **soft money** donations. These contributions are called "soft" because they are not given directly to any candidate. Instead, the money is given to a political party, either nationally, at the state level, or locally. These donations may be much greater than the amount an individual may give to a single candidate.

Federal Lobbyists

Federal lobbyists must register with the Clerk of the House of Representatives and the Secretary of the Senate, revealing what group they represent, and their salary and expenses. The courts have ruled that limits on lobbying are constitutional. Congress has restricted the value of gifts that lobbyists can give government officials.

Political Action Committees

Many citizens are concerned about the influence of PACs.

* Sheer cost prevents many talented people from running for office. Candidates supported by PACs can spend larger sums of money on their campaigns.

* Reformers have proposed limits on the amount of money an individual PAC can contribute to a candidate or the total amount the candidate can accept from all PACs.

Many members of Congress have hesitated to pass legislation on campaign finance reform. New laws would reduce the amount of money they have for their own campaigns.

Some special interest groups have formed to fight the power and influence of PACs. EXAMPLE: Common Cause is a 200,000-member group founded in 1970 that opposes "big money special interests." It believes that PACs should be prohibited altogether because they give well financed interest groups an unfair advantage.

Chapter 12 Wrap-up
PUBLIC OPINION AND INTEREST GROUPS

Many of the laws written and passed in this country are influenced by the opinion of the citizens who elect lawmakers. Legislators must stay in touch with their constituents and pay attention to issues that concern the voters. Propaganda techniques such as testimonials, name-calling, glittering generalities, and bandwagon are often used by public officials to shape public opinion. Polls are an important way to measure public opinion and to help legislators determine what actions they need to take, both to satisfy and influence the voters.

Special interest groups are organizations that take advantage of the power of numbers to influence lawmakers. People with similar interests or concerns join together to influence legislation, help each other stay informed, and help elect political candidates who will support their issues. Special interest groups hire lobbyists, create grassroots movements, form political action committees, and use individual membership activities, such as letter-writing, to achieve their goals.

approval rating—amount of public support for an official, such as a president. *p. 197*

conglomerate—huge corporation composed of several large companies. *p. 198*

enculturation—process of passing on the beliefs and values of a culture. *p. 194*

euphemisms—words or terms used to make something sound less unpleasant. *p. 195*

factions—groups of citizens with different interests. *p. 201*

generalities—broad, sweeping statements. *p. 195*

grassroots support—public popularity or endorsement of a candidate by large numbers of voters at the local level. *p. 197*

hard money—political donation that is given directly to an individual politician's election campaign. *p. 208*

lobby—group that tries to get legislators to vote a certain way. Used as a verb, this word also describes the persuasive activity that lobbyists do. *p. 201*

lobbyist—professional who represents an organization's interests by working to persuade legislators. *p. 205*

mass media—television, newspapers, radio, and magazines; media that reach large numbers of people. *p. 197*

muckraking—digging up dirt; uncovering unflattering facts about a candidate or issue. *p. 199*

name-calling—practice of using words that link a person or an idea to something perceived as negative. *p. 195*

opinion poll—survey of the views of a sample of the population on issues of public interest. *p. 200*

political action committees (PACs)—organized groups that raise money to support candidates and issues. *p. 206*

propaganda—communication of information to spread certain ideas, beliefs, or practices and to shape public opinion. *p. 194*

public opinion—feelings, thoughts, and positions that people collectively have on political or social issues. *p. 194*

soft money—political donations that are given to political parties rather than to individual candidates. *p. 208*

special interest group—public or private organization that tries to influence the public and lawmakers to support its special interests. *p. 199*

spin—way of describing an event or crisis to make a person's or group's role appear positive. *p. 198*

testimonials—statements by famous people in support of something—a candidate, a position, or a product. *p. 195*

transfer—propaganda method of creating a false connection between two ideas. *p. 195*

Law and Our Legal System

In this chapter, you will learn about:

- **how law is related to society**
- **what types of laws exist**
- **what the sources of American law are**
- **why basic rights come with responsibilities**

Imagine what would happen if all traffic lights just disappeared. Traffic would be in chaos. Accidents would be everywhere. Cars would be damaged, and drivers, passengers, and pedestrians would be hurt. No one would really be safe, except maybe drivers with the most powerful and heaviest vehicles. In short, travel would be a mess.

Laws are like traffic lights. We agree, as citizens, to set them up for the safety and order of society. We rely on specialists whom we employ to make sure that the lights are set up where needed, work properly, and are obeyed. We trade some liberty—the right to drive through intersections however and whenever we wish—to gain some order and safety, so we can go about our business and live our lives. We expect that everyone will obey the rules.

Laws help define what people can and can't do as they interact with other people in society. Good laws should prohibit behaviors that are harmful to others, including the public as a whole. As Americans, we agree that laws should not restrict anyone's rights unnecessarily. For centuries, societies have struggled to decide what and how many laws they need.

Laws and Society

A society is a group of people who share certain customs, practices, and relationships. People in a society agree to live by a common set of rules—a **legal code**. These rules spell out the ways that members of the group must behave toward one another.

Laws are our society's rules—the system of rules and principles made and enforced by the government. Because American society is a democracy, citizens can influence the law through their lawmakers, the officials they elect. By voting and communicating with legislators, citizens play an important role in the legal process.

Why We Need Laws

The end [purpose] of law is not to abolish or restrain, but to preserve and enlarge freedom. . . . where there is no law, there is no freedom.
—John Locke, British philosopher

You and society as a whole benefit from laws in many ways.

Keeping Order

People in a society need order so that they can do the things they want and need to do every day, such as shopping, working, or going to the doctor. Laws give society order. Many laws are designed to maintain order; for example:

* Littering laws keep trash from piling up and creating a health risk.
* Traffic laws allow traffic to flow smoothly for cars and for people walking.
* Criminal laws let people know what behavior is not allowed and how it will be punished.

Ensuring Safety

Laws also prevent one person or group, such as a business, from acting in a way that harms other people, intentionally or unintentionally. Laws designed to keep you and the rest of society safe include:

* Clean air laws, so you won't get sick from pollution.
* Food inspection laws, so you won't get sick from spoiled food.
* Laws against assault and battery, murder, and arson, so you and your property are freer from harm.

Protecting Property

Property is any *thing* that you own or have the right to possess. Property can also be the right to use that thing. Property can be divided into **three** general categories:

1. **Something You Can Touch or Feel.** This category includes most of the things in your room and house, including:
   * Your video games or books.
   * Your dog.
   * The furniture in your room.

2. **Something You Create.** This kind of property includes a story you write—not the paper that you write the words on, but the order and choice of words you used. No one else can copy or claim to own it. This ensures that only you can make money from a story you

sell. Examples of property that you create include:

* Song melodies and song lyrics.
* Images in a drawing or photograph.
* The content of CD-ROMs or the information you created and store in your computer files, as opposed to the storage devices.

3. **A Right to Do Something.** If you live in an apartment that your family rents, you don't own the actual apartment. But you *do* own the right to live in the apartment for a certain period of time. Other examples of this type of property include:

* The right to walk across someone else's property if it is the only way to get to your house.
* The right of an oil company to drill for oil in a particular place. The company doesn't own the land. They own or lease the right to take the oil out of the ground.
* Different types of laws are written to protect different kinds of property.

Did You Know?

You Could Own a Copyright

Copyright law protects the creators of "original works of authorship." Because this protection applies to both published and unpublished works, any original poem, song, or sketch you put down on paper is protected by copyright law. Copyright law also applies to works created in digital form—for example, on a web site. A copyright owner has the exclusive right to:

* Copy or reproduce the work.
* Distribute copies of the work to the public by sale, or by rental, lease, or lending.
* Perform the work publicly.
* Display the work publicly.

People and Their Property		
Person	**Property**	**Protection by the Law**
Grocery Store Owner	All the food in the store.	Criminal laws protect the grocer from theft and burglary.
Apartment Renter	Right to live in the apartment.	Housing laws protect the renter by requiring the owner to keep the apartment in good working order.
Songwriter	The melody and lyrics of a song.	Copyright laws protect the artist by preventing people from copying the song for profit.

Swapping Music on the Web

Students who don't have a lot of money love to get songs for free. But many recording artists and music publishers claim that some Internet services help people steal songs. In 2001, a federal appeals court in California decided that the online service called *Napster* was participating in the crime of theft by helping people get CDs and songs without paying the copyright owner. Napster had to remove all of the protected material. Here are the arguments for and against the court's decision.

Do you think the court was right? Why or why not? In your opinion, should Napster appeal its case to the Supreme Court?

Arguments <u>for</u> the Court's Decision

These services help millions of people steal music. They are guilty of helping people carry out crimes.

- - - - - - - - - - - - - - - - - - - -

These services violate copyright law by providing music and CDs for free.

- - - - - - - - - - - - - - - - - - - -

These services violate musicians' legal rights to make a profit from the works they create.

- - - - - - - - - - - - - - - - - - - -

If artists are not able to make money from their music, they will stop creating music. Society will suffer from this loss.

Arguments <u>against</u> the Court's Decision

These services don't actually copy the songs or send the songs to users. Therefore, they're not doing anything illegal.

- - - - - - - - - - - - - - - - - - - -

A phone company isn't guilty when someone uses phone lines to make a threatening phone call. Likewise, these services aren't guilty when users get together and decide to do something illegal.

- - - - - - - - - - - - - - - - - - - -

Individual users who swap music aren't charging money or making a profit. Therefore, they aren't violating the law.

Protecting Freedoms

Laws protect individual freedoms or rights. The Constitution, amendments, and other laws assure us that the government will not interfere with certain actions. These freedoms give us the right to enjoy being citizens.

Promoting the Common Good

The **common good** refers to things or services that are beneficial to the community. For example, order, safety, and public health are good for your community. Laws that protect these benefits promote the common good.

No one likes to pay taxes, but taxes help support the common good. The government collects taxes in order to pay for services that help everyone in society. These services include:

* Armies, to protect our safety.
* Social Security, to help people who cannot work.
* Public parks, to give children a safe place to play.
* Universities, to help educate people.
* Hospitals, to provide health care.

Laws, Morals, and Civil Disobedience

A person who leads a moral life lives according to certain standards of right and wrong. Within a society, some beliefs about helpful and harmful behavior are shared by almost everyone, including:

* Murder is harmful to society.
* Charity is helpful.
* Stealing is harmful.
* Respecting one's elders is helpful.

Laws, the rules that govern society, define some aspects of acceptable and unacceptable behavior for citizens. In a democracy, lawmakers are elected by a majority of citizens. So citizens directly influence society's legal code by their votes. Still, not everyone agrees with every law. We have laws that some people don't feel are right or just. Some of these laws deal with:

* **Capital punishment.** Executing people found guilty of murder is a form of punishment in some states, but many people believe it is wrong to kill for any reason, regardless of the crime.
* **War.** Our country has fought in wars, but some people believe war is always wrong.
* **Assisted suicide.** Most states do not allow doctors to help patients who are fatally ill to bring about their own deaths and an end of suffering. But some people believe this is a decision that an individual should be allowed to make.

Some people are so opposed to certain laws that they intentionally disobey those laws. When people break the law in order to express disagreement with the law, they are practicing **civil disobedience**. These people expect to be prosecuted for breaking the law, but they hope to focus the attention of other citizens on the laws they feel are bad. Sometimes a law is changed as a result of their actions.

EXAMPLE: The peaceful protests of the Civil Rights Movement of the 1950s and 1960s helped bring an end to racial segregation in the United States.

Acts of civil disobedience are peaceful and nonviolent. They never include rioting or hurting anyone in any way.

American Citizenship

Muhammad Ali: The Boxer Who Wouldn't Fight

The most famous American **conscientious objector** is Muhammad Ali, the former three-time world heavyweight boxing champion.

In 1967, Muhammad Ali, who had already won his first boxing title, was drafted into, or ordered to join, the United States Army to fight the war in Vietnam. Ali refused to join. He believed the war was wrong and, as a follower of Islam, he therefore could not fight or support it.

Ali became very unpopular. The press criticized him, and the boxing commission took away his title and refused to let him box. Because he wouldn't help with the war—even as a nonfighter—the government charged him with evading the draft. He was sentenced to five years in prison and fined $10,000.

In June 1970, the Supreme Court overturned Ali's conviction and he was allowed to box. But for four years, Ali couldn't earn a living and had to hire lawyers to fight his battle in court. He risked his career, his popularity, and his personal freedom because fighting in the war was against his personal moral code, even though it wasn't against the law. Today, Muhammad Ali is a hero to many Americans.

Characteristics of Good Laws

Is a law that promotes public safety always a helpful law? What's the difference between a "good" law and a "bad" law? Good laws share **four** basic qualities. Good laws are:

1. **Fair.**
2. **Reasonable.**
3. **Understandable.**
4. **Enforceable.**

Fair

If a teacher catches two students cheating on a test, he or she should treat both of them the same way. One function of the law is to ensure that people are treated fairly and those who commit the same crime receive the same punishment.

However, treating everyone the same way all the time may not always be fair either. Sometimes a punishment needs to reflect differences in the ages of people involved or their circumstances. A law may purposely treat two people who commit the same act differently. In these cases, different treatment makes the situation *more* fair.

EXAMPLE: In most states, when a child or **minor**—someone without the legal rights of an adult—and an adult commit the same crime, they receive different punishments. Society assumes that adults and children are different in their abilities to understand and take responsibility for their actions.

Reasonable

A law that is reasonable makes sense. A reasonable law isn't absurd or impossible for people to follow.

EXAMPLES: A law that says "Pedestrians cannot use the sidewalk" is not reasonable because it makes absolutely no sense. Sidewalks are designed specifically for the safety and convenience of pedestrians, or walkers. A law that orders "No person may breathe the air" is absurd as well as unreasonable.

Understandable

In order to follow a law, you have to understand it. Laws must include the information people need to understand exactly what they must or must not do.

EXAMPLE: Suppose your town has a law that says "All cyclists must wear a helmet that provides adequate protection." This law has a good purpose—to protect people who ride bicycles from head injuries. But the law is not understandable. What is *adequate protection* in a helmet? Does the helmet have a certain shape? Is it made of certain material? These questions leave too much uncertainty in the law. People don't know how to follow the law, and officials don't know how to enforce it.

Enforceable

An unenforceable law is a rule that most citizens won't follow or that police cannot make people obey. Law enforcement officials can't **enforce**—make people obey—laws that many people consider unreasonable or unfair, or do not believe will help society. **EXAMPLE:** A law that says "Every citizen must eat at least three servings of fresh vegetables every day" would be unenforceable. Eating vegetables is good for everyone, but how could such a law be enforced? Imagine what violations of privacy would be required to enforce it!

Did You Know?

Bad Laws in America

The United States and individual states have passed many "bad" laws in the past.

Chicago passed a law that said street gangs couldn't form groups and "remain in any one place with no apparent purpose." The law was designed to stop street gangs from bothering people. The law was not understandable, however, because, legally, street gangs *do* have the right to be together in "one place." More importantly, the term "no apparent purpose" isn't specific enough to let them (or anyone else) know when they were breaking the law and when they weren't.

Types of Law

Laws can be divided into categories: criminal, civil, constitutional, and administrative.

Criminal Law

Criminal laws are written by Congress and state legislators, and make certain behaviors illegal and punishable by fines and, possibly, imprisonment. The government's attorney must show that the person accused of the crime acted illegally and intended to act as he or she did. If the prosecution cannot prove guilt, the accused person is presumed to be innocent.

Criminal laws have **three** characteristics that distinguish them from other types of laws:

1. **Impact on Society.** The person's actions are so serious that they affect not just the victim, but society as a whole. The government considers the crime to be a threat to society's order and safety.
2. **Government Enforcement.** Because of the impact on society, the government enforces the law. Groups involved in enforcement include:
   * Police.
   * FBI.
   * Government lawyers, or prosecutors, who try to prove in court that the accused person is guilty.
   * Prison guards who make sure that criminals stay in jail.
3. **Serious Punishment.** People convicted of these crimes are punished by losing some or all of their freedoms. Punishments range from fines, community service, or required classes to imprisonment or worse for very serious crimes.

The most severe criminal punishment is the death penalty. In cases of murder, the state may execute the person who has broken the law.

Civil Law

A civil case is a noncriminal lawsuit, usually involving a dispute about relationships or private property. **Civil laws** are established by federal, state, and city governments and include cases dealing with such matters as:

* Divorce.
* Wills and inheritance.
* Broken contracts.
* Accidents and injuries.

Civil laws differ from criminal laws in **three** important ways:

1. **Limited Impact.** The person's actions affect only the person or group injured. Civil laws are designed to help the specific person or group injured when the rules are broken.
2. **Individual Enforcement.** The main enforcers of civil laws are the individuals themselves and their lawyers. These people try to work out a solution to the problem or disagreement. A judge only gets involved if one or both parties ask for help in resolving the dispute.
3. **Penalties.** Civil laws are not punishable by imprisonment. A person who breaks a civil law is usually required to pay for the damages caused by his or her actions. A judge can also issue an **injunction**, which prevents someone from committing damaging behavior.

In civil law, you may sometimes be responsible for your actions even though you did not intend to harm someone. For example, civil law makes you financially responsible for a car accident you caused but didn't intend.

Civil law and criminal law sometime prohibit the same behavior. This means that a person may face civil *and* criminal charges for the same crime. The government can charge the lawbreaker with a crime, and the person hurt can ask a court to command the lawbreaker to pay for the damages.

The Difference between Civil and Criminal Law				
Category	Lawmaker	Purpose of the Law	Punishment	Enforcer
Criminal	State legislatures, U.S. Congress.	Protect society's order and safety.	Execution, jail, fines, community service.	Police, FBI, prosecutors.
Civil	State legislatures, U.S. Congress, federal and state courts, city councils.	Compensate, or "make whole," the person injured.	Money and injunctions.	Individuals claiming injury or the lawyers they hire.

Constitutional Law

The United States Constitution is the foundation for all laws passed by federal, state, and local governments. The Constitution ensures:

* A balance of power among the branches of government.
* A division of power between state and federal governments.
* Protection for individual rights.

Balance of Power

The U.S. Constitution makes sure the three branches of government share power in the lawmaking and enforcing process.

* **The legislative branch,** Congress, is responsible for writing federal laws.
* **The executive branch,** which includes the president, is responsible for enforcing the laws.
* **The judicial branch,** which includes the federal courts, explains how laws should be understood and makes sure that laws don't violate the Constitution.

Division of Power

The Constitution also divides the power to govern between the federal government and the states.

* **The federal government** writes and enforces laws that apply to everyone living in the United States.

* **State governments** write and enforce laws that affect people living in or visiting their states. People in a particular state have to follow both federal and state laws.

The federal government has exclusive power over certain issues. The Constitution prohibits individual states from performing these acts. These duties include:

* Negotiating treaties with foreign nations.
* Coining money.
* Raising an army, except with permission from Congress.

Laws passed by the federal government are the supreme law of the land. If a state law conflicts with a federal law, the federal law overrules the state law in all but very rare circumstances.

Individual Rights

The most important job of the Constitution is to protect individual rights. The Bill of Rights and the other amendments to the Constitution identify specific rights that apply to all American citizens. These rights limit the power of the federal and state governments to control the citizens they govern. They ensure:

* The right to say and believe what you want.
* The right to practice any kind of religion.
* The right to form groups with whomever you want.

Supreme Court Case

Gideon v. Wainwright (1963)

The U.S. Constitution commands that "in all criminal prosecutions, the accused shall enjoy the right to have the Assistance of Counsel for his defense."

The state of Florida charged Clarence Gideon with the crime of breaking into a poolroom. Gideon was too poor to hire a lawyer to defend him, so he asked the judge to provide him with one. The judge refused. Gideon defended himself and was found guilty. He was sentenced to spend five years in prison.

Gideon appealed his prosecution to the U.S. Supreme Court. Claiming he was denied his constitutional right to counsel, he asked the Court to rule that his conviction was wrong.

The Supreme Court agreed with Gideon. The Court stated that both the criminal law code itself and the rules the court follows in a criminal trial are complicated. Because the law and court processes are so difficult to understand and use, a criminal defendant without a lawyer is at a huge disadvantage. He or she cannot get a fair trial. The Court declared that the guarantee of the right to counsel means that the government must appoint and pay for a lawyer to defend the person on trial if that person can't afford to hire a lawyer.

Administrative Law

Lawmakers set up administrative agencies to help people understand what the laws mean and how to carry them out.

Administrative laws are laws, rules, and decisions written by administrative agencies. Violation of these rules can result in criminal or civil prosecution.

EXAMPLE: The Securities and Exchange Commission (SEC) is an administrative agency that enforces the complicated rules that govern the stock market.

Sources of American Law

People have organized themselves into societies for thousands of years. Many societies developed legal codes, or a "rule book," that have ultimately impacted the laws of the United States.

Ancient Systems

Some of our most important laws are based on laws and moral codes created by ancient civilizations. The best known of the ancient codes is probably the **Ten Commandments**, the ten laws given, in the Bible, by God to Moses and the nation of Israel. Some of the Commandments, such as "do not steal" and "do not commit murder," are now part of our own legal code.

Hammurabi, who lived nearly 4,000 years ago, was a king of Babylonia, an empire that existed in what is presently the Middle East. The **Code of Hammurabi** was one of the first-known, written, legal codes. It regulated the relationships among his subjects in all areas of life, from murder to inheritance laws to personal injury. The United States today has many laws similar to provisions of the Code, although the punishments exacted under the Code were far more severe than they are in America today.

Primary Source

The Code of Hammurabi

Some provisions of the Code include:

Laws against Theft
* If anyone is committing a robbery and is caught, then he shall be put to death.
* If anyone steal cattle or sheep, or a donkey, or a pig or a goat, if it belong to a god or to the court, the thief shall pay thirtyfold therefore; if they belonged to a freed man of the king he shall pay tenfold; if the thief has nothing with which to pay, he shall be put to death.

Laws against Kidnapping
* If anyone steal the minor son of another, he shall be put to death.

Dividing the Property from a Marriage between the Couple
* If a man wish to separate from . . . his wife who has borne him children: then he shall give that wife her dowry and a part of the . . . field, garden, and property so that she can rear her children.

Roman Law

Ancient Rome's republican form of government influenced the founders of the United States. Rome also influenced our system of laws. Rome's written law code governed almost every aspect of life. The sixth-century Roman emperor Justinian created the **Justinian Code**. This code has shaped laws developed in the United States and Europe.

English Law

British judges have relied for centuries on **precedents**—decisions made in previous cases—from English common law to decide how the law applied to more recent disputes. Most American laws, whether delivered by a judge or a legislature, are based on traditional English rules of common law.

Basic Rights and Responsibilities

Although the Constitution lists your rights as a citizen, it is not specific about your *responsibilities* as a citizen, including:

* Obeying federal, state, and local laws.
* Paying taxes.
* Going to school until a certain age.
* Voting.

As a responsible citizen, by understanding, following, and influencing the law, you help create a safe, moral, and orderly society for everyone.

Spanish Law, Common Law, and Women's Rights

Texas was originally colonized by Spain, not England. Under Spanish law, married women could own property separately from their husbands. Property that the couple collected during the marriage belonged to both people: half to the husband and half to the wife.

Texas, after it separated from Spain and joined the United States, followed the Spanish property laws. Eventually, similar laws replaced the older English-based property laws of other states. English law gave a woman's property to her husband upon their marriage.

Chapter 13 Wrap-up
LAW AND OUR LEGAL SYSTEM

A society is a group of people who come together and agree to follow a set of rules. These rules limit individual members of society in ways that promote the good of the whole community. In other words, these rules or laws make society more safe, orderly, and efficient for everyone. Good laws are fair, reasonable, understandable, and enforceable.

United States law is based on the legal codes of past societies, including Roman law and British law. The two most common categories of United States laws are criminal and civil. The U.S. Constitution limits the government in the kind of laws it can pass. It also divides power between the federal government and states, and protects individual rights.

administrative law—laws, rules, and decisions written and enforced by administrative agencies of the government. *p. 221*

civil disobedience—act of breaking the law to express disagreement with the law; acts are nonviolent and are intended to cause a change in the law. *p. 216*

civil law—noncriminal law written by federal, state, and city governments, usually dealing with private property. *p. 219*

Code of Hammurabi—one of the first-known, written legal codes, developed by Hammurabi, a king of Babylonia nearly 4,000 years ago. *p. 221*

common good—good of the community at large. *p. 215*

conscientious objector—person who refuses to serve in the military based on a moral or religious belief that war is wrong. *p. 216*

copyright—right to own and copy intellectual or artistic property. *p. 213*

criminal law—law written by Congress and state legislators that make certain behaviors illegal and punishable by fines or imprisonment. *p. 218*

enforce—ensure that a law is obeyed; force someone to obey. *p. 218*

injunction—act of a court that commands a person to stop doing something or to keep doing something. *p. 219*

Justinian Code—written legal code developed by the Roman emperor Justinian. *p. 222*

law—rule or regulation requiring or forbidding certain conduct that is made by a governing body and applies to all members of a society. *p. 212*

legal code—systematic collection of laws that govern a society. *p. 212*

minor—someone who does not have the legal rights of an adult; in most states, a person younger than 18. *p. 217*

precedent—something done or said in a previous court case that serves as an example for a future court decision. *p. 222*

property—something owned or possessed; also the right to use that thing. *p. 212*

Ten Commandments—in the Bible, ten laws given by God to Moses and the nation of Israel. *p. 223*

CHAPTER 14

The American Justice System

In this chapter, you will learn about:

- the purpose of civil law
- what happens in a civil lawsuit
- the purpose of criminal law
- how a crime is prosecuted
- the juvenile justice system

Jane Bronstein attended the U.S. Open Tennis Championships as a spectator in New York in 1995. Television cameras videotaped spectators in the stands and taped Bronstein as she watched the tennis match and ate a peach. Then, for approximately two weeks, comedian and host David Letterman, who is known for his zany humor, showed the videotape on his late night comedy/talk show, adding funny comments about Bronstein. Bronstein did not find Letterman's joke so funny. In response, she filed a lawsuit stating that she was "repeatedly and publicly ridiculed and vilified" by Letterman. The dispute was eventually settled before it went to court.

What rights did Jane Bronstein have in this situation? What rights did David Letterman have? Civil law provides a way for private citizens to fairly settle disputes just like this one. Criminal law, in contrast, provides a way for the government to punish lawbreakers who are a threat to society. Civil and criminal law form the basis of the American justice system. They work together to protect citizens' rights and keep citizens safe.

Civil Law

Whose fault would it be if you went to someone else's house and accidentally tripped over some rollerblades that had been left lying on the front porch? What would you do if you took a bad fall and needed a trip to the emergency room of your local hospital? Who do you think should pay for the emergency room visit?

Civil law deals with this kind of question. Civil law deals with noncriminal disputes, providing a way to settle personal disputes that do not involve criminal activity—such as who should pay for your emergency room visit. Generally, people file civil lawsuits in court because they believe they have been harmed and should get **compensation**, some kind of payment to make up for it.

"I'm sorry, Your Honor, but I just don't have the time right now to go to prison."

Remedies

When one person sues another person, he or she asks the court to provide a **remedy**—a solution to the harm caused by the person accused. Judges and juries use laws to settle these conflicts and decide remedies. Civil law provides **two** kinds of remedies for breaking the law:

1. **Compensation.**
2. **Equity.**

Compensation

Civil law provides a way for you to get compensated for damage caused by another person. A **plaintiff**—the person suing—can ask the **defendant**—the person being sued—to pay:

* The amount of money needed to pay for medical treatment.
* The cost of fixing or replacing damaged property, such as a car or house.
* Income lost when the plaintiff had to miss work to recover from an injury.

Equity

Not every lawsuit can be settled with money. Judges use general rules of fairness, or **equity**, to create a remedy in some situations. Judges usually establish equity by ordering the defendant to do something or to stop doing something.

EXAMPLE: A homeowner wants the court to make her neighbor clean up his yard because the yard is a mess, with trash piled up everywhere. The garbage stinks and is attracting rats. If the court decides that the messy neighbor is doing something wrong—for example, creating a danger for people in the neighborhood—the judge can order him to clean up his yard.

Types of Civil Cases

Citizens file new lawsuits in United States courts every day. In the year 2000, more than 259,000 civil cases were filed in U.S. District Courts. The suits were filed for a wide variety of reasons, but most fell into **five** broad categories:

1. **Disputes about Contracts and Private Agreements.**
2. **Personal Injury or Property Damage Claims.**
3. **Disagreements over Property.**
4. **Consumer Protection Issues.**
5. **Domestic Relations.**

Contracts and Private Agreements

When you make a deal with a friend to trade video games, you and your friend make a **contract**. In other words, you promise to give your friend something and, in return, your friend promises to give something to you. Courts treat these contracts or agreements as if they were laws.
EXAMPLES: Contracts can be simple or complex. Examples might include:

* An employment agreement. You agree to mow a neighbor's lawn in return for money.
* A business agreement. Two large corporations agree to form one larger business.

Primary Source

The Business of Baseball

Professional sports are big business. Team owners want to make a lot of money, and players want to share in the profits. Complicated contracts ensure that both players and owners get what they want. The following is an example of just one small section of a 170-page contract between the major league players and the owners of the baseball teams.

The minimum rate of payment to a Player for each day of service on a Major League Club shall be as follows:

* 1996—at the rate per season of $109,000 from the beginning of the championship season up to and including July 30, 1996, and at the rate per season of $150,000 beginning on July 31, 1996, up to and including the end of the 1996 championship season;
* 1997—at the rate per season of $150,000;
* 1998—at the rate per season of $170,000;
* 1999—at the rate per season of $200,000;
* 2000—at the rate per season of $200,000.

Personal Injury or Property Damage

Personal injuries and torts account for nearly 40 percent of all civil cases filed. A **tort** is a damage caused to one person, other than a broken contract, for which someone who caused the damage is legally responsible.

A tort can be intentional, such as an angry punch in the nose, but most torts result from carelessness, such as riding a bicycle on the sidewalk and running into someone. The injury that forms the basis of a tort can also be damage to someone's reputation and image, or deliberately caused mental distress.

EXAMPLE: A tort can result if someone beats you up and physically injures you. This kind of behavior can also be prosecuted as a crime.

Disagreements over Property

Civil law also deals with disagreements about things people own, called property. These situations usually involve disagreement about who owns the property or how it can be used.

EXAMPLES: Common property disagreements involve land or buildings, inheritance rights (what happens to someone's property when he or she dies), and apartment rental agreements between landlords and tenants.

Consumer Protection

Consumers are people like you and your parents who buy things to own or to use, such as a house, a CD, or toothpaste. Consumer protection laws stop manufacturers, salespeople, and businesses from cheating or taking advantage of consumers. If sellers or manufacturers make claims about their products that are false, you, as a consumer, can take them to court.

EXAMPLE: If you buy a computer that does not work, and the store or manufacturer refuses to solve the problem, consumer law allows you to sue to get your money back.

Domestic Relations

Domestic-relations laws regulate disagreements among family members. Family disputes include:

* Divorce.
* Adoption.
* Child custody.

EXAMPLE: Two people decide that they want to end their marriage. They must go to family court to get divorced, or to legally undo their marriage, making arrangements for important issues such as care of any children and sharing of property and debts.

Civil Procedure

Both parties in a civil lawsuit must follow certain rules or procedures that describe every step of the trial. There are **three** stages in a civil lawsuit:

1. **Court Pleadings.** Both parties in the lawsuit give the court and each other **pleadings**—written explanations of their cases. The plaintiff must explain what the defendant did wrong. The defendant must explain how she or he will respond in court to the charges.

2. **Gathering Evidence.** Both parties collect **evidence**—proof that supports their claims. They may collect evidence in a number of ways, including interviewing witnesses before the trial and asking to see records such as private notes or financial information.

3. **Trial**. At trial, both parties present evidence to convince a judge or jury that their side is right and the opponent's side is wrong. In civil trials, the parties involved decide whether a judge or jury will make the final decision in the case.

Because the plaintiff brings the civil case to court, the plaintiff is responsible for providing enough evidence to prove the claim. In almost all civil trials, plaintiffs must show a judge or jury only that their case is more convincing than the defendants' arguments. The judge or jury has to be at least 51 percent sure that the plaintiff is correct. This is an easier standard, or basis for a decision, than in criminal trials.

Alternatives

Few lawsuits that are threatened or even started ever go all the way to trial. Many people decide to settle their disagreements before the trial, sometimes before the lawsuit is filed. Reasons for this practice include:

* *Money.* Filing and conducting a lawsuit is very expensive. Parties must pay for attorneys and the cost of gathering evidence.
* *Time.* Court cases can drag on for years as people take time to gather evidence, wait for the case to be scheduled, present their cases, and appeal the court's decision if they lose.

People can also settle lawsuits more quickly and less expensively when they agree to one of the following **two** alternatives:

1. **Mediation.** In mediation, an unbiased person meets with the parties involved to help them find possible solutions to their dispute, without taking up court time.

2. **Arbitration.** In arbitration, the parties agree to allow one or more people to review the dispute and decide the outcome.

Barbed wire and armed guards are part of the prison scene.

Criminal Law

Criminal law consists of laws written by Congress and state legislators that make certain types of behavior illegal and punishable by fines or imprisonment. In a criminal case, the actions of the defendant are considered to have been serious enough to make him or her a threat to the public good, not just to the victim in the case. The biggest differences between criminal and civil law are in **three** broad areas:

1. **Punishment.** Those who are found guilty of breaking civil laws do not go to prison.
2. **Proof of Guilt.** The burden of proving a person guilty in a criminal trial is greater.
3. **Victim.** In a civil case, a single person brings suit. In criminal cases, society is also considered the victim of the crime.

Civil vs. Criminal Law		
	Civil Law	**Criminal Law**
Punishment	Civil laws are not punishable by imprisonment.	Criminal laws are punishable by imprisonment.
Guilt	Plaintiffs must prove their cases by the weight of their evidence—the judge or jury must be 51 percent sure that the plaintiff is correct.	The prosecution must show enough evidence to prove that the defendant is guilty beyond a reasonable doubt.
Victim	A civil lawsuit is filed by the actual victim of the action.	A criminal lawsuit is brought by the government.

Types of Crimes

In general, criminal law includes:

* ***Crimes against a person,*** in which the criminal's aim is harm to the victim physically.
* ***Crimes concerning property,*** in which the criminal tries to steal or damage the victim's property.

Common Crimes		
Crime	**Definition**	**Example**
Murder	One person intentionally and without an excuse, such as self-defense, kills another person.	A terrorist kills a police officer as part of a plot. The terrorist carried out the killing of another person.
Manslaughter	One person kills another person without intending to do so, without demonstrating what is called expressed or implied intent.	Two fathers fight over a call at their daughters' softball game. The first father is so angry that he hits the second with a bat, killing the second father. The first father committed manslaughter because he lost control of his anger.
Battery	One person, without permission, touches and harms a second person as a result.	A father is watching his daughter play softball. She slides into home and the umpire calls her "out." The father disagrees with the call, gets angry, and punches the ump. The father committed battery.
Theft	One person takes away another person's property without permission or legal excuse.	A pickpocket quietly slips a wallet out of an unsuspecting man's back pocket.
Arson	One person intentionally and without legal excuse sets another person's building on fire.	A man is fired from his drugstore job. To get even, he burns down the drugstore.

Penalties for Crimes

Because a crime is considered an act against a community, not just against the victim, the government punishes criminals. A prosecuting attorney brings charges against the defendant for the government on behalf of all citizens.

The punishment handed down by the court is based on the seriousness of the crime. Punishments for crimes are designed to accomplish any or all of the following goals:

* To make criminals suffer for breaking the law and pay back society for the damage caused.
* To physically stop criminals from hurting anyone else. This may be done by putting criminals in jail.
* To convince criminals not to break the law again and to discourage anyone who is thinking about committing a similar crime.
* To make criminals see that they did something wrong and help them change their ways.

Criminal Justice System

You know from watching the evening news or reading your local newspaper that crime is an issue for society today. Police and other law enforcement agencies, such as the FBI, courts, jails, and prisons, work together to deal with crime in our communities by protecting:

* Society against people who break the law.
* The rights of people accused of crimes.

The Constitution and the Fourth, Fifth, Sixth, Seventh, and Eighth Amendments all play important roles in the legal system. The criminal justice system operates to ensure that the constitutional rights of all parties are protected.

Federal criminal case processing, 1994–2000

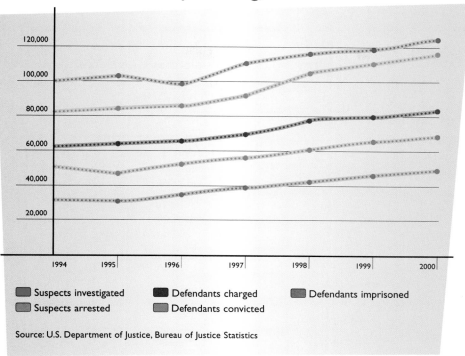

■ Suspects investigated		■ Defendants charged		■ Defendants imprisoned		
■ Suspects arrested		■ Defendants convicted				

Source: U.S. Department of Justice, Bureau of Justice Statistics

In our criminal justice system, many more suspects are investigated and arrested than are convicted and imprisoned.

What Happens When Someone Is Arrested

When law enforcement officials believe that someone is guilty of a crime, they place that person under arrest—meaning they hold him or her for trial by authority of the law. An arrest can be made if police:

* See a person commit a crime.
* Have a warrant to arrest a person.

A judge will give police a **warrant**—written authority to make an arrest or conduct a search—if he or she is shown enough reasonable evidence that the suspect committed the crime.

Initial Court Appearances

The arrest is only the first step in charging a person with a crime. Very soon after arrest, the prosecutor must bring the defendant before a judge. The judge then does the following:

* Describes the charges made against the defendant.
* Informs the defendant of his or her right to remain silent and right to a lawyer.
* Decides whether to set bail and the amount of bail. Suspects who commit very serious crimes or are likely to run away are usually denied bail and must stay in jail.

Arraignment

After the prosecutor files the charges with the trial court, the defendant appears in court for an **arraignment**—a session in which she or he pleads not guilty or guilty to the charges.

In some states, evidence for more serious crimes must first be presented to a **Grand Jury**—a group of citizens who decide whether there is enough evidence that the person may have committed a crime. The Grand Jury can then issue an **indictment**—a formal accusation that leads to trial.

Plea Bargaining

Criminal trials are expensive, and neither the prosecutor nor the defense can be sure how the trial will end. One way to limit the risk and expense is through a **plea bargain**. In a plea bargain, the defendant agrees to plead guilty to a less serious charge without going to trial. In return for the guilty plea, the prosecutor usually agrees to a lighter sentence. Parties may also agree to drop other charges made against the defendant.

What Happens at Trial

In a trial, the prosecution, the defendant with a lawyer, the judge, and usually a jury consider evidence and laws related to the case. Both sides present evidence, and the jury decides whether or not the defendant is guilty of breaking the law.

Jury Selection
The prosecutor and the defense attorney, with help from the judge, choose a jury of 12 unbiased citizens.

↓

Trial
The prosecution presents evidence to try to prove the defendant's guilt "beyond a reasonable doubt." The defense is not required to prove the innocence of the defendant, only that the prosecution has not proved the defendant guilty.

↓

Verdict
The jury decides if the defendant has been proven guilty.

↓

Sentencing
If the defendant is found guilty, the judge determines the punishment based on the law, the crime, and the person's background.

College Crusaders

No system works perfectly all the time. Juries make the best decisions they can from the evidence they are presented. But sometimes juries make mistakes and innocent people go to jail for crimes they did not commit.

Citizens can play an important role in the American justice system by taking part in "innocence projects." Many of these projects started in law schools and colleges all over the United States. Students volunteer their time to reinvestigate cases in which they believe a person was wrongly convicted of a crime. Students find new witnesses and evidence to support the claim of innocence.

A group of students at Northwestern University, near Chicago, succeeded in freeing an innocent person who had been wrongly convicted of murder and was on death row awaiting execution. The students identified the real murderer and got his confession on videotape.

The Corrections System

When someone is found guilty, or convicted, of a crime, the corrections system takes over. The corrections system treats offenders in a number of ways:

* *Probation.* Criminals granted **probation** are allowed to return to their communities to live and work. However, they have certain limits to their freedom. For example, they must be home by a certain hour, or they must not associate with certain people. If they break the rules, they can be sent to jail.
* *Fines.* Criminals must pay a fine or pay for the damage caused.
* *Community Service.* Criminals must do volunteer work in the community, such as picking up litter, counseling students, or serving meals to the homeless.

* *Prison.* Criminals lose their freedom and privacy, and must live in a prison for a specified period of time.
* *Death Penalty.* Some states allow the death penalty for the most serious crimes.

Prisoners may be let out of prison before they have served their full sentence. This is called being released on **parole**. Like probation, parole allows prisoners to live in society with certain limitations, such as curfews or regular meetings with parole officers. If the prisoner violates the rules of parole, he or she can be sent back to jail.

Prison Overcrowding

The number of criminals in American prisons and jails has tripled since the mid-1980s. By the early 2000s, the nation had two million people in prisons and jails at the federal, state, county, and city levels. The ACLU National Prison Project is one organization working to improve prison conditions. Some experts believe that overcrowded prisons expose prisoners to:

* Poorer medical care in prison.
* Less effective work, education, and treatment programs.
* Greater levels of violence from other prisoners.

Authorities have used the probation system and parole to help deal with overcrowding, but some citizens believe that too many prisoners receive parole before they are ready to return to society.

The Juvenile Justice System

In 1999, approximately one in six arrests involved a **juvenile**—a child or young person under the age set by law (usually 18 years) at which a person can be charged as an adult for a criminal act. The juvenile justice system is designed to deal with youths who break the law. While juvenile courts give young defendants most of the same basic constitutional rights as adult criminals, the goal of the system is very different.

History of Juvenile Justice

Before 1900, the law treated children like adults. Children and young people found guilty of crimes were:

* Prosecuted in criminal court.
* Given the same sentences as adults.
* Put in the same jails as adults.

Reformers of the 1800s believed that the real causes of juvenile crime were a lack of moral education and standards. They said the juvenile system should educate and **rehabilitate**—restore to useful life, usually through treatment and education—rather than punish. Youths should be helped to return to productive lives in society, not simply punished for their behavior.

Today, courts try to balance **three** factors when dealing with juveniles:

1. Helping youths avoid criminal behavior in the future.
2. Treating and rehabilitating youths who break the law.
3. Punishing youthful lawbreakers.

Court Procedure

Each state has its own juvenile justice system with its own laws and practices. In most states, juvenile court has authority over all people under the age of 18 who are charged with breaking the law. Juvenile courts generally operate the same way as regular courts.

Arrest

When a youth is arrested for a crime, the police have the authority to decide what to do next. Police may return the offender to his or her parents. Or they may hold the offender in detention or juvenile hall.

To determine if the case will go to the court system, juvenile court staff, probation officers, and social workers meet and review the evidence. Almost half of all juvenile cases are not sent to a judge, but are resolved more informally by:

* Dismissing the charges.
* Giving the juvenile an informal probation.
* Referring the young person to a treatment program.

Supreme Court Case

In re Gault (1967)

Gerald Gault was a 15-year-old boy who was accused of making obscene phone calls to his female neighbor. He was arrested and then tried in the juvenile courts. The judge sentenced Gerald to the State Industrial School, a juvenile reform school, until he turned 21.

Gerald and his parents appealed the decision, claiming that the judge conducted the hearing in a way that violated Gerald's constitutional rights. Before the juvenile hearing took place, the court did not provide a specific list of charges, so Gerald and his parents could not prepare for the hearing. The neighbor who accused Gerald of making the phone calls did not testify or appear at the hearing, so Gerald couldn't cross-examine her to find out if her story was true. No one told Gerald or his parents that he had the right to a lawyer or that he did not have to say anything that would make him appear guilty.

The Supreme Court ruled that children tried in juvenile court, like adults tried in criminal court, are entitled to certain rights. These rights include the right to written notice of the specific charges, the right to be represented by a lawyer, the right to refuse to say anything that could be used to incriminate them, and the right to cross-examine the witnesses testifying against them. "In re" means *as if against a thing*, rather than against a person. *In re* actions often occur when the defendant challenges a judicial process, as did Gerald and his parents.

Initial Hearings and Bail

If the court decides to send the case to a judge, the court holds a hearing. In this hearing:

* The judge describes the charges made against the defendant.
* The judge informs the defendant of his or her right to remain silent and right to a lawyer.
* The child pleads not guilty or guilty.

The judge decides if the child should be held in detention or released to a parent or guardian before the case is heard. Juveniles do not have the right to bail. If the crime is serious, the child may be transferred to an adult criminal court.

Delinquency Hearing

Juvenile courts give the defendant a delinquency hearing instead of a trial. As in criminal court, the defendant and his lawyer can present evidence and question witnesses, and the prosecutor must prove guilt beyond a reasonable doubt.

Juvenile hearings and records are not usually open to the public. This privacy helps give defendants a fresh start on the road to rehabilitation.

Judge's Decision

Juveniles do not have the right to a trial by jury. A judge decides whether the accused is innocent or not. In juvenile court, a conviction finds the accused **delinquent**, meaning the person has failed to do what the law requires, rather than guilty.

Adult criminals are held responsible, or guilty, for their actions. Delinquency suggests a lower level of responsibility. The court states only that the convicted juvenile failed to follow the law.

Sentencing

With the advice of social workers and psychologists, the judge decides the sentence for a delinquent. This sentence may include:

* Probation, which works the same as in criminal court probation.
* Counseling or drug treatment.
* A sentence to reform school or other residential facility.
* **Restitution**—act of making up in some way for the loss or damage caused.

JUVENILE COURT

Trying Juveniles as Adults

Between 1988 and 1994, the number of teens who committed violent crimes, such as murder, sexual assault, and armed robbery, more than doubled. In response, all states now allow juvenile offenders to be tried as adults in the criminal court system in certain circumstances. Whether a youth can be tried in criminal court depends on age, history of past run-ins with the law, and the seriousness of the crime. In most states, the young offender must be at least 14 years old to be tried in criminal court. Is this trend toward trying more youth in criminal court good or bad for society?

Are there certain types of cases in which juveniles should be tried as adults? How do you think youths who commit violent crimes should be treated in our legal system? You decide.

Arguments **for** Trying Juveniles in Criminal Court

Juveniles may be less mature than adults, but they know right from wrong. Violent crimes deserve serious punishment. These youths should be held responsible for their actions.

The juvenile justice system is too easy on youths who commit crimes. We need to deal with them more harshly to discourage other teen criminals.

The juvenile crime rate has been decreasing since the mid-nineties; obviously, the threat of criminal punishment has helped prevent crime.

Arguments **against** Trying Juveniles in Criminal Court

Juveniles, whatever they have done, are too young to fully appreciate the consequences of their acts. They should not be held to the same level of responsibility as adults.

Juveniles have most of their lives ahead of them. They should be given the chance to realize their mistakes and become productive members of society.

Prosecuting juveniles like adults does not deal with the real causes of violent juvenile crime, such as child abuse and poor parental supervision.

The American justice system is divided into criminal law and civil law. Civil law provides a way to settle fairly disputes between people, through such remedies as compensation for damages and equity, or fair remedy. Some of the most common civil cases deal with broken contracts, personal injury and property damage, disagreements over property, consumer protection, and domestic relations.

Criminal laws are designed to protect all citizens in the community from those who break the law, so the system may limit the freedom of convicted criminals. Criminal law is different from civil law in three important ways: the type of punishment, determination of guilt, and the victim.

The juvenile justice system is designed to deal with youths who break the law. Although juvenile courts give nonadults most of the same basic rights as adult criminals, the system focuses on rehabilitation. Sentences for juvenile offenders include probation, counseling or treatment, reform school, or restitution.

Civics in America

arraignment—pre-trial court appearance during which an accused person answers formal charges made against him or her with a plea of guilty or not guilty. *p. 234*

compensation—payment to make up for a loss, injury, and the like. *p. 226*

contract—agreement between two or more parties, written or oral, that can be enforced by law. *p. 227*

defendant—person being sued or accused of a crime. *p. 226*

delinquent—having failed to do what the law requires, according to a judicial ruling. *p. 238*

domestic-relations laws—laws regulating disagreements among family members. *p. 228*

equity—justice under the law that is influenced by fairness. *p. 226*

evidence—something that provides or tends to provide proof. *p. 229*

grand jury—group of citizens who decide if there is enough evidence of a crime to send the accused to trial. *p. 234*

indictment—formal accusation that leads to a trial. *p. 234*

juvenile—individual who is under an age set by law (usually 18 years) at which he or she can be charged as an adult for a criminal act. *p. 236*

parole—release from prison or jail before the full term is up on condition of lawful behavior and with the requirement of regular reporting to an officer of the court. *p. 235*

plaintiff—person who files a legal action or claim. *p. 226*

plea bargain—agreement in which a defendant pleads guilty to a lesser charge and the prosecutor, in return, drops more serious charges. *p. 234*

pleading—formal, written statement explaining the cause of action or the defense in a legal case. *p. 229*

probation—act of suspending the sentence of a criminal offender and giving him or her freedom under the supervision of an officer of the law. *p. 235*

rehabilitate—restore to a useful life, usually through treatment and education. *p. 236*

remedy—solution to the harm caused by the accused person. It is a legal order made by the court to make up for a wrong and may be money (compensation) or an order to do something (equity). *p. 226*

restitution—act of making up in some way for the harm caused by the accused person. *p. 238*

tort—damage, injury, or wrongful act caused to one person, other than breaking a contract, for which a civil lawsuit can be filed. *p. 228*

warrant—written authority to make an arrest or conduct a search. *p. 233*

CHAPTER 15

Economics and the American Economy

In this chapter, you will learn about:

- how the United States economy is structured
- how different economic systems distribute resources
- the operation of a free-market economy
- how businesses in the United States are organized
- the factors that drive basic economic decisions

Most Americans believe that, if you work hard, you can get ahead. Many successful business people have had to overcome obstacles in their lives. Dave Thomas, the founder of the Wendy's restaurant chain, was an adopted child who never knew his birth parents. His adoptive mother died when he was very young, and Dave spent most of his childhood moving from place to place so his adoptive father could find work. Thomas got his first job when he was 12. As a young man, he worked for a company helping restaurants that were having trouble making money. He was so good at this that he became a millionaire by the age of 35. In 1969, he opened his first Wendy's Old-Fashioned Hamburgers restaurant, naming it after his daughter. By 2001, there were more than 6,000 Wendy's restaurants.

Dave never forgot his roots. He created the Dave Thomas Foundation for Adoption to find homes for children in foster care. He died in 2002, but his restaurants, his foundation, and his example live on.

The American Economic System

Freedom is something we hold very dear in the United States. As our national anthem says, we live in "the land of the free."

We enjoy basic rights that guarantee our freedoms, including the freedom of our economy. The economy includes anything involving money, such as businesses, jobs, taxes, investments, and prices. Although it comes from an ancient Greek word meaning "home management," **economy** now means the system of material needs, expenses, and resources of a society.

Basic Economic Freedoms

Unlike in some other nations, our government does not try to control how citizens get the goods and services they need and want. Lawmakers set rules for how some economic activities in the United States take place, but even those laws are designed to protect the basic freedoms of citizens.

The U.S. economy is based on **capitalism**—a system that allows individuals and businesses to own and control their own property and create wealth with minimal government interference. Individuals and businesses are free to succeed—or fail.

Other economic systems include:

* *Communism:* a system directly opposed to capitalism, in which the government tries to protect individuals by controlling property and by sharing profits across the community as a whole.

* *Socialism:* a system that allows—but limits—private ownership and control of production and profits, in order to protect the well-being of the community.

In the United States, you enjoy several basic economic freedoms, including:

* freedom to buy and sell products and services.
* freedom to compete.
* freedom to work.
* freedom to make a profit.
* freedom to own property.

Freedom to Buy and Sell

A **market** is created when buyers and sellers exchange goods and services.

Our economic system is based on an idea called the **free market**—people buying and selling products and services according to their own wants and needs, without the government or some other authority planning and controlling what they do. In a free market, sellers and buyers decide whether or not to engage in a transaction. In this type of economy, nobody is forced to buy or sell anything, or to do so at a price set by the government.

In the United States, we value the democratic idea of **free enterprise**—allowing private industry to operate with as little control by the government as possible. But the free market is not a "free-for-all." Few Americans like the idea of **laissez-faire**—allowing the economy and free enterprise to be shaped only by the market, unrestricted by any government rules so businesses and citizens can operate as they wish. Most Americans *want* their government to protect its citizens from economic conditions that would limit or destroy their other freedoms.

As a result, our free enterprise system balances freedoms with the need to protect citizens by imposing some controls on what businesses can do.

Just as we balance our rights and responsibilities as citizens, or use a balance of powers in our government, free enterprise is really a compromise. Businesses and individuals in the free market can buy and sell as they wish, but they must obey certain laws.

EXAMPLES: Workplace safety for employees, accurate product labeling, and using agreed-upon weights and measurements for products.

Freedom to Compete

The freedom to compete helps both sellers and buyers.

As a seller, or someone who supplies a product or service, you can sell to anyone who wants to buy. And you can try to sell to the same customers as every other supplier.

EXAMPLE: You can try to sell your services to babysit kids in your neighborhood, but other babysitters may compete for the same business.

Competition also provides an important benefit for the buyer, or **consumer**. With competition, consumers have the freedom of choice. They are not forced to buy from only one seller or supplier. They can choose the best or the cheapest product or service, however they decide.

EXAMPLE: Thanks to competition, you can decide to buy CDs, clothes, or shoes from your choice of many stores, based on such factors as price, convenience, quality, and service.

▲
Shoppers in New York City

Freedom to Work

The freedom to work to earn a living is an important part of our economic system. Many laws protect your freedom to work.

EXAMPLE: The Equal Opportunity Employment Act makes it illegal for employers to discriminate against job candidates because of race or gender.

Hunt v. Washington Apple (1977)

U.S. interstate commerce laws are designed to protect competition among companies from different states. In Hunt v. Washington Apple Advertising Commission (1977), the Supreme Court ruled that one state could not use its lawmaking powers to protect in-state companies against out-of-state companies.

Some states, as well as the federal government, inspect fruits and vegetables and grade the product quality to protect consumers. North Carolina had passed a statute that required that all apples sold or shipped into North Carolina in closed containers be identified only by federal grades. In order not to lose their North Carolina customers, some apple growers in Washington had removed Washington State grade markings from containers bound for North Carolina. Washington's state grading standards were actually higher than the federal government's (and therefore better for consumers), but the Washington growers needed to compete.

The Supreme Court found (decided) that the North Carolina statute unfairly discriminated against out-of-state competition. The justices also declared that the statute reduced the grading protection that benefited American consumers.

Freedom to Make a Profit

We are free to work and to earn a **profit**—the amount of money left over after all of a business's expenses have been paid.
EXAMPLE: If you sell oatmeal cookies at a school bake sale, you might charge 25 cents each. If you sell 50 cookies, you make $12.50. But that is not your profit. You must subtract the money you paid for the oatmeal, butter, flour, and other ingredients. If you spent $5 to make the cookies, then your profit is $7.50.

In a free-market economy, the government is not permitted to interfere with your business if you obey business laws—except for collecting taxes. Individuals and companies must pay taxes on the profits they earn to help support government services.

Freedom to Own Property

Property can be something physical you own, such as a car or a CD, or it can also be something more abstract, such as song lyrics or a short story you wrote, or an idea for a product you invented. These things are called intellectual or artistic property.

The Constitution protects your economic or business property, including the right to prevent the government from taking or searching it without just cause.

Technology Gap

America has the largest and most technologically powerful economy in the world. American companies lead the way in technological developments, especially in computers and in the medical, aerospace, and weapons industries.

Some critics warn that the spread of technology is making it more and more difficult for people and workers *without* technology skills to get the better jobs that pay higher wages.

Since 1975, most raises and increases in earnings have been earned by people who were already members of the richest 20 percent of U.S. households, widening the gap between rich and poor people.

Scarcity of Resources

Have you ever tried to buy something and found that stores and online sellers had run out? **Scarcity** occurs when there is not enough of something available to all of the people who want to buy or use it. A **resource** is a supply of something or a support that is used to create economic activity, including capital (money), natural resources (such as water, timber, and oil), and human resources, such as labor.

Supply and Demand

When a resource becomes scarce, the free economy reacts to that imbalance of supply and demand.

* **Supply** is the amount of a particular good or service that producers are willing (and able) to provide at a given price.
* **Demand** is the amount of a particular good or service that people are willing (and able) to buy at various prices.

Supply and demand affect prices:

* When supply is greater than demand, prices tend to go down, or decrease.
* When demand is greater than supply, prices tend to go up, or increase.

  EXAMPLE: Your favorite band is playing in town next month. When you try to buy tickets, you find the concert is sold out. Tickets to that concert are scarce because there are more people who want to buy them than there are tickets for sale. Demand for tickets is greater than supply. To get a ticket for the sold-out concert, you might even be willing to pay more. Heavy demand makes prices increase. On the other hand, if tickets to the concert had not sold very well, the promoters might lower the price to encourage more people to buy.

Economic Systems

In the past and even today, people exchange, or trade, one kind of good or service for another in what is known as a barter system. The **barter** system works best in small societies or among friends because:

* To barter, one person has to find another person who wants to make the exact same trade.
* To trade, both people have to agree that one good or service has the exact same value as another good or service.

To make exchanges of goods and services easier, people long ago decided to use precious metals, such as gold or silver, and eventually money, as a medium for exchange. Today, the barter system is used primarily among people who know one another, when a country's money system breaks down, or when civil disorder creates chaos in a society.

Other kinds of economic systems have replaced bartering in most nations today:

* *Command Economy.*
* *Market Economy.*
* *Mixed Economy.*

Command Economy

In a **command economy**, the central government makes most of the country's economic decisions. Command economists believe that all the resources of a country should be managed by the government so they can be used by the government to serve its citizens. Critics say command economies do not work.

EXAMPLE: In the 20th century, the former Soviet Union and other Eastern European socialist countries used a government-managed command economy system to try to share resources and profits more equally among their citizens. Their economies did not grow naturally under government control, and ordinary citizens did not thrive. Most of those countries have now shifted to a less centralized economy.

Did You Know?

Capitalism vs. Managed Economies

Sir Winston Churchill, the former Prime Minister of Great Britain and a devoted friend of America and of Western democracy, was famous for his clever use of language and speech. He once said, "The inherent vice [the weakness] of capitalism is the unequal sharing of blessings; the inherent virtue [the strong point] of socialism is the equal sharing of miseries."

Market Economy

In a **market economy**, the government or any other authority does not try to manage the economy. Markets grow, shrink, and change only according to supply and demand, or what some economists call market-driven, or natural market, forces. Buyers and the costs of goods and services determine what prices can be charged.

EXAMPLE: The price of a music CD is set by music companies and stores, not by any government or organization. The owners of music industry businesses set prices based on:

* ***Their costs,*** such as artist royalties, manufacturing expenses, advertising, shipping, recording studio costs, store rents, and so on.
* ***What buyers will pay.*** If buyers like you think a CD is too expensive, they won't buy it. Eventually, the seller will drop the price to reach a level consumers are willing to pay.

Mixed Economy

As you might guess, **mixed economies** follow a combination of two factors:

1. Market-Driven Forces.

2. Centrally Planned Decisions.

Individuals, businesses, and the government all make economic decisions. Most countries today, including the United States, use a mixed economy. The U.S. government has passed antitrust laws to restrict any company from having a **monopoly**. That's when one company has exclusive control of sales of a product or service in a market. Monopolies have no competition. They usually result in higher prices and poorer service than would exist in a competitive market.

EXAMPLE: AT&T was once the only phone company operating in America. But as other companies developed the technology to deliver telephone service, the government broke up AT&T's monopoly to allow competition.

Economic Systems

Type of System	Who Makes the Decisions	Stated Advantages	Stated Disadvantages
Command Economy	The central government.	* More of a country's resources can be used for the public good. * A few rich people cannot exploit poorer people.	* Economies are difficult, if not impossible, to manage, especially for governments. * People are not rewarded for working harder to get ahead, so production drops. Shortages of basic goods or production of poor quality products are common.
Market Economy	Natural market forces.	* Prices are determined by supply and demand only. * Profit alone determines what economic activities continue, change, or stop. * People are rewarded for creating wealth, so they work harder.	* Economic activity can be distorted by monopolies or other unfair trade practices. * Uncontrolled markets cannot be concerned with the well-being of needy citizens. They can lead to more uneven or unfair distribution of wealth.
Mixed Economy	Central government *and* market forces.	* Tries to use the best of both other systems. * The government can limit possible harmful effects of the free-market system by, for example, stopping monopolies and giving tax relief to the poor.	* Governments should not interfere with the economy in any way because interference always brings unwanted results.

Amtrak: Public or Private?

Free enterprise works well in most parts of the economy, but some services are run or supported by the government because they require enormous investments and they are considered essential to the public good:

* Mail delivery: the U.S. Postal Service.
* Road travel between states: the Interstate Highway System.
* Management of air transportation: the Federal Aviation Administration.

Some people think that most government-run services should be operated by private businesses. Amtrak, the nation's passenger train system, is one example. Early in 2002, a Congressional panel said that Amtrak should be replaced, at least partly, by private companies.

What did Congress consider when deciding what to do with Amtrak? Was their thinking correct?

Arguments for Privatizing Amtrak

Amtrak costs the federal government money it needs for other services, such as national security.

Competition will drive down costs, improve service quality, and increase customer satisfaction.

People who use passenger railroad services should pay for rail service, not all taxpayers.

Private companies run airlines and interstate bus services successfully, yet are still regulated by the government to protect citizens.

Arguments against Privatizing Amtrak

Amtrak was created because passenger service cannot be run profitably and still ensure quality and safety. When passenger railroads were run by private companies, the service was awful.

Amtrak needs lots of money to improve its aging trains, tracks, and so on. Only the government can risk and manage that investment.

The interstate rail system is too important to the public to be run by private owners.

Subsidizing rail service reduces use of oil and gas and pollution. The government should encourage people people to use rail transportation by continuing to run Amtrak.

U.S. Business Organization and Management

Four different types of business organizations sell products and services:

1. **Sole Proprietorships.**
2. **Partnerships.**
3. **Corporations.**
4. **Not-for-Profit Organizations.**

Sole Proprietorship

A **sole proprietorship** is a business run by one person, without partners, and not set up, or incorporated, as a company. Money to start and grow the business usually comes from the owner-proprietor.

EXAMPLES: Many newsstands, convenience stores, and other small shops are sole proprietorships. So are writers, editors, artists, and consultants who work for themselves, not for a company, often out of their homes.

Advantages of sole proprietorship include complete control of the business and the ability to be your own boss. Sole proprietorships are also the simplest form of business to set up.

Disadvantages include unlimited **liability**—the legal responsibility to pay unsettled debts or damages. Customers who have serious complaints can sue a sole proprietor for her or his home and personal possessions. Sole proprietorships are also limited by the talents, skills, energies, and resources of the sole proprietor.

Partnership

Many business activities need the talents, skills, energies, and resources of more than one person. As a result, many sole proprietors form partnerships with other people, especially when their businesses grow.

A **partnership** is a business owned by more than one person. The partners are liable, or personally responsible, for the company's debts and damages, just as if they were sole proprietors (except in limited partnerships, which limit liability for some partners).

Advantages of partnerships are similar to those of a sole proprietorship, but partnerships also offer the added support provided by the other partners.

Disadvantages are also similar to those of sole proprietorships. Partnerships are also slightly more complicated in terms of ownership and decision-making because more owners are involved.

Corporation

Incorporation is a complicated idea that basically means that a business has been made a legal entity or **corporation**, with the approval of the government, for its owners' benefit.

* A corporation is considered by the law to exist as something separate from its employees or owners.
* Because a corporation is a kind of "being" or "thing," owners set up corporations so "they" can become an "it."
* Some corporations sell stock to raise money, so owners can avoid using their own or borrowing the money they need.
* Corporations protect their owners from personal liability for the debts or mistakes of the business.

Most medium-sized and large businesses and many small businesses are corporations.

Some towns also incorporate to gain legal status and municipal rights for their citizens.

When an owner starts a corporation, or when its owners and managers want to expand into new types of businesses or markets, they can raise money from individuals and institutions in **two** ways:

1. **By Selling Stock. Stocks** represent shares of ownership. You can think of stocks as pieces of the total corporate pie. When you buy a company's stock, you become an owner of some portion of the company. (In fact, all ownership of a corporation is in shares—even that of the original owners.) As a shareholder, you may even be able to vote on major decisions the company makes. Investing in stocks is risky: If the company does well, and the stock price goes up, your investment becomes more valuable. But if the stock price plunges, you lose money.

Did You Know?

Stock Market

Approximately 51 million Americans own stock in companies. Stocks are bought and sold through stock exchanges, including the New York Stock Exchange and the National Association of Securities Dealers exchange (known as the NASDAQ).

Indexes that track the ups and downs of the stock exchanges are published in newspapers, on the Internet, and elsewhere.

When investors put their money in stocks, the stock market indexes go up. When investors sell their shares, the indexes go down. Many people consider the stock market to be an early measure of the overall health of the economy.

EXAMPLE: When the stock market plunged in April 2000, it was an early sign of the tough times that came in 2001.

2. By Issuing Bonds. <u>Bonds</u> are interest-bearing instruments issued by corporations or government agencies. In other words, bonds are loans that investors make to corporations and governments in exchange for a set amount of interest, which is money paid for the use of money. The amount of **interest** you will get is guaranteed when you buy a bond, so bonds are a safer investment than stocks.

Like sole proprietorships and partnerships, there are pluses and minuses to setting up a business as a corporation.

Advantages of corporations for their principal owners are protection from liability and the right to sell shares.

Disadvantages include extra set-up time and expense, and more legal and tax reporting requirements than partnerships or proprietorships have.

Not-for-Profit Organizations

Sole proprietorships, partnerships, and corporations all try to earn profit for their owners and investors. But some business-like organizations, such as charities or some educational and scientific foundations, try not to keep more money than they need to operate and fulfill their missions. They do not aim to make a profit. Some examples of **not-for-profit organizations** are:

✳ Charities, such as the American Red Cross, the YMCA, and the Salvation Army.
✳ Schools, universities, and some private educational agencies.
✳ Churches, mosques, and synagogues.

Basic Economic Decisions

You probably try to use your time to get as many things done and to have as much fun as possible. Every economic system aims to use its **factors of production**—the resources used in the production of goods and services—as efficiently as possible.

Junior Achievers

Why wait until you are out of school to learn about business, or even to start your own company? Headquartered in Colorado Springs, CO, the Junior Achievement organization teaches students about business, economics, and free enterprise using classroom volunteers from the business community. The group's mission is to "ensure that every child in America has a fundamental understanding of the free enterprise system."

Here are some of the things students in Junior Achievement programs are doing throughout the country:

* A California student started her own company making and selling hair clips. All the money she makes goes to buy teddy bears for children with cancer and chronic blood diseases.
* Students in Kentucky developed a plan to get funding for a family activity center. Thanks to their efforts, $5.1 million was raised to open the center.
* A New York City student spent a day accompanying and job-shadowing a telephone company executive. He learned "how to be a true leader" by watching the executive in action.

Factors of Production

Factors of production can be a complicated idea. Think of them as things that can be used to create goods or services that have value. They can be broken down into **three** areas:

1. **Capital**—human-made means of production, such as tools and machinery, a factory's buildings and property, or money.
2. **Land**—natural resources, such as water, minerals, or timber, as well as land used for developing resources, for farming, or for building on.
3. **Labor**—human work effort and people employed in production.

Factors of production are limited, which means every society and business has only a certain amount of them. So using them efficiently is important. To stay in business, companies must make wise decisions about how to use these resources.

EXAMPLES: If a clothing manufacturer uses all its factories, machines, and employees to make jeans, it cannot make T-shirts. If a city uses all its land for buildings, there will not be any land for parks. If a company spends all its profits on employee holiday bonuses, it will not have enough money to invest in new computers.

Managing and balancing its factors of production are the major challenge of any business.

Production, Distribution, and Consumption

Other areas of basic economic decision-making include:

* **Production**—what and how many goods and services to make.
* **Distribution**—how to move goods and services to consumers.
* **Consumption**—what goods and services to buy.

Maintaining and growing the economy of a country for the good of its citizens is a balancing act. Many countries now believe what the government of the United States believes: The natural market forces of supply and demand are the best ways to balance production, distribution, and consumption—with a little help from government.

Primary Source

Adam Smith's *Wealth of Nations*

Adam Smith published his *Inquiry in the Nature and Causes of the Wealth of Nations,* more commonly called *The Wealth of Nations,* in 1776. In his famous book, Smith described what would later be called *free market economics.* Smith believed that a country's wealth can be measured by calculating the total value of all the goods that its citizens' labor produced.

"The annual labor of every nation is the fund which originally supplies it with all the necessities and conveniences of life which it annually consumes, and which consists always either in the immediate produce of that labor, or in what is purchased with that produce from other nations.

"According therefore as this produce, or what is purchased with it, bears a greater or smaller proportion to the number of those who are to consume it, the nation will be better or worse supplied with all the necessaries and conveniences for which it has occasion [what it needs and wants].

"But this proportion must in every nation be regulated by two different circumstances [conditions]; first, by the skill, dexterity, and judgment with which its labor is generally applied [the quality of its labor]; and, secondly, by the proportion between the number of those who are employed in useful labor, and that of those who are not so employed. Whatever be the soil, climate, or extent of territory of any particular nation, the abundance or scantiness [scarcity] of its annual supply must . . . depend upon those two circumstances."

An important aspect of our democratic political system is a capitalist, mixed free market economy, which allows the market—the exchange of goods and services—to react naturally to supply and demand with little interference from governments. Capitalism depends on certain freedoms, including the freedoms to buy and sell, compete, work, make a profit, and own property.

The major challenge of any economic system is to use its scarce resources to meet supply and demand and to balance the use of capital, land, and labor with production, distribution, and consumption.

Civics in America

barter—exchange of one kind of good or service for another. *p. 247*

bonds—interest-bearing instruments issued by corporations or government agencies. You are paid back within a specified period of time at a fixed rate of interest. *p. 253*

capital—human-made means of production, such as machinery, money, or buildings. *p. 254*

capitalism—economic system based on private property and private enterprise; allows individuals and businesses to own and control their own property and profits with little government interference. *p. 243*

command economy—economy in which most major decisions are made by the central government. *p. 247*

communism—political and economic system of public ownership of property and production based on Marx's theories. The Soviet Union was the world's leading Communist regime. *p. 243*

consumer—person who buys the goods and services produced. *p. 244*

consumption—act of using up goods and services to satisfy wants and needs. *p. 255*

corporation—type of business established as a legal entity, separate from the individuals making up the corporation. *p. 252*

demand—amount of a particular good or service that people are willing (and able) to buy at various prices. *p. 246*

distribution—process of moving goods and services to consumers. *p. 255*

economy—system of the material needs, expenses, and resources of a human society. *p. 243*

factors of production—resources (capital, land, and labor) used in the production of goods and services. *p. 253*

free enterprise—economic practice of permitting private industry to operate with a minimum of control by the government. *p. 243*

free market—type of market in which sellers and buyers decide, with the aid of prices, whether or not to engage in a transaction. Free markets follow the forces of supply and demand rather than government plans. *p. 243*

interest—money paid for the use of money. *p. 253*

labor—human work effort, the people employed in the production of goods and services. *p. 254*

laissez-faire—policy of complete non-intervention by government in the economy, leaving all decisions to the market; the economy and free enterprise are shaped only by the market, without any government rules. *p. 243*

land—natural resources as factors of production, such as oil, acreage, or timber. *p. 254*

liability—legal obligation to pay debts or damages. *p. 251*

market—activities that occur when and where buyers and sellers meet. *p. 243*

market economy—system in which supply and demand, not the central government, shape the exchange of goods and services. *p. 248*

mixed economy—system in which both government and market forces shape the economy. *p. 248*

monopoly—exclusive control (or right to control) of sales of a product or service in a market. *p. 248*

not-for-profit organization—organization, such as a charity, that does not intend to make a profit. *p. 253*

partnership—business owned by more than one individual. *p. 251*

production—use of resources to create goods and services. *p. 255*

profit—amount of money remaining after all of a business's operating expenses have been paid. *p. 245*

resources—factors of production that include natural resources, human resources (labor), and capital. *p. 246*

scarcity—situation in which there are not enough resources available to satisfy existing needs or wants. *p. 246*

socialism—economic system in which many basic factors of production and key industries are under government ownership and control, some private ownership of businesses and profits are permitted. *p. 243*

sole proprietorship—business owned and run by one person. *p. 251*

stocks—shares of ownership in a company. *p. 252*

supply—amount of a particular good or service that producers are willing (and able) to provide at a given price. *p. 246*

Government's Role in the Economy

In this chapter, you will learn about:

- how the government tries to maintain economic stability
- what business cycles are
- how government manages businesses and the banking system
- how government protects consumers and workers

The Great Depression of the 1930s ruined many businesses and created widespread poverty and unemployment for many Americans. This devastating collapse of world trade and industry also challenged the idea that the economy should be allowed to operate on its own, with no interference from the government. A British economist named John Maynard Keynes became the best-known spokesman of the need for government to step in to coordinate the economy, especially in times of high unemployment. He wrote about his recommendations for large-scale government planning in his 1936 book, The General Theory of Employment, Interest, and Money. Keynes' ideas influenced economic theory for years to come. They still have an impact on how the U.S. government interacts with the economy.

Government and the Economy

In a capitalist economy, the market, or what people and businesses want to buy, determines the prices of goods and services. As a rule, no central planning authority, such as a federal government, decides what the prices of gasoline, bread, or other products and services should be. Instead, purchases and sales between buyers and sellers throughout the country (and around the world) cause prices to move up, or down, or stay flat.

In that kind of a free market, the government tries to interfere in the economy as little as possible. But government still guides the economy.

EXAMPLE: The government's role in the economy is like the conductor of an orchestra. Like a conductor, the government does not actually play the economic instruments or write the music. But it interprets how the economic "notes" sound, measures the overall performance, and encourages the players in one direction or another.

Constitutional Framework

The U.S. government's role in our economy begins with the Constitution. The Constitution gives several economic powers to Congress, including the powers to:

* Collect taxes.
* Borrow money.
* Regulate commerce with other countries, among the states, and with Native American tribes.
* Coin money.

Limits of Free Enterprise

The U.S. Constitution does not guarantee Americans the right to free enterprise, and free enterprise is not entirely "free." Government laws limit how businesses can operate in several ways. Business enterprises:

* *Must pay taxes* to federal, state, and local governments.
* *Cannot compete unfairly* with each other.
* *Cannot harm consumers* with unsafe products or deceptive selling practices.

The Economy in the Constitution

The U.S. Constitution lists the rights and duties of government concerning the economy.

From Article 1, Section 8:

The Congress shall have Power

To lay and collect Taxes, Duties, Imposts [taxes on imports] and Excises [taxes on manufacturing or use], to pay the Debts and provide for the common Defense and general Welfare of the United States; but all Duties, Imposts and Excises shall be uniform throughout the United States;

To borrow Money on the credit of the United States;

To regulate Commerce with foreign Nations, and among the several States, and with the Indian Tribes;

To establish an uniform Rule of Naturalization, and uniform Laws on the subject of Bankruptcies throughout the United States;

To coin Money, regulate the Value thereof, and of foreign Coin, and fix the Standard of Weights and Measures;

To provide for the Punishment of counterfeiting the Securities and current Coin of the United States;

To establish Post Offices and post Roads;

To promote the Progress of Science and useful Arts, by securing for limited Times to Authors and Inventors the exclusive Right to their respective Writings and Discoveries. . . .

From Article 1, Section 9:

No Preference shall be given by any Regulation of Commerce or Revenue to the Ports of one State over those of another; nor shall Vessels bound to, or from, one State, be obliged to enter, clear, or pay Duties in another.

No Money shall be drawn from the Treasury, but in Consequence of Appropriations made by Law; and a regular Statement and Account of the Receipts and Expenditures of all public Money shall be published from time to time.

From Amendment XVI:

The Congress shall have power to lay and collect taxes on incomes, from whatever sources derived . . .

In addition to regulating the actions of companies, the government can also influence the economy by using its powers of taxing and spending. The government's economic policies can influence the economy to:

* *Grow* or be more active.
* *Shrink* or be less active.

  EXAMPLE: If the economy is slow or weak, the government may lower the amount of taxes it collects, so citizens can keep and spend more of their income. Or the government may spend more of the money it has collected (on new public projects and purchases). Either way, more money is available to stimulate economic activity.

Maintaining Economic Stability

An economy that is running well helps the public good. As the saying goes, "Money makes the world go around." The government, therefore, tries to steer the economy through ups and downs.

Business Cycles

Unfortunately, the economy is not always healthy. Business activity in the United States goes through periods of growth, or expansion, and shrinkage, or contraction. Some economists think that these ups and downs in the economy—**business cycles**—repeat regularly every few years. Although no two business cycles are exactly the

same, economists identify **four** stages of economic changes:

1. **Expansion,** or growth.
2. **Peak,** or the highest point of growth.
3. **Recession** or a contraction (slowing or stopping of growth).
4. **Depression.**

The Business Cycle

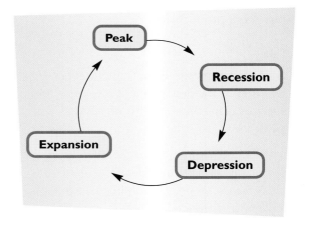

Expansion

During an **expansion**, a period in which demand for products, services, and labor is growing, also called a boom, several conditions occur:

* People and businesses increasingly believe that their short-term economic futures will be secure and prosperous.
* They want to buy more goods and services. They often borrow money to do so.

* The demand for goods and services grows. The first sign of a period of expansion may be a shortage in the supply, or inventory, of certain goods and services.
* The drop in inventory, in turn, makes businesses want to produce more goods and services.
* To produce more, companies hire more workers to fill the increased demand.

Workers earn more money, so they can buy more products and services.

Peak

An expansion cannot continue forever. Eventually, the new demand for goods and services is met, and expansion hits its **peak**, or highest level.

* Demand for new investments to keep businesses and lifestyles growing increases, so people and businesses seek to borrow money.
* Demand for money causes interest rates—the costs of borrowing money—to go up.
* Businesses cannot find enough workers to hire, so they raise salaries to attract workers. These higher expenses reduce company profits or cause companies to raise prices.
* If rates and prices get too high, companies stop borrowing money to make new investments.

The period of expansion comes to an end.

Recession

What goes up must come down. The natural movement of the cycle continues:

* As fewer businesses make fewer new investments, companies stop hiring new workers. Some current workers may lose their jobs if the company loses business.
* Workers are laid off. New workers hired earn lower salaries. Wages overall stay flat or go down.
* With more people out of work, the demand for products and services declines.
* As people have less to spend, companies lower prices to continue to sell their products.
* Momentum gathers again, but this time it moves downward.

When the United States economy has experienced low demand, low production, and rising unemployment, resulting in decline or no growth for six months, economists say that the economy is in a **recession**. Often, economic growth can resume at this point:

* As demand for new investments and purchases drops, interest rates and prices begin to fall.
* The lower rates and prices stimulate new investments and spending.
* Eventually, the economy begins to expand again, and a new business cycle starts.

Depression

A serious recession that lasts significantly longer than six months is called a **depression**.

EXAMPLE: The worst depression ever was the Great Depression of the 1930s. It followed a major expansion in the 1920s. During the Depression, more than one quarter of the U.S. workforce could not find jobs because so many businesses had closed.

In economic terms, a depression can be seen as a very severe recession, and even after a depression, which is characterized by so much human suffering, the business cycle of expansion and contraction will resume.

Managing How the Economy Performs

Economists believe that the business cycle is a natural process, caused by billions of people and businesses around the world buying and selling what they need. But the governments try to influence the natural fluctuations of the economy in order to:

✳ Protect their citizens and businesses in the short term, or near future.
✳ Encourage the economy to grow steadily, but not too quickly, over the longer term.

▲
Unemployed men wait for free soup, coffee, and doughnuts outside a soup kitchen in 1931.

Measuring Economic Performance

During a medical check-up, your doctor gathers information about how healthy you are: your pulse, your blood pressure, your reflexes, and other signals. Before the government can even try to guide the economy, economists must gather information about the economy's health, called **economic indicators**. These include:

* *Gross Domestic Product (GDP)*—the value of all goods and services produced in a country for one year. The 2001 GDP of the United States was more than $10 trillion. Economists use the GDP to measure the size and growth of a country's economy from year to year.

* *Consumer Price Index (CPI)*—list of the prices of approximately 400 selected ordinary goods and services used by consumers, such as milk, jeans, cable TV, haircuts, pet care, and phone service.

    Government economists watch for (and report) monthly changes in the index to see if prices are going up or down.

* *Inflation*—an increase in the overall level of prices for goods and services. Economists consider high inflation a sign of an unhealthy economy.

* *Deflation*—the opposite of inflation, is a period in which the value of assets and price levels decrease.

    EXAMPLE: During the Great Depression of the 1930s, values of such assets as farm property, homes, and minerals fell sharply, wiping out the life savings of millions of people. Because the value of their real assets was lower than the amount these people owed in, for example, mortgages, they could not obtain new loans. Many people lost their homes.

* *Unemployment rate*—the number of people looking for work divided by the number of people in the civilian (non-military) workforce. Economists consider high unemployment a sign of a weak economy.

Adjusting Economic Performance

A doctor can use medical tools, including drugs, surgery, and advice about exercise, to improve your health. The government uses several tools to improve the health of the economy. The **two** most important are:

1. **Fiscal Policy,** which is the government's plan for how much it collects and spends. To put more money back into a weak or sluggish economy, the government may decide to hire more workers, to give raises to its employees, to start new building projects, or to reduce taxes, leaving citizens with more of their own money to spend.

2. **Monetary Policy,** which is the government's plan for how much money or credit it makes available. Lowering federal bank lending rates makes it easier for more people and companies to borrow and lend money.

Managing the Federal Budget

You, your friends, and your family are consumers. The federal government is a huge consumer that buys a lot of goods and services. What the government buys and how much money it spends have an enormous influence on the economy.

At the beginning of each year, the president submits a federal budget to Congress for approval. Creating the federal budget is one of the powers that the office of the president uses to shape legislation for Congress to pass. In the proposed budget, the president outlines:

* How much money government agencies need to spend on existing programs.
* Ideas for spending on new programs that the president proposes.
* Estimates of how much money the government will collect in taxes and other revenues.

Congress must approve the budget, a lengthy process of negotiations and compromises.

"And on my left is 'The Great Fantino,' who takes the position that the deficit will disappear by magic."

Balancing the Budget

The money the government can spend comes mainly from **two** sources:

1. **Taxes,** or revenues.
2. **Loans,** or borrowing.

When the federal budget is balanced, the government does not spend more money than it receives in taxes. But the federal government often decides to spend more than it earns, resulting in a **budget deficit**—more spending than income. The government plans to borrow money to make up the difference. Some government leaders have tried to pass laws to stop Congress from approving deficit budgets, but, so far, these attempts have been ruled unconstitutional.

The National Debt

Since around 1940, federal spending has grown enormously, largely on military and social expenses. Government income has not grown as quickly, so the **national debt**—the amount of money the country owes—is now more than five trillion dollars!

The economic boom of the 1990s, combined with efforts to cut spending, reduced the federal deficit. Before 2002, there were four consecutive federal **budget surpluses**—more income than spending. Some of this money was used to reduce the national debt. However, after the events of September 11, 2001 and the economic downturn, government spending increased and again exceeded income.

Government and Banking

Besides taxing and spending, the federal government also affects the economy by influencing the supply of money and the cost of borrowing money.

Federal Reserve System

Established by Congress in 1913, the Federal Reserve System, usually called simply the Fed, works as the central banking system of the United States. The 25 Federal Reserve Bank branches, located in 12 Reserve Districts across the country, serve:

* The federal government.
* Other banks and banking institutions.

Federal Reserve Banks deposit money *from* and lend money *to* other banks. They are banks for other banks. People keep their money in (and maybe borrow money from) commercial banks; those banks keep their money in a Federal Reserve Bank and borrow money from the Fed.

"I told you the Fed should have tightened."

Federal Reserve's Duties

The Federal Reserve has **four** main duties. The Fed must:

1. **Carry out the federal government's monetary policy** by controlling:
   * The interest rates that other banks must pay to borrow money from the Fed.
   * Reserve requirements—the percent of their deposits other banks must keep in Federal Reserve banks.

2. **Make and enforce rules for banking institutions** and protect consumers' credit rights.

3. **Keep the banking system stable** by watching over how other banks operate.

4. **Serve the U.S. government, the public, financial institutions, and foreign official institutions** in financial matters.

Controlling the Money Supply

The Fed can control the money supply and therefore influence the economy in **three** ways, by:

1. **Changing the reserve requirement**— the formula for determining the amount of cash that member banks must keep on deposit in their regional Federal Reserve bank. This reserve requirement ensures that member banks are financially sound and safe for consumers to use.

   EXAMPLE: If the reserve requirement is raised, banks have less money available to lend to individuals and corporations.

2. **Adjusting its <u>discount rate</u>**—the interest rate that member banks must pay to borrow money from a Federal Reserve Bank.

   EXAMPLE: If the Fed lowers its rate, member banks are more likely to borrow from the Fed, and then lend money to customers. Loans to customers support new investments that can make the economy grow. In 1993, when the Fed lowered its interest rates, economists credited it with pulling the economy out of recession.

3. **Buying and selling <u>government securities</u>**—instruments of government debt, such as U.S. Treasury notes and bonds that are sold to raise money for the federal government.

   EXAMPLE: When it buys back securities, the Fed spends and puts more money into circulation. When it sells securities, it takes money out of circulation, leaving less money for others to borrow.

Political Independence

The Federal Reserve System is run by a board of seven governors who are appointed by the U.S. president and approved by the Senate, one governor every 2 years, for a term of 14 years. The president also appoints one of them to be the chair for a 4-year term, whenever the previous chair's term ends. Ideally, the chair and governors make decisions in the public interest, without interference by the president, Congress, or political parties.

Did You Know?

Fed Chair Alan Greenspan

Some people think that the chair of the Federal Reserve Board is the second-most-powerful person in the world, behind only the president of the United States.

Alan Greenspan became chairman of the Fed Board in 1987 and has been reappointed since then by different presidents from both parties.

Greenspan believes in the free market and generally opposes government intervention in the economy. As Federal Reserve chairman, he has supported controlling inflation, often by adjusting interest rates, a policy that has earned him widespread praise.

In December 1996, Greenspan used the phrase "irrational exuberance" (enthusiasm without common sense) to describe how some people were investing in the stock market. At the time, his words were shocking, but when the stock market fell significantly in the spring of 2000, and a recession followed, Greenspan seemed very wise.

Government and Business

Government regulation of businesses protects **three** things:

1. **Fair Competition.**
2. **Consumers and Workers.**
3. **The Environment.**

Protecting Fair Competition

Americans both admire and distrust large corporations. Large companies may have wellknown products and brands that consumers buy and depend on, for example, in baby-care products or medicines. On the other hand, some large companies have forced smaller companies out of business or bought them, leaving consumers with less choice or higher prices.

Americans place a high value on fairness, in business and elsewhere. **Antitrust laws** were developed to restrict monopolies, promote fairness, and ensure open and honest competition among companies.

Trust Busting

The U.S. government first tried to regulate big businesses in the late 1800s by controlling, or *busting,* trusts. A **trust** is an alliance of individual companies whose owners agree to combine their resources. They use the trust's size and power to overpower competitors. One example is the Standard Oil Trust, which was formed in 1882.

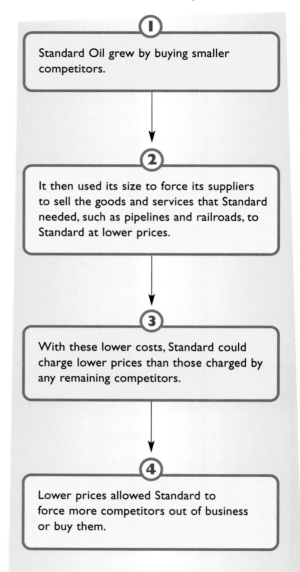

How a Trust Reduced Competition

1 Standard Oil grew by buying smaller competitors.

2 It then used its size to force its suppliers to sell the goods and services that Standard needed, such as pipelines and railroads, to Standard at lower prices.

3 With these lower costs, Standard could charge lower prices than those charged by any remaining competitors.

4 Lower prices allowed Standard to force more competitors out of business or buy them.

The business practices of the Standard Oil Trust and other trusts were not illegal, but they were considered unfair. Congress passed new laws, such as the Sherman Antitrust Act of 1890 and the Clayton Antitrust Act of 1914, to allow the government to break up the trusts. In 1911, the Supreme Court forced Standard Oil Trust to break up its operations.

Federal Trade Commission

In 1915, the U.S. government set up the Federal Trade Commission as an independent agency to protect consumers and smaller businesses by:

* Enforcing antitrust laws.
* Eliminating advertising that was false or deceptive.
* Investigating suspicious business practices.
* Keeping Congress, consumers, and citizens informed about existing (and needed) antitrust laws.

Protecting Consumers

Antitrust laws primarily protect companies from other companies. The government also protects consumers from companies.

Three federal agencies or departments are involved in safeguarding customers.

1. **Consumer Product Safety Commission.**
   * Works with businesses to protect users and consumers from accidental injury and death caused by products.
   * Sets and enforces safety standards for many products, such as car seat belts.
   * Orders recalls and alerts on products that might be defective or dangerous.

Did You Know?

Microsoft and Antitrust Laws

In 1998, the Justice Department and 20 states filed an antitrust lawsuit against software maker Microsoft. The suit charged that, by giving away its web browser for free—by bundling it with the popular Windows operating system software owned by Microsoft that was installed in 80 percent of new computers—Microsoft was competing unfairly and acting as a monopoly. Browser rival Netscape, who had developed a web browser before Microsoft created its own, claimed that this bundling was unfair.

Government lawyers argued that having such a dominant position in a market gave Microsoft too much control over pricing, computer manufacturers, suppliers, and competitors. This amount of control was not, the government argued, good for the public or for business. Ultimately, the court ruled in April 2000 that Microsoft *had* competed unfairly and hurt consumers. The judge ordered the company to change some of its business practices.

2. **Food and Drug Administration.**
   * Oversees safety of foods, drugs, and cosmetics by inspecting products being sold to consumers.
   * Enforces food labeling laws, to ensure that consumers can tell what they are buying.
   * Tests and certifies that new drugs are safe to use.
3. **Department of Agriculture.**
   * Inspects, grades, and sets safety and production standards for meat, poultry, and canned fruits and vegetables.
   * Manages food programs for people in need.
   * Publishes information for consumers to use.

Protecting the Environment

The government also protects citizens and consumers by safeguarding the environment from harmful practices by businesses. The Environmental Protection Agency is a federal group that:

* Enforces environmental laws.
* Determines air and water quality standards to detect pollution.
* Monitors businesses to make sure they follow environmental laws, such as those involving dumping and waste disposal.
* Oversees safe disposal of hazardous waste, such as toxic chemicals that are by-products of manufacturing.

Government and Labor

Over the years, government economic policy has been extended to protecting workers from the companies that employ them. The government sometimes acts as a mediator between labor—workers—and business management.

Organized Labor

A **labor union** is an organization of workers formed to achieve shared goals, such as higher wages, shorter work weeks, and better working conditions. Like other interest groups, labor unions use the power of the many to influence and persuade. Workers who negotiate with management as a united group have more power than individuals to get what they want. Negotiating as a group through representatives is known as **collective bargaining**. Tactics used by labor unions include:

* *Boycotts.* Workers may stop buying all products made by their company and urge others to do the same.
* *Pickets*, or peaceful protests and demonstrations against a company or organization. Workers may march in front of the company headquarters carrying signs critical of the company.
* *Strikes*, or work stoppages. All workers in the union refuse to work. Sometimes workers "phone in sick" or take turns staying away from work to slow production without stopping it completely.

The Endangered Species Act

The Endangered Species Act protects specific varieties of plants and animals that are in danger of becoming extinct. The act makes it illegal for people to harm them or change the habitats in which they live. For example, to protect a certain kind of owl, laws prevent the cutting down of trees in some forests.

Since the act took effect in 1973, Americans have disagreed about how to balance the need to protect wildlife with the needs and rights of businesses and home-owners. For example, in 2001, some federal officials tried to limit the ability of environmental groups to add additional endangered species to the list. The action was never passed by Congress. In early 2002, the Bush administration reviewed several already-protected species that lived in the western United States, including a songbird called the California gnatcatcher. Developers wanted to build on land that was reserved as "critical habitat" for the gnatcatcher.

How do you think land owners' rights to use their own land should be balanced against preventing a species from becoming extinct?

Is protecting a species more important then helping people? How far should the government go to protect species from extinction?

Arguments for the Endangered Species Act

Without protection, many species would die out. Humans have an obligation to protect nature and have no right to destroy a species.

We need to consider the environment as a connected whole. Dams and bridges can affect habitats.

Extinctions have an unknown impact on the environment or an ecosystem.

Arguments against the Endangered Species Act

The Act is unfair to landowners and workers. It can take away their freedom to make choices about the use of their property. It endangers profits and jobs.

Environmental groups use endangered species laws to stop or delay needed projects, such as dams and airport expansions.

People and progress are more important than plant and animal species which come and go in nature without human involvement.

Early Labor Unions

Labor unions have existed in the United States almost since the country was founded. In the 18th and 19th centuries, skilled craftspeople, including printers, carpenters, tailors, and weavers, formed local unions with two primary goals:

1. **To make sure that the quality of their products was kept high.**
2. **To keep untrained workers and non-members out of the trade.**

During the 19th century, the American workforce started to change with the arrival of factories and industrialization. New industrial unions, such as the Knights of Labor, were formed to fight for the rights of laborers, the unskilled workers who manned the factories. Many of the craft unions joined together in 1886 to create the American Federation of Labor, which merged with the Congress of Industrial Organizations to form the AFL-CIO in 1955.

American Citizenship

United Mine Workers of America

Citizens actively take part in American democracy every day. Few have done so as bravely as the workers of the UMWA, the labor union formed in 1890 to secure rights for miners.

The dangerous and unfair working conditions that coal miners endured in the 19th and early 20th centuries have been recognized by American artists in songs and movies. George Gershon Korson (1899–1967) created a collection of hundreds of coal-mining folksongs that was first published in the UMW Journal and is now available from the Library of Congress. *Coal Miner's Daughter,* starring Sissy Spacek, is based on the life of country singer Loretta Lynn, whose coal miner father died of a lung disease caused by breathing coal dust in unsafe mines. *Matewan,* directed by John Sayles, tells the heroic struggles of workers and their families against acts of intimidation, violence, and murder that mine owners used to try to stop the union.

The UMWA led bitter strikes to win the right to an 8-hour workday in 1898. Violence that resulted from strikes in 1919 and 1920 resulted in the creation of a U.S. government commission to oversee the mining industry. In 1933, the union established collective bargaining rights. Health and retirement benefits were gained in 1946. The brave leaders and members of the UMWA helped the cause of the entire American labor movement.

Department of Labor

During the 19th century, labor unions began to pressure their government representatives to take actions to improve working conditions, which often included danger to life and limb, long hours, and very low pay.

* The U.S. Department of Labor was established in 1913 to protect the rights and welfare of workers.
* In 1914, the Clayton Antitrust Act was passed, stating that "the labor of a human being is not a commodity or article of commerce," meaning that workers were not just raw materials or tools for businesses to use as they wished.
* The Clayton Act also made peaceful strikes, picketing, and boycotts legal.

Labor Today

Labor unions still protect workers in America, but they are not as powerful as they once were. Unions were weakened by scandals surrounding illegal practices by the trucking industry's Teamsters Union. In 1957, after a Senate investigation that uncovered widespread corruption, the Teamsters were expelled from the AFL-CIO.

While labor unions continue to play an important role in the American scene, many people feel they're responsible for the high cost of American-made goods over foreign ones, and that in some professions, they make it nearly impossible for employers to get rid of incompetent employees.

Nonetheless, history has proved that, united, workers can gain better treatment from employers than individuals can do on their own. The right of workers to form a union is an accepted American right.

Supreme Court Case

NLRB v. Jones & Laughlin (1937)

In the case of the National Labor Relations Board v. Jones & Laughlin Steel Corp., the Supreme Court ruled that the steel company had treated the union unfairly, including firing union leaders and discriminating against union members when hiring employees. The Supreme Court upheld the rights of workers that had been described in the National Labor Relations Act of 1935.

The Court declared that the freedom "to self-organization, to form, join, or assist labor organizations, to bargain collectively through representatives of their own choosing, and to engage in concerted [acting together] activities for the purpose of collective bargaining or other mutual aid or protection" was a fundamental right of workers.

Chapter 16 Wrap-up
GOVERNMENT'S ROLE IN THE ECONOMY

Americans enjoy the right to live in a free-market economy that operates with minimal interference from the government, but the government still oversees the economy, gently directing it one way or another.

Taxing and spending are two of the tools the government uses to influence the economy. If the economy slows, the government can lower taxes to give people more money to spend, or it can hire more government workers so that more people are employed and earning wages. The government, using its Federal Reserve System, can also lower interest rates to make investing by citizens and businesses more attractive.

In addition, the government helps protect companies from unfair competition, consumers from unfair business practices, the environment from industrial pollution, and workers from companies.

Civics in America

antitrust laws—laws developed to restrict monopolies and trusts and ensure fair competition among companies. *p. 268*

budget deficit—shortage in a budget between estimated income and the cost of planned expenditures. *p. 265*

budget surplus—excess of income over spending in a budget. *p. 265*

business cycle—period of growth and shrinkage of business activity. *p. 261*

collective bargaining—negotiating in a group, such as a labor union, often with business management. *p. 270*

Consumer Price Index (CPI)—list of the prices of approximately 400 goods and services used by consumers. The CPI measures price changes. *p. 264*

deflation—period in the economic cycle characterized by a decrease in the overall level of prices for goods and services and in the value of assets. *p. 264*

depression—severe recession that lasts significantly longer than six months; prolonged period of low economic activity and employment. *p. 263*

discount rate—interest rate that the Federal Reserve Bank charges member banks to borrow money. *p. 267*

economic indicators—signs of the economy's performance, such as the value of goods produced or changes in the prices of certain products. *p. 264*

expansion—period in the business cycle when demand for products, services, and labor grows; also called a "boom." *p. 261*

government securities—government obligations, such as U.S. Treasury notes and bonds, through which the government borrows money. *p. 267*

Gross Domestic Product (GDP)— value of all goods and services produced in a country for one year. *p. 264*

inflation—period characterized by an increase in the overall level of prices for goods and services. *p. 264*

labor union—organization of workers formed to promote the economic interests and well being of its members, such as salary and working conditions. *p. 270*

national debt—amount of money a country owes to residents and foreign lenders. *p. 265*

peak—highest point in a period of economic expansion. *p. 262*

picket—peaceful protest or demonstration. *p. 270*

recession—period of at least six months of no growth in the economy. (An ongoing depression.) *p. 262*

reserve requirement—formula for determining the percent of their deposits that member banks must keep in a regional Federal Reserve Bank. *p. 266*

strike—refusal to work in order to obtain improved working conditions and wages. *p. 270*

trust—alliance of firms formed by legal agreement to gain competitive advantage. *p. 268*

unemployment rate—the ratio of people who can't find work to those in the civilian (non-military) labor force. *p. 264*

United States Foreign Policy

In this chapter, you will learn about:

- **what foreign policy is**
- **who decides foreign policy**
- **the tools used in making foreign policy**
- **the history of America's foreign policy**
- **what U.S. foreign policy is today**

Some of the grandparents of your classmates can probably remember where they were when the news of the attack on Pearl Harbor was announced in 1941. They can all tell you where they were when President Kennedy was assassinated in 1963. Now your generation has its own day of tragedy to remember: September 11, 2001. Where were you when you heard the news?

The terrorist attacks reminded everyone how closely America is connected to the rest of the world. When President Bush created his antiterrorism campaign, he consulted advisors at home and abroad. His advisors examined international intelligence information collected by U.S. agents. U.S. ambassadors and diplomats met with foreign leaders and urged other countries to commit to the fight for world security. Americans representing the United States in other countries reacted to the new dangers. While our government was using emergency foreign policy tools to pursue the terrorists, our usual foreign policy activities continued to protect world trade, humanitarian aid, and peacekeeping efforts throughout the world.

What Is Foreign Policy?

Foreign policy is the plan that a government develops and the actions it takes in its relationships with other countries. Like other nations, the United States develops foreign policy to protect its interests. Our foreign policy has several goals.

It Protects American Citizens

One of the first jobs of any government is to protect its people. Foreign policy includes plans to keep our borders secure and to keep our citizens, wherever they may be, safe from foreign enemies. Foreign policy preserves national security. It includes the actions we take to defend ourselves. **Two** examples of foreign policy for national security include:

1. **Directing the armed forces.** Decisions about how our armed forces will react to events in the world are a part of our foreign policy. Will we help another country with its battles? Will we send advisors to train foreign troops? Will we give weapons? Will we send in our own troops? These are difficult questions. Our policy helps answer them.
2. **Developing new weapons to protect against new threats.** Some in the world view our strength as a protection to help bring world peace. Others see new weapons, especially nuclear ones, as increasing world danger. We have treaties with other countries about weapons development. What are we willing to agree to? How do we make agreements? These questions are answered by foreign policy.

It Works for Peace in the World

We need a peaceful world. You will hear people say, "We are not the world's policeman," and that may be true. But our quality of life depends on the people, resources, and ideas that come from all over the world. Our businesses are international. Our communication systems are international. Our lives and those of our allies require world peace. Our foreign policy, therefore, involves making treaties, forming alliances, and maintaining relations with other countries.

It Supports Democracy

American foreign policy supports other democratic nations. We believe that a democratic form of government is the best form humans have been able to put together. Through democracy, the world has achieved the greatest degree of human freedom and the highest standard of living for the greatest number of people ever in human history. Our foreign policy works to help other nations move toward democracy.

It Provides Humanitarian Assistance

America recognizes it has a special role in the world. We have enormous resources. Where there is suffering in the world, Americans reach out to help. When we provide that help through our government, then it becomes a part of our foreign policy. Some areas we work in include:

* *Disaster relief,* including bringing aid to the victims of floods, hurricanes, and droughts, as well as to refugees escaping warfare.
* *Global environment,* working with other nations to fight air and water pollution.
* *Health,* fighting epidemics, providing medicines, helping to build hospitals and train health care workers.
* *Hunger,* providing food from our farms for people starving around the world.

Our government provides help with donations of needed items, with gifts or loans of money, and with programs that send people who have specialized knowledge to work on problems.

Who Decides Foreign Policy?

The Constitution divides the responsibility for deciding and implementing foreign policy between the executive branch and Congress. Other groups try to influence decision-makers in order to advance their own interests and opinions.

The Executive Branch

The president has the primary responsibility for deciding U.S. foreign policy. He selects and uses expert advisors to gather information and to advise him. These experts work in **four** executive departments and organizations:

1. **The State Department** is led by the Secretary of State, who is a Cabinet member. The Secretary of State acts as chief diplomat for the United States. Other diplomats include the ambassadors and their staffs that work in our **embassies**—the official U.S. government offices in foreign countries. The State Department connects America with the rest of the world.

2. The National Security Council (NSC)

The NSC is a group of top advisors who help to coordinate the activities of the different parts of government in their dealings with national security issues. It consists of the president, the vice president, the secretaries of defense and state, and other advisors such as the CIA Director, the White House Chief of Staff, and the National Security Advisor. The NSC also provides the president with **intelligence**—information about the activities of our enemies and our allies. By combining all of this information from all these sources, members of the NSC can give a very accurate picture of what is going on.

3. The Central Intelligence Agency (CIA)

analyzes and gathers intelligence from numerous sources about foreign nations, organizations, and people. It uses methods that are both *overt* (public or open) and *covert* (hidden or secret), such as spying.

4. The Department of Defense (DOD) has

its main offices in the Pentagon in Washington, D.C. It is managed by the Secretary of Defense and oversees all military activities. In its foreign policy role, it provides expert military information and advice.

Congress

The Constitution gives Congress important responsibilities in **four** significant areas. Only Congress may:

1. **Declare War.** Although the president is military Commander-in-Chief, only Congress can commit the nation to going to war.

2. **Approve Treaties.** The U.S. Senate has to ratify all **treaties**—agreements with other countries made by the executive branch. A proposed treaty needs a two-thirds Senate vote to be approved.

3. **Ratify Appointments.** The Senate has the power to approve key foreign policy appointments, including:
   * Secretary of State.
   * Secretary of Defense.
   * Ambassadors—chief U.S. diplomats in other countries.

4. **Approve Funds.** Congress approves all federal spending. When the president and his foreign policy advisors want new weapons, or money to pay for foreign policy activities, they must seek approval from Congress.

At times, in response to emergencies, the president has sent troops into areas without a formal declaration of war. Often, this leads to debate about whether he has overstepped his power. In 1973, Congress passed the War Powers Act. It requires the president to notify Congress within 48 hours after he has sent troops into a dangerous situation. Congress then has 60 days to approve the operation, or the troops must be withdrawn.

Groups Outside Government

U.S foreign policy affects the lives and business activities of many people. As a result, citizens, business and interest groups, and foreign governments and companies try to influence it.

Domestic Groups

Many domestic groups lobby Congress on foreign policy issues, including:

* **Farmers,** who want to sell crops to foreign countries and reduce <u>domestic</u>—U.S. made—competition for their products.
* **Labor unions,** who want to keep jobs from going abroad and foreign-manufactured goods from being less expensive to American consumers than those they make. Unions lobby for trade agreements that help sell American goods to other countries.
* **Manufacturers,** who want to be able to make and sell American products overseas and who also want protection against cheaper, competing foreign imports. Businesses also want their operations in foreign countries—including investments, factories, and workers—to be safe.
* **Think tanks,** that employ scholars and researchers to work on policy issues. They gather information, study data, and make proposals that suggest directions U.S. policy might take.

Public Opinion

The president and other elected lawmakers pay attention to the opinions of American voters. But American lawmakers also need to be aware of how people in *other* countries view the actions and policies of the United States, because those opinions influence how foreign leaders and governments act.

Mass Media

United States lawmakers who decide foreign policy are affected by the media and what the media reports to the voting public. U.S. foreign policy makers, however, are also influenced by how the foreign press, or the media in other countries, shapes public and government opinions in those nations.

Foreign Countries

Many foreign nations lobby the United States government to:

* Obtain foreign aid or loans.
* Get favorable tariff and trade terms for their products.
* Receive military assistance to protect their borders and to deal with internal strife.
* Convince the United States to purchase goods or raw materials from them.

Foreign Companies

Many foreign companies also lobby American lawmakers because they want to:

* **Sell their products** in the United States.
* **Operate** in the United States—have business offices and factories here, and sometimes move their managers to the United States.
* **Obtain loans** to start up or expand their businesses.

The Elian Gonzalez Case

Politics, immigration policy, and foreign policy came together in a historic case about a young Cuban boy. In 1999, Elian Gonzalez was five years old when his mother and stepfather escaped from Cuba in a small boat. When the boat sank, 11 people drowned, including Elian's mother and stepfather. Elian was rescued, and his American relatives in Miami, Florida, took him into their home. His father in Cuba wanted him back. The community of Cuban Americans in Miami believed he should be allowed to stay.

American politicians came out on both sides of the argument. Elian and his Miami relatives were seen on TV nearly every night for weeks. People all over the country debated the issue. Finally, the U.S. Immigration and Naturalization Service agreed that Juan Gonzalez was Elian's lawful guardian and should decide where Elian would live. Juan Gonzalez was allowed to come and take Elian home to Cuba. Did the INS make the right decision? You decide.

Elian Should Stay in America

His mother had wanted Elian to live in freedom in America.

Elian was seeking **political asylum**—safety from an unfriendly government. The United States has given asylum to other children of foreigners.

Elian would enjoy a better life growing up in the United States than in Cuba.

Elian was loved and cared for by his relatives. Elian wanted to stay with his relatives in America.

Foreign policy has opposed Cuba's communist government for many years. America should protect Elian's freedom. Miami's Cuban community is an important voting group. Politicians should support them.

Elian Should Return to Cuba

With his mother's death, legal custody of Elian went to his father, Juan Miguel Gonzalez, not his Miami relatives. Elian's father was entitled by law to decide where his son would live.

Elian's father loved him, followed proper procedures, and requested that his son be returned to Cuba to live with him.

Elian was too young to make such an important decision.

Cuba's premier Fidel Castro asked the U.S. government to return Elian.

Cuban relations are not friendly. Allowing Elian to remain in the United States would make them worse.

How to Influence Foreign Policy

United States citizens can influence foreign policy in several ways:

* **Through a career choice.** If you are interested in travel to foreign countries, meeting people from other parts of the world, and being part of American foreign policy, you might want to consider a job in the State Department, the U.S. Foreign Service, journalism, or international business.
* **By electing officials.** Most candidates for national office let the public know where they stand on important foreign policy issues. You can choose people who believe as you do.
* **By joining with others.** There's strength in numbers. Join groups whose views are the same as yours. Participate in their activities to influence government.
* **By boycotting foreign products.** The practice of **boycotting**—refusing to buy a particular product—was used by the American colonists against English tea. It still works as a way to express disagreement with a nation's policies.

Peace Corps worker encourages a student in an adult literacy class in Guatemala. ▶

Tools of Foreign Policy

Foreign policy is part of a political process that uses different tools or strategies. **Four** of the most effective methods include:

1. Diplomacy

The most basic activity of foreign policy makers is **diplomacy**—the process of reaching a peaceful agreement with a foreign nation through discussion. All sides have to give a little for negotiations to be successful.

2. Alliances

One result of diplomatic success is an **alliance**—an agreement between two or more nations, in which the countries involved agree to defend each other in a time of war. Potential enemies know that the allies will aid one another if attacked. An alliance can also be formed to encourage trade among nations.

EXAMPLE: The North American Free Trade Agreement (NAFTA) promotes and regulates trade among Canada, Mexico, and the United States.

3. Foreign Aid

Foreign aid can take the form of money, arms, or goods given by the United States to another country. Sometimes, foreign aid is given in exchange for something the U.S. government wants, such as permission to set up a military base in a foreign country, purchase of American products, or a promise to stop human rights violations.

EXAMPLE: During the Afghanistan conflict, the U.S. provided tons of food to the starving Afghan people to stabilize the situation, create goodwill towards the United States, and reduce human misery.

4. Intelligence

Information about foreign governments— what they are doing and what they are capable of doing—is called intelligence. Intelligence informs our policy makers. It is used to protect the American homeland and U.S. interests overseas from terrorist and other enemy threats.

History of Foreign Policy

U.S. foreign policy has changed over time from **isolationism**—avoiding involvement in foreign military alliances and wars—to active involvement in world issues and peacekeeping.

Ben Franklin and the French

From the very first days of our nation, the country has needed the support of other nations. When the colonies fought the American Revolution, Benjamin Franklin went to Europe to get support against England. France, England's trade and military rival, secretly supplied weapons and cash to the American war effort and eventually agreed to a formal open alliance with the new nation. America's first foreign policy effort was a success.

Isolationism

After the Constitution was put into place, **three** significant factors shaped America's goals in foreign policy:

1. Washington's Farewell Address

President George Washington advised the new nation to avoid involvement in European political and military issues that did not directly involve it. He knew America had plenty of its own problems to solve. Generally, U.S. foreign policy followed this approach for about 150 years.

2. The Monroe Doctrine

In 1823, President James Monroe proclaimed the Monroe Doctrine. He warned European nations not to interfere in the affairs of Central or South American countries. He said:

* America considered anything that happened anywhere in the Western Hemisphere to be connected with its own national interests.
* The United States was prepared to use military force to stop European interference.
* In return, America would continue to stay out of European affairs.

3. Fear of Foreigners

In the 1840s and 1850s, American policy allowed people to immigrate to the United States to help the nation grow, but the feelings of many Americans caused foreign policy to change and become more isolationist.

The Monroe Doctrine

"As a principle in which the rights and interests of the United States are involved, the American continents are henceforth not to be considered as subjects for future colonization by any European powers.

"We consider any attempt on their part to extend their system to any portion of this hemisphere as dangerous to our peace and safety. With the existing colonies of any European power we shall not interfere. But we view any [new action] for the purpose of oppressing them, or controlling their destiny, by any European power, as the manifestation of an unfriendly disposition toward the United States."

EXAMPLE: By 1860, more than 1.5 million Irish people had come to the United States.

The new immigrants competed with native-born citizens for jobs and places to live. Many Americans resented their arrival and argued that foreigners, especially the Irish and later the Chinese, should be kept out of the country.

Teddy Roosevelt and the American Empire

President Theodore Roosevelt wanted America to become more involved in world affairs. As a young man, he had led a cavalry unit, known as the Rough Riders, against the Spanish in Cuba. Victory in the Spanish-American War (1898) gained independence for Cuba and the Spanish colonies of Puerto Rico and the Philippines for the United States.

As president, Roosevelt argued for the building of the Panama Canal to improve the transportation of American goods and troops between the Atlantic and Pacific oceans.

His "Roosevelt Corollary" to the Monroe Doctrine proclaimed that the United States had the right to police the Caribbean.

Roosevelt sent the U.S. Navy on a world tour to show off American military power. He also won the Nobel Peace Prize for negotiating the end of a war between Russia and Japan.

Supreme Court Case

Dorr v. the United States (1904)

Fred L. Dorr and Edward F. O'Brien owned a newspaper in the Philippines. They were charged with libel by one of the U.S. officials appointed to govern the new Philippines territory after the Spanish-American War. Though they asked for a jury trial, it was denied and their case was tried by a judge.

Dorr and O'Brien then appealed to the U.S. Supreme Court. They claimed that, since they lived in a U.S. territory, they should have been allowed the right to a jury trial guaranteed by the U.S. Constitution.

The Supreme Court ruled that the U.S. Constitution does not automatically grant rights to people living in territories acquired by the United States. The Court declared that Congress, and only Congress, had the power to decide if a territory was *incorporated*, meaning that it was a full part of the United States with all the rights protected by the Constitution. The Philippines, at the time of this trial, was not yet incorporated, so the Court rejected the appeal.

Ships in the Panama Canal

The World Wars

Have you ever tried to stay out of an argument that didn't involve you? The military and political conflicts in Europe that led to World War I and World War II did not directly involve the United States. But, when American trade and shipping with its European trading partners were disrupted during World War I, United States lawmakers decided that America had to end its isolationist foreign policy and enter the war. When World War I ended, America returned to isolationism—until a direct attack on the American naval base at Pearl Harbor in 1941 brought us into World War II.

American isolation ended for good after World War II when the United States, now a major world power, changed its foreign policy, began an active leadership role, and:

* *Helped set up the United Nations* in 1945 to maintain world peace.
* *Joined in founding the North Atlantic Treaty Organization (NATO),* to protect the western nations against the aggressive expansionist activities of the Soviet Union and the spread of communism.

American Foreign Policy 1780 to 1950

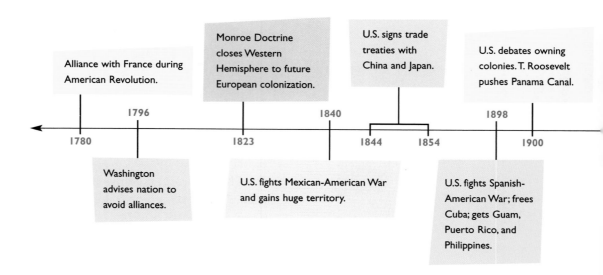

Alliance with France during American Revolution.

Monroe Doctrine closes Western Hemisphere to future European colonization.

U.S. signs trade treaties with China and Japan.

U.S. debates owning colonies. T. Roosevelt pushes Panama Canal.

1796   1840   1898

1780   1823   1844   1854   1900

Washington advises nation to avoid alliances.

U.S. fights Mexican-American War and gains huge territory.

U.S. fights Spanish-American War; frees Cuba; gets Guam, Puerto Rico, and Philippines.

The Cold War

The **Cold War** was the long period of tension between the communist Soviet Union and the United States following World War II. The two nations never went to war against each other, but the world lived under the fear that they would wage a nuclear war. During this time, the United States adopted a foreign policy of **containment** aimed at stopping communism from spreading into more countries.

Cold War Confrontations

One aspect of the Cold War was a series of confrontations between the United States and the Soviet Union. In some cases, U.S. policy led to military involvement, but more often it did not:

* ***Greece.*** America provided aid to prevent Greece's post-war government from being overthrown by communists.
* ***Turkey.*** The United States gave aid and support to a struggling government.
* ***Marshall Plan.*** The United States provided billions of dollars to help Europe rebuild after Word War II.
* ***Berlin Airlift.*** The Communist Soviet Union tried to force the United States to abandon West Berlin in 1948 by closing roads and railroads into the city. America responded with an airlift of supplies to keep the city going. Thirteen months later, the blockade ended.

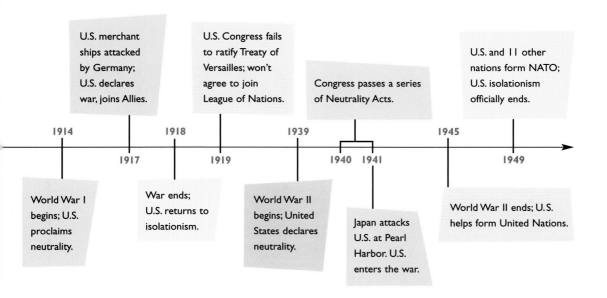

U.S. merchant ships attacked by Germany; U.S. declares war, joins Allies.

U.S. Congress fails to ratify Treaty of Versailles; won't agree to join League of Nations.

Congress passes a series of Neutrality Acts.

U.S. and 11 other nations form NATO; U.S. isolationism officially ends.

1914   1918   1939   1945

1917   1919   1940 1941   1949

World War I begins; U.S. proclaims neutrality.

War ends; U.S. returns to isolationism.

World War II begins; United States declares neutrality.

Japan attacks U.S. at Pearl Harbor. U.S. enters the war.

World War II ends; U.S. helps form United Nations.

* **Korea.** When communist North Korea invaded noncommunist South Korea, the United Nations, led by the United States, defended South Korea. The conflict lasted from 1950–1953, and South Korea remained independent.
* **Vietnam.** After World War II, North Vietnam was under communist control, while South Vietnam was supported by democratic countries. As North Vietnam became more aggressive, the United States became more involved in the conflict. After years of fighting in which the American public increasingly protested U.S. involvement, America left the conflict, and the country was unified under a communist government.
* **Arms Race.** Both the United States and the Soviet Union built stockpiles of nuclear weapons during the Cold War in order to deter an attack by the other. This arms race threatened world peace and cost both sides billions of dollars. In a sense, the arms race led to the downfall of the Soviet Union because its economy was not strong enough to pay for the weapons and also provide the comforts of life in an industrial society. The arms race ended with the break up of the Soviet Union in 1991.

Russian Federation president Boris Yeltsin speaks during a meeting of the UN Security Council in 1994. ▶

The United Nations

The United Nations (UN) played a role in the Cold War and continues to play a large international role today. The UN was created in 1945 after World War II, with full United States support, to help achieve foreign policy goals of the United States and many other nations.

Creation

The UN Charter spells out **four** goals.

1. **To maintain international peace** and security.
2. **To develop friendly relations** among nations.
3. **To cooperate in solving international problems** and in promoting respect for human rights.
4. **To coordinate the actions of the member nations** in securing peace.

UN Structure

To accomplish its goals, the UN has **five** main organizations:

1. **The General Assembly** is a forum of the nearly 200 nations in the U.N. Every member nation has a seat and a vote. The General Assembly makes recommendations to the Security Council for action.

2. **The Security Council** includes 15 members, 5 of which are permanent (United States, Britain, France, Russia, China). This group responds to international conflicts and crises. It coordinates negotiations between disputing nations, provides peacekeeping forces, and imposes <u>sanctions</u>—nonviolent penalties that prevent a country from doing something, such as selling oil.

3. **The Economic and Social Council** consists of 54 members of the General Assembly who carry out and monitor many UN programs.

4. **International Court of Justice.** This 15-member international court hears cases submitted to it for advice and judgment. UN members agree to accept its decisions.

5. **Secretariat.** Like the United States' federal bureaucracy, it carries out the policies of the Assembly and Council as directed by the Secretary General, the chief spokesman for the UN.

The Trusteeship Council, which helped trust territories become self-governing nations, suspended operations in 1994.

Did You Know?

UN Peacekeeping Efforts

In 2001, the UN had peacekeeping missions in 15 nations: 4 in Africa, 4 in the Middle East, 2 in Asia, and 5 in Europe. Since 1948, there have been 54 UN peacekeeping operations. As the UN has no peacekeeping troops of its own, member nations voluntarily loan or assign personnel to the UN.

Peacekeeping Work

The UN, using troops and observers, has helped to stop or prevent conflicts between hostile groups or nations. Neutral UN peacekeepers have acted as observers, policed ceasefires and troop withdrawals, and protected assistance organizations, such as the Red Cross, in such trouble spots as Kosovo, East Timor, and Iraq.

Humanitarian Work

Besides peacekeeping, the UN runs more than 10 different programs and funds, providing humanitarian aid, protecting human rights, and helping developing nations. **EXAMPLE:** UNICEF, the United Nations Children's Fund, helps children and mothers in developing countries.

Through its membership in the UN, the United States seeks its foreign policy goals and works cooperatively with other nations to promote peace and human rights in the world.

Other International Organizations

U.S. foreign policy requires relationships with many nations, some of which are secured by treaties, alliances, and international agencies other than the UN. Some of the most important are:

1. **The North Atlantic Treaty Organization (NATO).** Today, NATO has 19 members and provides peacekeeping and crisis support.

2. **Organization of American States (OAS).** Originally set up in 1948 to safeguard member nations against communism, the OAS is now used by the United States for economic partnerships and to fight drug trafficking.

3. **World Bank.** In 2001, the Bank loaned more than $17 billion (expressed in U.S. dollars) to poor countries that needed money for health care, education, and other programs. The money is provided to the Bank by donations from wealthier countries such as the United States.

4. **World Trade Organization (WTO).** Since 1995, the WTO has helped promote trade among nations by, for example, helping to settle tariff disputes.

Foreign Policy Challenges Today

Foreign policy is formed in the continuing face of new challenges. Some include:

* *Ethnic conflicts.* When people of different cultural groups within a nation go to war, life and business in the nation are disrupted. Refugees flee to neighboring lands that are unprepared to provide for them. People everywhere are shocked and outraged. The question for America is—how much should we get involved?

* *Developing nations* are attempting to modernize their technologies, become players in the global marketplace, and raise the standard of living for their people. The foreign policy question is—how much should we help direct their growth?

* *Trade competition* involves the U.S. businesses in battles for workers and markets. The low cost of hiring foreign workers and the very poor conditions in which many work pit business and moral interests against each other. Another issue is protective import laws and taxes that hurt our ability to compete. The foreign policy question is—how do we balance these different interests?

* *Resources,* such as oil, are needed by the United States. The question is— how can we make sure that supplies are available and affordable?

* **Hostile nations and groups** that resent American power and influence. The question for America is—how do we deal with countries that threaten the United States or our allies or that support terrorism?

Europe

The challenges of our foreign policy in Europe include:

* **The Economic Transition of Eastern Europe.** Since 1991, many formerly communist Eastern European nations are struggling to change from a controlled, socialist economy to a freer, capitalist economy. Their people are impatient to have the "good life" they see in the West.
* **Ethnic Conflicts.** After years of oppressive communist rule, some new governments in Eastern Europe are now torn apart by ethnic rivalries. Often, these involve groups whose religion differs from that of the group in power, or who historically think of themselves as a different people. This part of Europe includes the countries of Serbia and Montenegro, Bosnia and Herzegovina, and Albania.
* **NATO.** It was originally created as an alliance against the Soviet Union. Russia's relations with western Europe and the United States have improved, and now the purpose, membership, leadership, and financial support of NATO by the United States need to be reevaluated.

* **The European Union,** or EU. This association of 15 countries works to advance European economic, political, and social progress, and to assert Europe's role in the word. It has recently become very successful in achieving its goals. Today a common currency, the eruo, replaces the different kinds of money that used to bog down economic activity in the region. Thirteen eastern and southern European countries are looking to join the Union. And increasingly, the European nations speak to the United States with one voice, making the EU an important concern of U.S. foreign policy.

Did You Know?

European Union Members

* Belgium
* Denmark
* Germany
* Greece
* Spain
* France
* Ireland
* Italy
* Luxembourg
* The Netherlands
* Austria
* Portugal
* Finland
* Sweden
* United Kingdom

The Middle East

The Middle East presents some of the greatest challenges facing U.S. foreign policy. These challenges primarily revolve around **four** main areas:

1. **Oil.** America and other industrialized countries depend on oil and petroleum products. The Organization of Petroleum Exporting Countries, OPEC, consists of 11 (mostly Middle Eastern) countries that have large reserves of oil and influence the price of oil that international customers pay. America negotiates with OPEC and other nations to secure reliable and fairly priced sources of oil.

2. **Arab-Israeli Conflict.** The Israelis (with American support) and the Palestinians (and their Arab and Middle Eastern supporters) have engaged in a bitter struggle for many years, both seeking to secure their own safe homelands in the same region. The United States has tried many times to help resolve the conflict, knowing it is a cause of many other Middle Eastern and world problems.

3. **Iraq.** The United States considers Saddam Hussein's government in Iraq a threat to world peace. Historically, Iraq is among those nations that fought Israel. During the Cold War, it pursued a policy of friendship with the USSR. When it attacked Kuwait in 1991, the six-week Persian Gulf War followed. Iraq's development of biological and chemical weapons, its efforts to get nuclear weapons, and its support of terrorists represent a real danger.

4. **Iran.** In 1953, as a part of Cold War foreign policy, the U.S. and Britain supported the overthrow of Premier Mossadeq by the Shah of Iran. While the Shah's government helped modernize Iran, it was also very brutal. In the 1970s, a revolution installed the Ayatollah Khomeini as ruler and held the staff of the U.S. embassy there hostage for more than a year. Some groups in Iran still have strong anti-American feelings.

Africa

The huge continent of Africa has not traditionally been a focus of U.S. foreign policy. Until the mid-1900s, much of it was colonized by European nations. Now, the United States is becoming more involved.

* *South Africa.* South Africa's movement toward democracy is viewed by the United States as a positive development, and its former leader, Nelson Mandela, still has popular support among American people.
* *Civil Wars.* Earlier European empires had little concern for the native tribal groups and cultures within their African colonies. As these former colonies became independent nations, many were composed of rival ethnic groups. Conflicts within and across their borders have caused terrible suffering and instability. The United States has little involvement and trade with modern Africa, but struggles to decide how best to assist the emerging nations.

The Americas

The Western Hemisphere has been a major concern of U.S. foreign policy ever since the Monroe Doctrine. **Four** policy areas include:

1. **North America Free Trade Agreement (NAFTA).** This foreign policy tool aims to increase U.S. trade with our closest neighbors, Canada and Mexico, by gradually lowering tariffs. Supporters of the policy hope to create new markets for our businesses without causing companies to move manufacturing jobs to Canada or Mexico, where labor costs are generally lower.

2. **Cuba.** In 1959, when the government of Cuba became communist and an ally of the Soviet Union, the United States ended relations with Cuba. Trade and travel between the U.S. and Cuba almost completely stopped. Now that the Cold War has ended, some foreign policy experts urge our government to develop a new policy. Steps toward change have begun.

3. **Illegal Drugs.** Some South American countries, such as Colombia, are major sources for illegal drugs. Stopping the illegal drug trade is a major goal of U.S. foreign policy in the Western Hemisphere. The United States offers assistance to Colombia and other countries that are fighting powerful criminals engaged in the trade.

4. **Poverty and Political Instability.** The economies of some countries in Latin America are weak, and some nations are torn by civil strife. The United States has made mistakes in the past, when working for political stability led us to support governments that do not support their own people. Helping to make this region stable is a continuing challenge.

Asia and the Pacific Rim

Several challenges face U.S. foreign policy in Asia:

* **China.** China's enormous population is a huge potential market for American businesses, but the communist Chinese government has not granted its citizens full democratic rights. American foreign policy has tried to expand opportunities for trade while pressuring Chinese leaders to address human rights issues.
* **North Korea.** North Korea has a very weak economy, and starvation often threatens its people. It has rich natural resources but not the industrial strength to develop them. Its communist government is repressive, and its people are not free. In 2002, U.S. president George W. Bush announced there was reason to believe that the leaders of North Korea were linked to terrorists and the development of weapons of mass destruction, and the foreign policy of his administration remained one of deep suspicion of North Korean intentions.
* **Japan.** After World War II, Japan experienced decades of amazing economic growth (despite a recent slowdown). Japan remains an important ally and trading partner for the United States. Japanese protective tariffs on American imports, especially in view of the many Japanese exports sold in the United States, is an issue U.S. foreign policy works at solving.

Chapter 17 Wrap-up
UNITED STATES FOREIGN POLICY

America's foreign policy protects citizens, works for peace in the world, supports democratic governments, and provides humanitarian assistance worldwide. It is developed in the executive branch. Congress plays an important role. Interest groups and individual citizens also help to shape our government's relations with other countries.

Diplomacy, foreign aid, and intelligence gathering, as well as military, trade, and cultural alliances, and memberships in international organizations are the foreign policy tools that advance U.S. goals in the modern world. In the past, from the time of George Washington until the modern era, much of American foreign policy was isolationist. But since World War II, the United States has been an active world leader.

The Cold War of the latter half of the 20th century shaped many policy decisions. Some laid the groundwork for challenges our world faces today. Through the United Nations and in other partnerships with friendly nations, the United States works to meet these challenges, protect our interests, and secure peace.

alliance—special agreement among nations for military or trade purposes. *p. 283*

boycotting—acting together to refuse to use, deal with, or buy as an expression of protest. *p. 282*

Cold War—period of increased tension between the Soviet Union and the United States, lasting from the late 1940s to the early 1990s. *p. 287*

containment—U.S. Cold War policy of preventing the spread of communism. *p. 287*

diplomacy—process of handling international relations through negotiation. *p. 283*

domestic—opposite of foreign or international; related to internal issues. *p. 280*

embassy—official government office and staff that represents one country in another; also, the buildings used for their duties. *p. 278*

intelligence—information, especially about political or military matters. *p. 279*

isolationism—former U.S. policy of avoiding alliances or involvements with other nations. *p. 283*

political asylum—shelter granted by a country to refugees from a foreign country who are escaping persecution by their government. *p. 281*

sanctions—nonviolent penalties imposed on a nation or group by others; sanctions aim to force the offender to act according to a prior agreement. *p. 289*

treaty—trade, military, or other formal agreement between nations. *p. 279*

Global Issues

In this chapter, you will learn about:

- how the global economy works
- why environmental issues are important
- that terrorism is not a new threat
- what nations can do about world health and human rights
- how citizens can make a difference

Imagine that you are the president of the United States. Five of your closest advisors ask to see you immediately about several global issues.

One advisor asks you to meet with labor leaders who are worried about how many companies are moving factory jobs from the United States to Mexico. The second advisor reviews Canadian concerns about acid rain. The third advisor informs you that 80,000 refugees are starving in central Africa and need assistance. The fourth warns of a terrorist plot to kidnap Americans overseas. Finally, the American ambassador wants to tell the Chinese government that the United States supports recent Chinese student protests.

In the past, major events in other countries were not as important to American citizens as they are today. The world's nations were not as connected as they are now. In the 21st century, the United States and other nations must find solutions to global issues that affect the entire world.

A Global Economy

The world today is the same size it always has been, but it seems much smaller because many countries are connected through communications, international business, and trade. The United States and its citizens will benefit if a greater number of countries can prosper from trade relationships.

Economic Development

The world today is economically divided into **two** parts:

1. **Wealthy, developed, industrialized countries**—modernized nations that are supported by a complex economic base that includes the manufacture of many goods and services and that produces enough goods and services to sell to other countries. Only about 24 countries today are considered industrial nations, including the United States, Canada, Australia, Japan, Great Britain, France, Italy, Germany, and Sweden.

Most industrialized countries enjoy the following advantages:

* *High GDPs*—Gross Domestic Products, the value of all goods and services bought in one year.
* *Low birth rates.* Families are generally small.
* *High literacy rates,* the percentage of the population over age 15 that can read and write.
* *Small percentages of the population working in agriculture* to grow food. A relatively small percentage of people can produce enough food for everyone.
* *Long life spans.* People live long, safe, healthy lives.
* *Low child labor rates.* Only a small percentage of children aged 10 to 14 are in the labor force. In industrialized nations, very few children must work to support themselves and their families.
* *Access to technology.* Many citizens and workers use computers and the Internet.

2. **Poor, developing countries**—less wealthy countries that do not have much industry. The other countries of the world, more than 165 nations, are considered developing nations. Many developing nations have:

* *Low GDPs.*
* *High birth rates.*
* *Low literacy rates.*
* *High proportions of the population working in agriculture.*
* *Short life spans.*
* *High child labor rates.*
* *Little access to technology.*

Many developing nations try to industrialize by allowing new (often foreign-owned) businesses to set up within their borders.

Transnational companies, or multinationals—companies, including many U.S. businesses, that operate in more than one country—set up offices, factories, and other production facilities in foreign countries. Transnationals, like all companies, want to make profits, either by reducing their production costs or by finding new customers. They expect a host country to offer them:

* *Infrastructure*—the support framework of a society that allows further development, such as roads, railways, high-speed Internet access, running water, electricity, law and order, and stability so businesses can operate efficiently.
* *Natural resources*—minerals, land, sources of water, and so on, so the materials the company needs are easy to buy and use.
* *A trained or trainable workforce*— people who can work for the company as employees.

The governments of many developing (and developed) nations are eager to attract new industry, including transnational businesses, and the new jobs they create. Governments then earn business taxes, which they can use to improve the daily lives of their citizens.

Culture Clash

Trading partners need to communicate, so world trade has brought the people of different countries closer together. Unfortunately, industrialism has also created conflict, especially over culture and values.

Western Values and Capitalism/Consumerism

Industrialization often introduces the people of developing countries to a Western, consumerism culture that values the following:

* *Material wealth.* People work hard to earn money to purchase things that help define themselves and improve their lives.
* *Modernization.* People enjoy the conveniences (and gadgets) that technology has brought. Scientific achievements in medicine, too, add value to life.
* *Profit-making.* Business owners and investors have a right to benefit from their talents and efforts.

These values are not universally shared. In many developing nations, people believe:

* Material goods are not important to who one is. People should be satisfied with what they have, even if they are poor.
* Quality of life depends on your relationships with others, not on how easy your life is.
* Industrialization destroys traditional values. Profit-making only benefits the rich.

To Industrialize or Not

National leaders try to decide what is best for their citizens. Many leaders of developing countries want their countries to industrialize so there will be new jobs, more money from new taxes that can be used for health care and education, and better lives for more citizens.

Think about the following options for a developing country. Its government spent a lot of money trying to industrialize and modernize the country, but it failed. The government's money is almost gone, and no successful industry has developed. Fifteen percent of the people are hungry and not enough food is being grown.

Should the country return to traditional ways but become self supporting, or should the country push to modernize, knowing there will be hardships along the way? You decide.

Arguments for Industrialization

One national leader wants to invite a transnational company to build a factory in the country.

To do so, the country will have to spend most of its remaining resources (and even borrow money) to create infrastructure and provide training that the company will need.

The number of hungry people in the country will go up for the next 5 to 7 years until the industry is established. The citizens will also have to live with fewer government services such as health care and education.

If all goes well, in 8 to 10 years the country and its citizens will begin to enjoy a higher standard of living.

Arguments against Industrialization

Another national leader wants to focus on the needs of the people. All efforts at modernizing will be dropped.

Land and resources used for industry will be used to encourage farmers to grow food crops instead of cash crops.

The little money that the government has left will be used to buy fertilizer and farm machinery to be loaned out to farmers.

Within a year, all hunger will disappear, but the country will give up the chance to industrialize and modernize. The people will remain poor, but their basic needs will be met.

The country's traditional culture will be preserved.

Japan: A Case Study

Japan has become industrialized like the West, but it has still maintained much of its own traditional culture and values.

Starting in the 1920s, when there was a shortage of skilled workers, large Japanese companies recruited workers for industrial jobs. The companies offered to:

* Train all workers.
* Provide recreational facilities, inexpensive housing, benefits, and bonuses.
* Give the workers jobs for life.

The companies asked the workers to:

* Work hard.
* Accept low pay to start, and then receive higher pay for more responsibility.
* Be loyal to the company.

This system was like a trusting family relationship. It was based on harmony, a concept that most Japanese people valued. Japan was industrialized by *using*, not changing, traditional cultural beliefs and values. Japanese industry grew very rapidly and successfully.

American Citizens and World Trade

America's economy is tied to almost every other country in the world. Several factors affect our global trade:

* *Tariffs.* All countries use tariffs, or taxes charged on imported goods, to protect their own domestic industries and products. When a foreign nation's tariff makes your import products more expensive, you lose customers in that nation and you might yell "Foul!" Tariffs create conflict.
* *Open Markets.* A country that lets a foreign business sell its products into that country is an **open market**. The opposite situation is a **closed market**.

  EXAMPLE: Japan does not allow U.S. rice producers to sell rice into Japan freely, because doing so would compete with Japanese domestic rice producers. Japan is closed to American-grown rice.

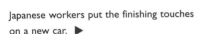

Japanese workers put the finishing touches on a new car. ▶

NAFTA Agreement

The North American Free Trade Agreement (NAFTA) of 1994 was designed to create the world's largest free trade area by 2003.

The United States, Canada, and Mexico each agreed to open their own domestic markets to the others. The preamble, or opening section, of the NAFTA document lists the goals of the trade partners.

STRENGTHEN the special bonds of friendship and cooperation among [the NAFTA partners];

CONTRIBUTE to the harmonious development and expansion of world trade and . . . broader international cooperation;

CREATE an expanded and secure market for the goods and services produced in [the partners' countries];

ENSURE a predictable commercial framework for business planning and investment;

ENHANCE the competitiveness of their firms in global markets;

FOSTER creativity and innovation, and promote trade in goods and services that are the subject of intellectual property rights;

CREATE new employment opportunities and improve working conditions and living standards in their respective territories;

UNDERTAKE each of the preceding in a manner consistent with environmental protection and conservation;

STRENGTHEN the development and enforcement of environmental laws and regulations; and

PROTECT, enhance, and enforce basic workers' rights.

American companies (and foreign-owned companies) want to be able to make and sell their products in other countries. But governments have to consider the advantages and disadvantages of open markets and lowered tariffs, including:

* ***Jobs and competition.*** Governments who open their markets to multinational companies create competition for their own domestic businesses. A foreign-owned factory in the United States creates new jobs for American citizens.

An American-owned company that sets up a factory in another country moves jobs to that country.

* ***Costs.*** Wages and working conditions in many foreign countries are much lower than in the United States. As a result, some American-made products cost more to make and are more expensive for people to buy than similar foreign products.

Although the economics of competitive global trade are complicated, free trade generally creates:

* New markets for U.S.-produced goods and services.
* American jobs.
* Prosperity for U.S. citizens (and people in other countries).

Creating international business rules that let U.S. companies compete fairly is a global issue for the United States.

Environmental Issues

Citizens of all nations need a healthy global environment.

Natural Resources

The earth provides a wealth of natural resources.

* Resources, such as oil and minerals, that cannot be recreated, are called **nonrenewable resources**.
* Resources that can be replaced or regrown, such as trees or fresh water, are called **renewable resources**.

Renewable Resources

Renewable resources are valuable because they can be used for everyone's benefit, then replaced.

EXAMPLE: In America, wood is used in construction, and in making furniture and paper. In many developing countries,

billions of people use wood for heating and cooking. Many developing countries do not have the money and opportunity to replace their wood supplies.

All countries must find ways to replace the renewable resources they are using.

Nonrenewable Resources

Fossil Fuels—fuels formed by decaying organic matter—are among the most important nonrenewable resources. They cannot be replaced when they are used up.

Fuel	Remaining Supply in Years
Oil	40 years
Natural Gas	60 years
Coal	200 years

Source: National Wildlife Federation

Not all countries have supplies of fossil fuels, nor do they use fuels equally.

EXAMPLE: The industrialized countries have only 25 percent of the world's population, but they use 70 percent of the fossil fuels produced.

All countries, including ours, need to find ways to recycle and conserve fuels. Many conservationists want to find alternate, low-cost fuel sources, such as wind, solar, and nuclear fission and fusion energy.

Pollution

Pollution of the earth's air, land, and water is largely caused by:

* The effects of burning fossil fuels to power industry, propel vehicles, heat homes, and so on.
* Industrial pollutants, the leftover wastes of industrial production.
  EXAMPLE: Mexico City issued pollution alerts on 354 out of 365 days in 1991. Just breathing the air there is said to be as harmful as smoking 40 cigarettes a day!

Air pollution may be contributing to **global warming**—the increase in the average temperature of the earth's climate. Many scientists believe that "greenhouse" gases, such as carbon dioxide, are building up in the earth's atmosphere as a result of burning fossil fuels.
EXAMPLE: Some gases are natural, meaning they normally exist in nature, but in the 1900s carbon dioxide levels increased 30 percent.

Some experts warn that, if this trend continues, disasters such as coastal flooding, prolonged heat waves, droughts, and an increase in severe storms could occur around the globe.

American Citizens and the Global Environment

America needs and uses more energy than any other country, about one-quarter of the world's commercial energy.
EXAMPLE: The average person in Bangladesh uses energy equal to about 3 barrels of oil per year. The average American uses energy equal to about 55 barrels of oil per year.

Conserving energy resources will save money and the environment. You can help through:

* Recycling.
* Using energy efficiently.
* Reducing pollution.
* Supporting alternative energy sources.

Terrorism

How did you feel after September 11, 2001? Afraid? Shocked? Threatened? Angry? Confused?

Terrorists create fear and terror among citizens and their leaders. They try to scare the governments they oppose into supporting terrorist goals. The September 11 terrorists created the opposite effect: Instead of fear, their actions stirred outrage, patriotism, and determination in many Americans, and in our many good friends around the globe.

Terrorism—the unlawful use of violence or the threat of violence to create fear among civilians—is a weapon that desperate groups and individuals use to achieve their goals.

Terrorism Is Not New

Terrorism is an old way of attacking people and governments.

* A thousand years ago, a secret group in Syria and Persia called the Assassins murdered political and religious enemies.
* World War I broke out after a Serbian terrorist group assassinated an Austrian noble.

Terrorism and the United States

Americans have been the victims of terrorism for many years.

* **November 1979.** Our American Embassy in Iran was attacked, and 53 Americans were held hostage for more than a year.

* **April 1983.** A U.S. military barracks in Beirut was attacked by a truck bomber, killing 63 people.
* **February 1993.** The World Trade Center was damaged, and six people were killed by a car bomb planted by foreign terrorists.
* **August 1998.** A bomb exploded at the U.S. Embassy in Kenya, killing 291 people, including 12 Americans.
* **September 2001.** Terrorists used hijacked airliners to attack the World Trade Center and the Pentagon.

Terrorism Is a Global Threat

Terrorism is not just an American problem.

* **July 1972.** An Irish Republican Army (IRA) bomb killed 11 and injured 130 people in Belfast, Northern Ireland.
* **September 1972.** At the Munich Olympics, 11 Israeli athletes were held hostage by terrorists. In a later rescue attempt, 9 hostages and 5 terrorists were killed.

▲
Terrorist kidnapper at the Munich Olympic Games, 1972.

Firefighters at the scene of the attack on the World Trade Center, September 11, 2001. ▶

* **November 1979.** Terrorists took over the Islamic Grand Mosque in Saudi Arabia. In a battle to retake the complex, 250 people were killed.
* **June 1985.** An Air India plane was destroyed by a bomb, and 329 people were killed.
* **March 1995.** A terrorist nerve gas attack killed 12 and injured 5,700 people in Tokyo, Japan's subway system.
* **2001–2002.** Palestinian suicide bombers killed hundreds of Israelis. In retaliation, Israeli raids into Palestinian territory killed an even larger number of Palestinians. Each side accused the other of terrorism.

Today terrorists can strike anywhere in the world.

Keeping World Peace

World trouble spots such as the Middle East threaten world peace. These disputes:

* Create misery for the people directly involved.

* Threaten to get worse and to involve other nations in a larger war.
* Provide hiding places for terrorists.

The United Nations has helped to bring an end to many global conflicts. However, ongoing conflicts have also spread terrorism among peoples and nations. Terrorists threaten:

* **Security** of individual nations and their citizens.
* **Ways of life** of all civilized nations and societies. Terrorists try to change values and institutions illegally, rather than through political and democratic ways.
* **Life on earth.** Terrorists may have access to weapons of mass destruction, such as nuclear weapons, "dirty" bombs, and biochemical weapons.

No country is safe from terrorism. Many nations have improved their own security systems and have joined forces with the United States to protect the global community from terrorism. This effort is expected to be long, costly, and difficult.

World Health

The United Nations and individual countries have focused on world health issues in three areas in particular:

1. **Hunger and Nutrition.**
2. **Infectious Diseases.**
3. **Drug Use and Abuse.**

Hunger and Nutrition

The United Nations reports that, between 1997 and 1999, 815 million people in the world were undernourished. Most of them lived in developing countries. **Three** separate problems exist.

1. **Population Growth vs. Food Production.** If populations, especially in developing countries, continue to grow rapidly, and if more people continue to live longer, the world may need more food than it can produce.
2. **Food Distribution.** Together, the countries of the world could grow enough food to feed everyone, but some regions of the world cannot grow or afford to buy what they need. In some developing countries, the systems or infrastructures needed to distribute food to people do not exist.
3. **Land Use.** Many farmers have chosen to use their land to grow profitable cash crops, such as tobacco or coca, instead of food. Countries have also used precious farmland for factories.

World hunger causes human misery and can create conflict among nations. America and all of the nations of the world will have to deal with the issue through:

* Lower population growth.
* Increased food production.
* Better food distribution.

Disease

The UN World Health Organization (WHO) tracks the spread of many diseases. **Three** of the most troubling are:

1. **HIV.** Some experts estimate that, today, more than 30 million people worldwide are infected by the HIV virus, which causes AIDS. Most are in developing and less developed nations with poor health care. In recent years, almost 12 million people have died of AIDS and AIDS-related diseases.
2. **Hepatitis C.** This virus is transmitted through blood transfusions and some forms of drug abuse. Of all reported cases, 90 percent are in developed countries.
3. **Cholera.** Recently, cholera has reappeared in South America and Africa, where it had been previously eliminated. Cholera spreads wherever water and sewage systems are poor.

Diseases kill and bring misery to millions of infected people, especially citizens of developing nations that lack health services. Diseases can also spread and cause international conflicts. They are a problem for every nation.

Drug Abuse

Drug abuse is a global issue that:

* *Ruins human lives and health,* especially among poorer people.
* *Causes crime and conflict,* especially in poorer areas.
* *Supports terrorists* and criminal organizations.
* *Costs every citizen money,* by using up government tax resources in treatment and prevention.

People all around the world are hurt by illegal drugs. Many drugs are manufactured from products often grown as cash crops by farmers in poorer, developing countries:

* *Cannabis (marijuana).* The world's most widely used illegal drug has around 141 million users.
* *Amphetamines.* The use of drugs such as Ecstasy increased significantly in the 1990s in developed nations.
* *Cocaine.* The second most abused drug (after cannabis), cocaine is used by about 13 million people worldwide. The U.S. Justice Department estimates that United States citizens illegally spent more than $36 billion on cocaine in 2001.
* *Heroin.* Heroin is abused in the United States, but it is more widely used in Europe and parts of Asia.

The governments of some countries such as Colombia have worked with U.S. officials to fight the illegal drug production and trafficking.

EXAMPLE: Worldwide coca cultivation was reduced by 14 percent between 1990 and 1999.

Despite some successes, drug abuse and drug-related crime are problems for all nations, inside and beyond their own borders, and can only be solved by a partnership of nations.

Human Rights

The U.S. Constitution guarantees to you rights and freedoms that are unknown to people in many other countries.

Prejudice and Equality

Many nations are not democratic or do not treat all citizens fairly or equally.

* Governments seize and maintain power without election by voters.
* Many minority, racial, or ethnic groups suffer discrimination.
* Women are not full citizens.
  EXAMPLE: In many countries, women have fewer rights, are less educated, earn lower wages than men for the same jobs, and are more likely to live in poverty than men. According to the UN, of the more than one billion people worldwide who live in poverty, the great majority are women.
* Children are not protected.

America and other democratic nations work to encourage all nations to end prejudice and inequality in order to:

* Protect human dignity and human rights.
* Prevent conflict that could threaten world peace.
* Extend democratic values.

Refugees

Refugees are people who flee military conflict or oppression in their own country and seek safety in another country.

Refugees are a issue in many nations:

* Large groups of refugees usually enter a neighboring country.
* Individual refugees or families sometimes seek refuge in countries far away, possibly with relatives.

Most countries try to follow guidelines set by the United Nations and provide humane treatment for refugees, including protection, food, shelter, clean water, and a place to live with other refugees. However, some governments are overwhelmed by large numbers of refugees. Their own citizens do not have adequate food and housing, so they resent the refugees' use of land and resources.

EXAMPLES: At the end of 2000, Iran hosted nearly 1.9 million refugees, mostly from Afghanistan, Iraq, Palestine, Turkey, Somalia, and Sudan. Most of the 6 million refugees in the Middle Eastern countries are Palestinian people. Israel also hosts millions of refugees.

Refugee issues are a global problem because they can:

* Create ethnic and political tensions.
* Cause resource shortages in the host country.
* Grow into larger, international crises.

Individual Rights

As an American, you probably believe that government policies should reflect certain basic rights, but not all governments agree. Nations such as the United States encourage less democratic nations to extend human rights. Promoting human rights raises human dignity and helps promote peace and democratic values.

Did You Know?

Tiananmen Square

In May 1989, Chinese students gathered in Tiananmen Square in Beijing, China. They came to mourn the death of a former Chinese leader who had supported student rights in that Communist nation. The gathering turned into a rally for democratic reforms that lasted for weeks. The students even built a replica of the Statue of Liberty, a symbol of American democracy.

The Chinese government eventually lost patience with the courageous students and ordered the army to use force to clear Tiananmen Square. In a brutal confrontation, the army obeyed its orders. As many as 2,000 or more unarmed students were killed. The Tiananmen Square Massacre is now a symbol of the struggle for human rights in China and around the world.

Making a Difference

The many global issues in the world today are complicated, to say the least. As a result, you may think that an individual cannot do much to help. But anything is possible for those who try.

Power of Individuals

Many people change the world, or at least, their corner of it, in significant and visible ways. Some change-makers are:

* *Distinguished leaders.* Leaders of government, businesses, and other organizations in many nations do exceptional things that change the world, for better or for worse. Who are some leaders you admire?

* *Scoundrels.* Terrorists, their supporters, criminals, people who abuse human rights, and people who don't care change peoples' lives for the worse. Sometimes, the same person is considered a leader and a hero by some people and an evil-doer by others.

* *Citizen heroes.* Every day, the world benefits from "average" citizens who volunteer their money, their time, their teaching, and their talent. Organizations like the International Red Cross, supported by citizens, make the world a better place.

American Citizenship

The Red Cross

When you think about the Red Cross, you may think of disaster relief, which is a major service the Red Cross provides through its network of trained staff workers. But you can be part of the Red Cross, too. Students can become international Red Cross pen pals, assemble Red Cross friendship boxes and school chests, or make international exchanges with a Red Cross chapter (or Red Crescent society, the organization in Islamic countries) in another nation. If you take part in any Red Cross activities, you will not only help other people. You will learn more about both the world around you and yourself. (For information on Red Cross programs, go to www.redcross.org)

Staying Informed and Involved

All citizens, including you, should stay informed by following the news. The informed students of today might be the leaders and heroes of tomorrow.

You can also take a more active role in global and local issues:

* Raise and discuss global issues at school.
* Exchange letters and e-mails with English-speaking students in other countries.

* Volunteer to help in your local community in places such as free food banks or senior centers.

Perhaps the most important thing you can do is to fight prejudice by trying to understand other people, regardless of their race, religion, gender, or ethnic background. If students all over the world work toward this one goal, the world will become a better place.

Chapter 18 Wrap-up
GLOBAL ISSUES

The global issues faced by America's leaders today become more complicated as the world community becomes more connected. Developing nations struggle with poverty, lack of current technologies and resources, and cultural change. The developed, industrial nations face the challenge of staying current and competitive. They also debate how to help the less developed nations in order to maintain world trade and security. Environmental issues have become more important as resources dwindle and industrialization increases. Health issues are also more complicated. New treatments and medicines are available, but only some nations can afford them. Human rights concerns have also been raised because some nations try to take shortcuts to success and modernization. Then there is terrorism. Can conflict ever be completely eliminated?

The nations of the world will not resolve all of these global issues in the near future, but you and people like you in other countries must try to find solutions. People like you will, step by step, make the world a better place.

closed market—market that is closed to foreign companies; goods and services produced in other countries may not be offered for sale. *p. 300*

developing countries—poor countries without much modern industry or infrastructure. *p. 297*

fossil fuels—burnable material, such as oil or gas, formed from decayed organic material over hundreds of thousands of years. *p. 302*

global warming—increase in the average temperature of the earth's climate. *p. 303*

industrialized countries—modernized countries supported by the manufacture of many goods and services. *p. 297*

infrastructure—network of facilities that allow a community to function and that support development; roads, bridges, power lines, water supply, and the like. *p. 298*

literacy rate—percentage of the population over age 15 that can read and write. *p. 297*

nonrenewable resource—natural resource, such as oil, that cannot be replaced after it is taken. *p. 302*

open markets—markets into which non-domestic or offshore companies are allowed by the government to sell goods and services produced in foreign countries. The U.S. is an open market for Canadian-produced automobiles. *p. 300*

refugees—people who flee into another country for safety, often in times of conflict or persecution. *p. 308*

renewable resource—natural resource that can be regrown, replaced, or restored. *p. 302*

terrorism—unlawful use of fear or violence, frequently against civilians, to achieve a political goal. *p. 304*

transnational companies (also called multinationals)—businesses that have facilities and do business in more than one country. *p. 298*

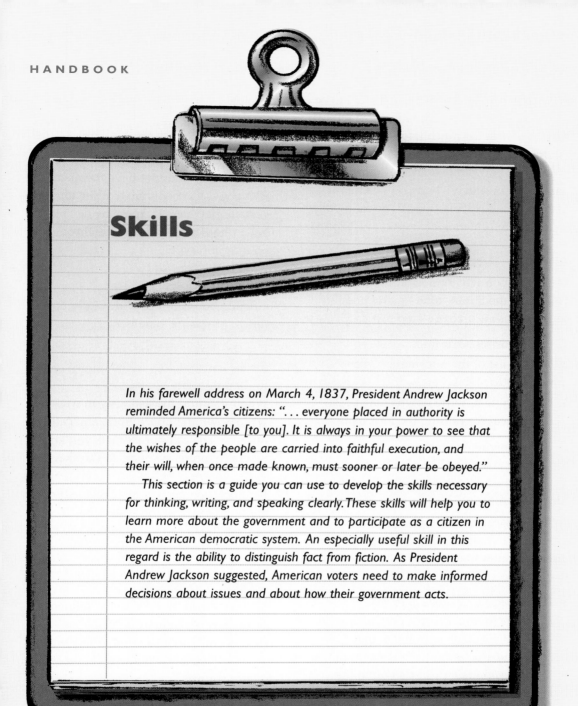

Skills

In his farewell address on March 4, 1837, President Andrew Jackson reminded America's citizens: ". . . everyone placed in authority is ultimately responsible [to you]. It is always in your power to see that the wishes of the people are carried into faithful execution, and their will, when once made known, must sooner or later be obeyed."

This section is a guide you can use to develop the skills necessary for thinking, writing, and speaking clearly. These skills will help you to learn more about the government and to participate as a citizen in the American democratic system. An especially useful skill in this regard is the ability to distinguish fact from fiction. As President Andrew Jackson suggested, American voters need to make informed decisions about issues and about how their government acts.

Getting Information

To make informed decisions, you need to be able to find and use information. Sometimes there is almost too much information to use. Finding the *right* information takes skill.

Luckily, you can use certain sources to narrow your search when you need information on a particular topic. The following sources of information are especially helpful.

Library Resources

Depending on what kinds of information you need, the library offers many possible sources. Follow a **three-**step process:

1. Plan your research first.
2. Make a list of the information you will need.
3. For each item, write down some possible sources for finding the information.

The following sources are available at the library. Ask your librarian for help.

Newspapers and Magazines

To find information about a particular event that happened on a specific date, go directly to newspapers and magazines for that date.

* Use the *Reader's Guide to Periodical Literature* for articles on a particular topic. *The Reader's Guide* is an index that lists magazine articles under subject headings.
* *The Periodical Index* directs you to the latest information on any subject, as well as provides summaries of the information.

* Newspaper indexes tell you where to find recent information on most subjects in a detailed way.
* If the library does not have the magazine or newspaper you need, it may have a copy of it on microfilm.
* If the library does not have the microfilm copy, another branch of the library system may have it. You may be able to get a photocopy of the article through an interlibrary loan.

Nonfiction Books

Nonfiction books can provide either broad coverage or specific details.

* Use the library catalog on a computer (or the card catalog) in the library to find appropriate books.
* When you find the listings you want, write down the title, author, and call number. The call number lets you know where to locate the book on the shelves in the library.
* If a book you need is unavailable but another library in the system has it, you can ask the librarian to get you the book through interlibrary loan.

Reference Works

Libraries contain many kinds of reference works. Some of them are available on CD-ROM and online, as well as in print form. These are a few of the main types of reference sources:

* **General encyclopedias** have articles on thousands of topics.

* **Specialized encyclopedias** focus on particular subject areas, such as science or art.
* **Biographical dictionaries** and indexes provide brief articles on specific people and often list other sources for more detailed information.
* **Almanacs** provide statistics and data on current events.
* **Atlases** contain maps and geographical data, such as average annual rainfall, elevation, and population.

* **Vertical files** contain a variety of pamphlets, booklets, and government publications that provide current information.

Online Research Sources

The following web sites provide information about our government and political system. Web site addresses sometimes change, but these well known web addresses have been helpful to many other students.

What You'll Find	Address
A useful basic link to almost all U.S. government web sites.	http://www.lib.umich.edu/govdocs/federal.html
Historical documents, including the Declaration of Independence, the Constitution, and the *Federalist Papers*.	http://www.law.emory.edu/FEDERAL
Information on the Constitution.	http://www.constitutioncenter.org
Information on civil rights issues.	http://www.aclu.org
Supreme Court constitutional law decisions and a virtual tour of the Supreme Court.	http://oyez.nwu.edu
Information on women's issues.	http://www.now.org
Information about the Democratic Party.	http://www.democrats.org/index.html
Information about the Republican Party.	http://www.rnc.org
Details on elections and election law from the Federal Election Commission.	http://www.fec.gov
Reports on campaign funding and spending.	http://www.opensecrets.org
Voting records and campaign-finance information.	http://www.vote-smart.org
The White House homepage.	http://www.whitehouse.gov
Information on state issues from the National Governors Association.	http://www.nga.org

Interpreting Graphics

Graphics include such tools as tables, charts, line graphs, bar graphs, circle or pie graphs, maps, and even cartoons. Communicators often present certain types of information in graphics because:

* Amounts, quantities, and other specific facts located in paragraphs of text can be hard to find.
* Pictures sometimes describe an idea more easily than words can.
* Information in graph form is often easier to locate, especially if you want to compare numeric data about places, groups, quantities, dates, or amounts.

Of course, you have to be able to read and interpret graphics in order for them to be useful.

Graphs

A graph is a chart or diagram that shows how one quantity compares to others. **EXAMPLE:** Graphs can be used to show how one state's population compares to the populations of other states, or how one state's population has grown over the years.

Graphs make it easier to understand numbers and statistics—information consisting of numbers. Graphs can be in the form of connected lines, curves, bars, or circles (pie charts).

Line Graphs

Line graphs show trends—how something changes. They present a lot of information in a small amount of space. The line graph below shows how much money (grants-in-aid) the federal government has given to state and local governments each year from 1969 to 2000. To interpret the information, you first must read what the graph "says":

Federal Grants-in-Aid of Education

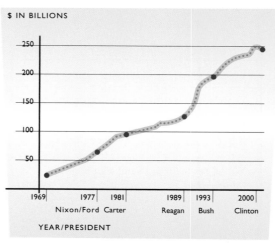

Source: U.S. Department of Commerce, *Statistical Abstract of the United States* (Washington, D.C.: U.S. Government Printing Office, 2000)

* First read the title. It tells you what the topic of the graph is.
* Next look at the horizontal labels along the bottom. They indicate the names of presidents and the years that they were in office.
* The vertical label tells you that the numbers running up along the left side of the graph represent amounts of federal grants-in-aid in billions of dollars.
* The sources of information shown indicate the organization that prepared the data. Is the source trustworthy and reliable? How could you find out?
* Now read the graph from the lower left corner, where it starts. As you follow the line from left to right, notice the steady progression upwards until, just before the end, at 2000, there is a slight dip.
* Now that you have read the information in the graph, you can interpret—decide what this graph tells you. The amount of funds given to state and local governments in the form of grants-in-aid has increased steadily from 1969 to the late 1990s, and then dipped slightly in 2000. The graph also shows that the greatest increases occurred when the first George Bush was president.

Bar Graphs

Bar graphs present information in the shape of bars. You read it the same way that you read a line graph.

* Read the title of the graph. It tells you what the graph represents—the growth in the number of people over 65.
* Look at the information measured vertically and horizontally.

* What do the numbers on the left mean? The words at the top tell you that the numbers represent millions of people 65 and older.
* Notice that the numbers at the bottom represent specific years, beginning in 1900 and going as far into the future as the year 2030.
* Now interpret the information. What does the graph tell you? The number of people older than 65 has been increasing since 1900. A huge increase is projected—expected based on data—during the next 30 years. Ask yourself questions:
  1. What do you conclude from this data?
  2. What effects might a larger population of seniors have on issues, such as health-care costs, or the outcome of elections in the future?

Growth of Population 65+

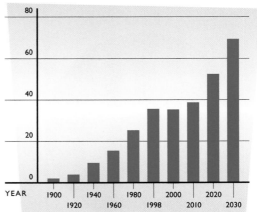

Source: U.S. Census Bureau (1998)

Circle (or Pie) Graphs

The area of a circle or pie graph represents 100 percent. It can be divided into segments or wedges that represent parts or percentages of the whole.

* The circle shape indicates that this is a circle or pie graph. The whole circle represents 100 percent of something.
* Read the title. The pie shows all sources of school funding.
* Notice that the pie is divided into four parts. Each is labeled to tell you **two** things:
  1. A source of school funding.
  2. The percent of funding contributed by that source.
* As you interpret this graph, what conclusions can you draw? Which source contributed the least to public schools? Which contributed the most?

Sources of School Funding

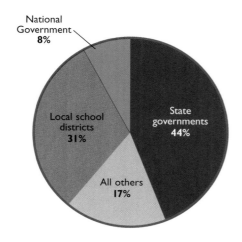

Source: U.S. Census Bureau

Maps

Maps can present complex political information in a graphic way. Notice that the sizes and shapes of many of the states in the map below have been changed. For example, Alaska, the nation's largest state by far, is tiny on this map. Texas has also shrunk so that it is not much larger than Florida.

Electoral Votes Per State, 2000

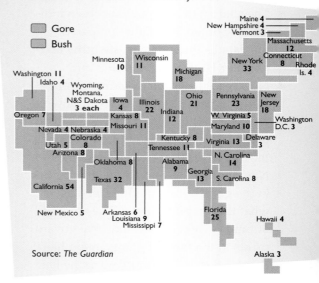

Source: *The Guardian*

* The title at the top tells you why the map is not an ordinary map of the United States. The map is distorted to show how many Electoral College votes each state had in 2000. A presidential candidate must win 270 electoral votes to be elected. So candidates often focus on states from which they can get the most electoral votes.

  EXAMPLE: Democrat candidate Al Gore made many trips to California, a state with a lot of electoral votes, during the 2000 presidential campaign.

* Now look at the key in the upper left corner. It tells you that the electoral votes from the darker states went to George W. Bush, and those from the lighter states went to Al Gore.
* How might you interpret this information?
  1. What does this say about the voters of the various states?
  2. Which states had a majority of Republican voters?
  3. A majority of Democratic voters?

Charts

Charts or graphic organizers present information in a visual way. Flow charts show information in square or rectangular boxes that are connected by arrows or lines to show next steps, directions, or connections. Some charts contain boxes within boxes or other shapes. Venn diagrams consist of two overlapping ovals, each containing a specific category of information. The area formed by the intersection of the two ovals—the area where the ovals overlap—shows something both ovals have in common.

To read the Venn diagram below, first look at the title at the top. This tells you that the chart shows the distribution of power between the federal and state governments.

The left oval, under the label National Powers, lists powers of the federal government. The right oval, under the label State Powers, lists powers of the state governments.

The area of overlap, under the label Concurrent Powers, lists the powers shared by federal and state governments.

How might you interpret the information in this chart? The chart shows you that federal and state governments both have the power to tax, for example, and that only the federal government has the power to declare war. In other words, the chart shows you, at a glance, which level of government is responsible for what areas of laws and services.

Federal and State Powers

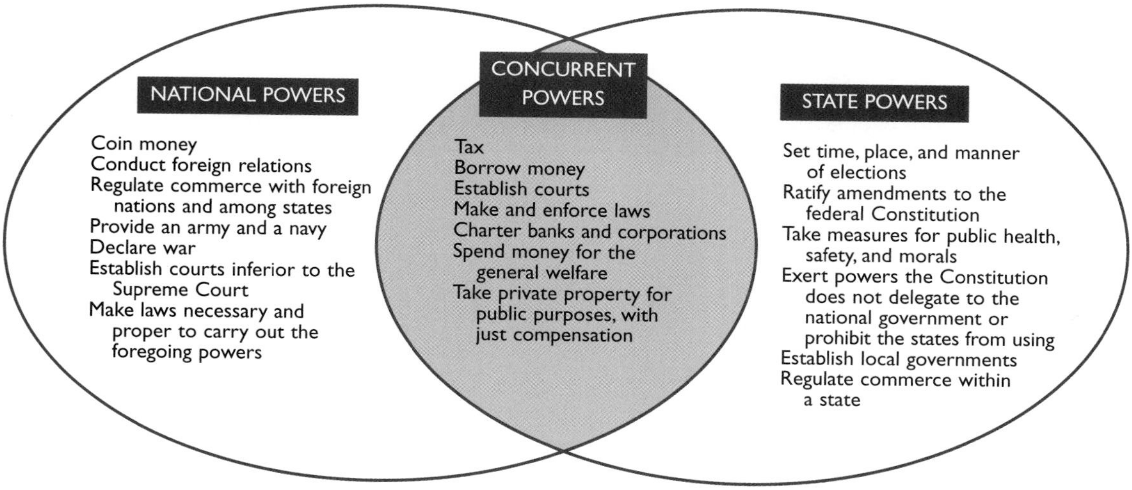

NATIONAL POWERS

Coin money
Conduct foreign relations
Regulate commerce with foreign nations and among states
Provide an army and a navy
Declare war
Establish courts inferior to the Supreme Court
Make laws necessary and proper to carry out the foregoing powers

CONCURRENT POWERS

Tax
Borrow money
Establish courts
Make and enforce laws
Charter banks and corporations
Spend money for the general welfare
Take private property for public purposes, with just compensation

STATE POWERS

Set time, place, and manner of elections
Ratify amendments to the federal Constitution
Take measures for public health, safety, and morals
Exert powers the Constitution does not delegate to the national government or prohibit the states from using
Establish local governments
Regulate commerce within a state

Tables

Tables organize information so you can easily make comparisons. To read this table, follow **three** steps:

1. **Look at the title at the top.**
2. **Read the labels above each column.** The labels tell you that the table lists various political issues and the percentages of males and females supporting them.
3. **Interpret the information.** What type of family makes up the largest percentage of American homes? What type makes up the smallest percentage? Were you surprised by these numbers? How might a politician use this information to his or her advantage?

Imagine you are a politician. You want voters in your district to like the work you are doing to protect their interests. You are invited to talk about family to a group of your constituents. Given the information below, what types of issues do you think would appeal to your audience?

Households by Type: 2000		
Household type	Number	Percent
Total households	**105,480,101**	**100.0**
Family Households	71,787,347	68.1
Married-couple households	54,493,232	51.7
Female householder, no husband present	12,900,103	12.2
Male householder, no wife present	4,394,012	4.2
Nonfamily households	33,692,754	31.9
One person	27,230,075	25.8
Two or more people	6,462,679	6.1

Source: U.S. Census Bureau, 2000.

Cartoons

Political cartoons work differently from other graphics, but they also convey complicated information visually. Cartoons express ideas that cannot be said the same way in written or spoken language, even if the language is humorous. Cartoons use simplicity, suggestion, brevity, and surprise to create an impact on their readers. Some political cartoons poke fun at political personalities, groups, or issues, with humor but with serious intent. Some cartoonists use biting satirical humor to make a critical point.

EXAMPLES: The first two cartoons make fun of how money is used to influence politics. Does Tom Toles think Congress really wants to change how politicians get money for their election campaigns?

What do you think Joseph Farris means by "special interest" in this cartoon?

"A _very_ special interest to see you, Senator."

This cartoon by Henry Payne pokes fun at the low level of voter interest in serious political issues. How well do the characters in Payne's cartoon represent the typical American voter?

"At last, a campaign about the _real_ issues!"

Evaluating Sources

Unfortunately, not all sources are equally reliable. For example, some information may present a point of view that is not entirely accurate or is based on only some of the facts. Consider the following when you evaluate sources:

* *Bias.* If you think a source might be biased, double-check the information using other sources.
* *Expertise.* Determine what you can about any "experts" you use. Might their information be less convincing because they are associated with a certain interest group?
* *Source date.* If you are using a source that is old, especially if it deals with a rapidly changing topic, the information may be out of date.
* *Reliability.* Some newspapers, magazines, and other sources have a reputation for the quality and accuracy of their information.
* *Reputation.* Information in publications or on web sites that are not well known or have bad reputations may not be reliable.
* *Objectivity.* A publication or web site may deliberately include opinions and facts to promote its group's own interests. EXAMPLE: A trade magazine, journal, or web site published by a particular special interest group or organization will portray its own industry favorably.

Distinguishing Fact from Opinion

You are probably familiar with these expressions:

* Don't believe everything you hear.
* Don't believe everything you read.

Statements of opinion are sometimes easily confused with statements of fact. People often express opinions—their personal beliefs, feelings, judgments, attitudes, or values, which cannot be proved or disproved. A particular opinion might turn out to be true or false, but it is not a factual statement. Different people may have different opinions about the same topic. EXAMPLES: Since neither of the following statements can be easily proved, neither is a statement of fact. Both statements are opinions. Either might or might not be correct. Intelligent people could argue that either is correct:

1. *William McKinley was one of the greatest presidents.*
2. *William McKinley was one of the worst presidents.*

The information in the following statement, on the other hand, can easily be checked in any reliable source, so it is a statement of fact. When checked, the statement cannot be argued:

3. *William McKinley was the 25th president of the United States.*

Statements of fact may be incorrect, either because the writer was careless or the writer's source was incorrect.

The following statement is incorrect, but it is still a statement of fact. It can be disproved by checking in a reliable source.

4. *William McKinley was the 24th president of the United States.*

If you are ever unsure whether a factual statement is correct, don't hesitate to check another source, preferably two.

Here are some tools to help you distinguish fact from opinion:

* Opinions are often emotional expressions. Look for signal words, such as: *best, most, favorite, biggest, cheapest, dumb, stupid, boring, worst, awful.*
* Words such as *feel, think,* or *believe* indicate that a statement is a judgment or evaluation and, therefore, an opinion.
* Words that show uncertainty or probability, such as *might, may,* and *probably,* indicate that a statement is an opinion.
* If a statement is supported by evidence, it is probably a statement of fact.

* If you can argue the statement or have an opposite point of view, then the statement is an opinion.

Identify the statements of opinion in the following paragraph. Explain why you think they are opinions, rather than statements of fact.

"On Election Day, I'll have the chance to vote on propositions regarding local issues in our county. *Proposition A* calls for a special tax to pay for building new bicycle trails. I'm going to vote NO on Proposition A. I don't own a bicycle, and I'm not interested in riding one. Furthermore, I think most bicyclists prefer to use the existing roads. After all, if a road is good enough for a car, it is certainly good enough for a bicycle. Proposition B calls for a special tax to beautify our town by planting trees along the streets. I suppose it would be nice to live on a tree-lined street, but I refuse to pay for it. I can live without the trees. After all, the trees are mainly for the birds!"

How would you verify the information in the factual statements?

The Writing Process

Often, participation as an active citizen requires you to communicate your ideas. You may want to persuade a senator to vote according to your views. You may want to protest some plan your community is proposing. You may want to persuade others through a letter to the editor of your local paper. Writing to explain or convince involves a four-part process:

1. **Planning your writing.**
2. **Expressing the main idea.**
3. **Using evidence to support the main idea.**
4. **Making generalizations and drawing conclusions.**

Planning Your Writing

Before you begin to write, you need to:

* *Choose your topic.*
* *Research the topic* to gather information.
* *Consider your audience.* How interested are they in the topic? How much do they already know about it?
* *Consider your purpose.* Are you writing to persuade, to educate or inform, or perhaps to entertain your audience?
* *Create an outline* to help you organize your thoughts and to help you make sure you include all of the important information.

Expressing the Main Idea

Begin your writing by expressing the main idea using a concise statement that sums up what you want to say. The main idea tells your readers the main point of your paper.

* Know what you plan to say before you write your paper.
* In stating your main idea, give readers a sense of what you plan to cover and why it is important.
* In your main idea, give a brief overview of evidence and arguments your paper will include.

Using Evidence to Support the Main Idea

Effective writing to persuade or inform needs evidence to support the main ideas.

* Make sure that all of your sources of information are reliable.
* Make sure that the details you present as evidence are based on factual information, not opinion.
* Remember that factual details answer questions such as *where, when, how, who, what, which,* or *why.*
* Present evidence you gathered from other sources by summarizing, paraphrasing, or quoting. When you paraphrase—say the same thing in different words—another person's work, credit the source in the body of your paper. Identify the work you have paraphrased. Use quotation marks when you directly quote another author's words.

Making Generalizations and Drawing Conclusions

After you have presented your evidence or arguments, add **two** more elements:

1. **Make generalizations**—statements or ideas based on information and facts that you apply to a broader situation or set of circumstances.

    EXAMPLE: If you were protesting an ordinance that would require trains to sound their horns as they passed near your school, you could generalize about the effects of the noise that would result: *Students would not be able to hear their teachers, classroom discussions would be disrupted, students would have difficulty concentrating.*

2. **Draw your conclusions**—decisions, predictions, or understandings that are reached through a process of reasoning.

    EXAMPLE: In this example, your generalizations would result in the conclusion that *the ordinance would be bad for the education of students in our community.*

These suggestions may help you build your case:

* Review your conclusions and generalizations. Do they follow logically from the particular details you have used to support your main ideas?
* Review your evidence. Do your details and examples actually lead to the conclusions that you make?

* Use your prior knowledge—what you already know about the topic—and your common sense to decide if your evidence and conclusions "fit" together.
* Do not make exaggerated claims that are difficult to prove in your conclusion. Use words such as *most, many,* and *usually,* rather than *every, no,* or *all.*
* Avoid drawing a conclusion that ignores evidence that you neglected to present.
* Use the conclusions you have drawn to make a broader generalization, but be careful not to overgeneralize and make sweeping statements that you cannot support.

Persuasive Writing

Any written communication in which you try to convince others to believe that something is true (or to do something) is a form of persuasive writing.

* Election ads.
* Persuasive letters, such as a letter to the editor of a newspaper.
* Newspaper editorials.
* Essays.
* Position papers written to agency officials to try to shape policy.
* Campaign speeches.

Points to Consider before Writing Persuasively

These **four** tips will help you to be a more persuasive writer.

1. **Choose your topic carefully.** Pick one that you feel strongly about, that other people will find interesting and important, and for which you can find evidence for to support your opinion.
2. **Narrow your topic to focus on a particular aspect of it.**
   EXAMPLE: Broad topic: Popularity. Narrow topic: *Popularity among politicians.* Narrower topic: *Why politicians cannot always be popular.*
3. **Anticipate your audience.** Expect your audience to challenge your position. Anticipate and address its arguments.
4. **Gather evidence and organize details.** Take notes as you read. Organize notes in the order you believe will make an effective argument. End with a strong point. Outline before you write.

Points to Consider When Writing Persuasively

In your introduction, make your position clear right away. Begin with a strong and convincing opening line.

* Use an example, a quotation, a statement, a fact, or an opinion to introduce your point of view.
* Capture your readers' attention and appeal to their interests.
* Acknowledge the opinions they may already hold.

In the body of your paper:

* Support your argument with clear reasons, facts, examples, and statements from authorities.
* Write a separate paragraph for each point you wish to make.
* Present your ideas using a cause-and-effect organization or a pro-and-con organization.

Cause-and-Effect Organization

Use a **two**-step, cause-and-effect relationship order to explain why or how something happened or will happen.

1. **State a cause**—evidence that something has happened or will happen.
2. **Follow with the effects** that have occurred or will occur as a result of that cause.
   EXAMPLE: The weaknesses in the Articles of Confederation shaped many of the ideas in the Constitution. The Articles did not give enough power to the central government. The states tried to revise it, and ended up creating a whole new plan.

Or you can state a series of related effects, and then state the cause that shows your evidence is or will be responsible for those effects.

EXAMPLE: Slavery was allowed to continue when the Constitution was debated. As a group, the founders were more interested in saving the nation than they were in dealing with the issue of slavery.

Pro-and-Con Organization

Use a pro-and-con organization to compare opposing arguments. This method of organization follows **four** steps:

1. **Present the evidence that supports your opinions and ideas**—the pros.

2. **Then mention the cons**—the opposing arguments.

3. **Follow up with further evidence** against the opposing arguments (more pros).

4. **In the conclusion, restate the issue and your position.** Summarize your most important reasons. Tell your audience what you think they should do or tell them how they will benefit.

    EXAMPLE: You may not yet be old enough to vote, but you can still use persuasive writing to get people thinking about key issues. Write a letter to the editor or an article for your school website or community newspaper to persuade readers that special interest groups should be allowed to donate money to candidates.

First, list the pros, the arguments that support why politicians should be allowed to accept donations. Then list the cons, the reasons why they should not, and offer evidence against each con. Conclude by restating your arguments why donating should be allowed.

Things to Avoid When Writing Persuasively

As you write, make sure your evidence accurately supports your position. Avoid the following types of faulty logic and emotional appeals:

* *Overgeneralization*—a statement that is too broad for the evidence that backs it up.
* *Circular reasoning*—the attempt to support an argument just by restating it in other words.
* *Either/or argument*—an extreme statement that allows for only two possibilities, when there may be several.
* *Questionable cause-and-effect statement*—a statement that identifies a cause-and-effect relationship that isn't necessarily there.
* *Propaganda techniques,* such as bandwagon appeal or loaded language— the use of words that influence an audience's thinking by appealing to their fears or prejudices.

Speaking Effectively in Public

If you can speak effectively in front of a group—whether in your classroom, in the school auditorium, before some community organization, or at a meeting at the town hall—you improve your effectiveness as a citizen.

Planning Your Speech

Although some situations call for an impromptu speech (or ad-lib speaking)—a speech that is not prepared in advance—in most cases, you will be able to prepare your speech ahead of time.

Determine the Subject of Your Speech

Most of the same rules that you use to pick a writing topic apply to planning your speech topic: personal interest, your own knowledge and experience, audience needs, and so on.

Establish the Purpose of Your Speech

The purposes of a speech are the same as the purposes for writing:

* *Exposition* to inform your audience, or to deliver factual information to them.
* *Argument* to affect the opinions of your listeners.
* *Description* to give an impression of something.
* *Narration* to tell a story.

Consider Your Audience

When planning your speech, think about the people in your audience.

EXAMPLE: If the audience will be made up of a lot of young children, your language should be easy to understand.

Organize Your Remarks

Your speech needs an opening, a body, and a conclusion.

* Begin with an attention-getting device, such as a joke or story, a question, a command, or a surprising or impressive fact.
* Make a brief overview statement, expressing what you are going to say and why the topic is important.
* Plan the length of your remarks to fit the occasion. Take time to develop your points, but don't run on and on.
* Plan the wording of your closing so you know when and how your speech will end.

Writing Your Speech

List the important points you want to cover in your speech. Research your topic to gather information. Plan your words precisely. Use the following tips:

* Understand the difference between fact and opinion.
* Beware of overstating your case. Be careful with words such as *always* or *never*.
* If you use statistics, keep them simple enough to be understood.
* Use and quote authorities.

Rehearsing the Speech

The more you practice your speech:

* The better prepared you will be.
* The more confident you will feel.
* The less nervous you will be.

These **four** useful tips may help.

1. **Practice reading the speech, word for word.**
2. **If the speech is not too long, memorize all or parts of it.**
3. **Stand while you practice the speech.**
4. **Experiment with different gestures that seem natural to you as you speak.** EXAMPLE: Occasionally extend or stretch your arms, point, and pound your fist for visual interest. Make eye contact with different people in your audience.

Presenting the Speech

When you deliver your speech, follow **six** basic rules:

1. **Don't worry if you forget a word or two.** Vary the speech if necessary. The audience will not notice.
2. **Use and refer to an outline or notes** on note cards or pages.
3. **Use a lectern or speaker's stand.** Rest your papers or notes on it, or stand behind it to feel more comfortable.
4. **Vary your voice and show emotion and interest.** Don't rush.
5. **Be yourself.** EXAMPLE: If you never tell jokes, avoid them in your speech.
6. **Pay attention to your audience.**

Audiences appreciate effort. Show them you have worked hard to deliver your speech.

The Declaration of Independence

In Congress, July 4, 1776.

A Declaration by the Representatives of the United States of America, in General Congress assembled.

When in the Course of human events, it becomes necessary for one people to dissolve the political bands which have connected them with another, and to assume among the powers of the earth, the separate and equal station to which the Laws of Nature and of Nature's God entitle them, a decent respect to the opinions of mankind requires that they should declare the causes which impel them to the separation.

We hold these truths to be self-evident, that all men are created equal, that they are endowed by their Creator with certain unalienable Rights, that among these are Life, Liberty and the pursuit of Happiness; that, to secure these rights, Governments are instituted among Men, deriving their just powers from the consent of the governed; that whenever any Form of Government becomes destructive of these ends, it is the Right of the People to alter or to abolish it, and to institute new Government, laying its foundation on such principles and organizing its powers in such form, as to them shall seem most likely to effect their Safety and Happiness. Prudence, indeed, will dictate that Governments long established should not be changed for light and transient causes; and accordingly all experience hath shewn that mankind are more disposed to suffer, while evils are sufferable, than to right themselves by abolishing the forms to which they are accustomed. But when a long train of abuses and usurpations, pursuing invariably the same Object, evinces a design to reduce them under absolute Despotism, it is their right, it is their duty, to throw off such Government, and to provide new Guards for their future security.

Such has been the patient sufferance of these Colonies; and such is now the necessity which constrains them to alter their former Systems of Government. The history of the present King of Great Britain is a history of repeated injuries and usurpations, all having in direct object the establishment of an absolute Tyranny over these States. To prove this, let facts be submitted to a candid world.

He has refused his Assent to Laws, the most wholesome and necessary for the public good.

He has forbidden his Governors to pass Laws of immediate and pressing importance, unless suspended in their operation till his assent should be obtained; and, when so suspended, he has utterly neglected to attend to them.

He has refused to pass other Laws for the accommodation of large districts of people, unless those people would relinquish the right of Representation in the Legislature, a right inestimable to them, and formidable to tyrants only.

He has called together legislative bodies at places unusual, uncomfortable, and distant from the depository of their public Records, for the sole purpose of fatiguing them into compliance with his measures.

He has dissolved Representative Houses repeatedly, for opposing with manly firmness his invasions on the rights of the people.

He has refused for a long time, after such dissolutions, to cause others to be elected; whereby the Legislative powers, incapable of Annihilation, have returned to the people at large for their exercise; the State remaining in the mean time exposed to all the dangers of invasions from without, and convulsions within.

He has endeavoured to prevent the population of these States; for that purpose obstructing the Laws for Naturalization of Foreigners; refusing to pass others to encourage their migration hither, and raising the conditions of new Appropriations of Lands.

He has obstructed the Administration of justice, by refusing his Assent to Laws for establishing Judiciary powers,

He has made judges dependent on his Will alone, for the tenure of their offices, and the amount and payment of their salaries.

He has erected a multitude of New Offices, and sent hither swarms of Officers to harass our people and eat out their substance.

He has kept among us, in times of peace, Standing Armies, without the Consent of our legislatures.

He has affected to render the Military independent of and superior to the Civil power.

He has combined with others to subject us to a jurisdiction foreign to our constitution and unacknowledged by our laws; giving his Assent to their Acts of pretended Legislation:

For quartering large bodies of armed troops among us;

For protecting them, by a mock Trial, from punishment for any Murders which they should commit on the Inhabitants of these States;

For cutting off our Trade with all parts of the world;

For imposing Taxes on us without our Consent;

For depriving us, in many cases, of the benefits of Trial by jury;

For transporting us beyond Seas to be tried for pretended offenses;

For abolishing the free System of English Laws in a neighboring Province, establishing therein an Arbitrary government, and enlarging its Boundaries so as to render it at once an example and fit instrument for introducing the same absolute rule into these Colonies;

For taking away our Charters, abolishing our most valuable laws, and altering fundamentally the Forms of our Governments;

For suspending our own Legislatures, and declaring themselves invested with power to legislate for us in all cases whatsoever.

He has abdicated Government here, by declaring us out of his Protection and waging War against us.

He has plundered our seas, ravaged our Coasts, burnt our towns, and destroyed the lives of our people.

He is at this time transporting large Armies of foreign Mercenaries to complete the works of death, desolation, and tyranny, already begun with circumstances of Cruelty & perfidy scarcely paralleled in the most barbarous ages, and totally unworthy of the Head of a civilized nation.

He has constrained our fellow Citizens, taken Captive on the high Seas, to bear Arms against their Country, to become the executioners of their friends and Brethren, or to fall themselves by their Hands.

He has excited domestic insurrections amongst us, and has endeavoured to bring on the inhabitants of our frontiers the merciless Indian Savages, whose known rule of warfare is an undistinguished destruction of all ages, sexes and conditions.

In every stage of these Oppressions We have Petitioned for Redress in the most humble terms. Our repeated Petitions have been answered only by repeated injury. A Prince, whose character is thus marked by every act which may define a Tyrant, is unfit to be the ruler of a free people.

Nor have We been wanting in attentions to our British brethren. We have warned them from time to time of attempts by their legislature to extend an unwarrantable jurisdiction over us. We have reminded them of the circumstances of our emigration and settlement here. We have appealed to their native justice and magnanimity, and we have conjured them by the ties of our common kindred, to disavow these usurpations, which would inevitably interrupt our connections and correspondence. They too have been deaf to the voice of justice and of consanguinity. We must, therefore, acquiesce in the necessity, which denounces our Separation, and hold them, as we hold the rest of mankind, Enemies in War, in Peace Friends.

We, therefore, the Representatives of the United States of America, in General Congress Assembled, appealing to the Supreme judge of the world for the rectitude of our intentions, do in the name, and by the Authority of the good People of these Colonies solemnly publish and declare, That these United Colonies are, and of Right ought to be, Free and Independent States; that they are Absolved from all Allegiance to the British Crown, and that all political connection between them and the State of Great Britain is, and ought to be, totally dissolved; and that as Free and Independent States, they have full Power to levy War, conclude Peace, contract Alliances, establish Commerce, and do all other Acts and Things which Independent States may of right do.

And for the support of this Declaration, with a firm reliance on the protection of divine Providence, we mutually pledge to each other our Lives, our Fortunes, and our sacred honor.

Signed by

John Hancock [President of the Continental Congress]

GEORGIA:
Burton Gwinnett
Lyman Hall
George Walton

RHODE ISLAND:
Stephen Hopkins
William Ellery

CONNECTICUT:
Roger Sherman
Samuel Huntington
William Williams
Oliver Wolcott

NORTH CAROLINA:
William Hooper
Josheph Hewes
John Penn

SOUTH CAROLINA:
Edward Rutledge
Thomas Heyward, Jr.
Thomas Lynch, Jr.
Arthur Middleton

MARYLAND:
Samuel Chase
William Paca
Thomas Stone
Charles Carroll

VIRGINIA:
George Wythe
Richard Henry Lee
Thomas Jefferson
Benjamin Harrison
Thomas Nelson, Jr.
Francis Lightfoot Lee
Carter Braxton

PENNSYLVANIA:
Robert Morris
Benjamin Rush
Benjamin Franklin
John Morton
George Clymer
James Smith
George Taylor
James Wilson
George Ross

DELAWARE:
Caesar Rodney
George Read
Thomas McKean

NEW YORK:
William Floyd
Philip Livingston
Francis Lewis
Lewis Morris

NEW JERSEY:
Richard Stockton
John Witherspoon
Francis Hopkinson
John Hart
Abraham Clark

NEW HAMPSHIRE:
Josiah Bartlett
William Whipple
Matthew Thornton

MASSACHUSETTS:
Samuel Adams
John Adams
Robert Treat Paine
Elbridge Gerry

The Constitution of the United States

Preamble: Purpose of the Constitution

We the people of the United States, in order to form a more perfect Union, establish justice, insure domestic tranquility, provide for the common defense, promote the general welfare, and secure the blessings of liberty to ourselves and our posterity, do ordain and establish this Constitution for the United States of America.

Article I.
The Legislature

Section 1: Congress

All legislative powers herein granted shall be vested in a Congress of the United States, which shall consist of a Senate and House of Representatives.

Section 2: The House of Representatives

Clause 1: Elections

The House of Representatives shall be composed of members chosen every second year by the people of the several states and the electors in each state shall have the qualifications requisite for electors of the most numerous branch of the state legislature.

Clause 2: Qualifications

No person shall be a Representative who shall not have attained to the age of twenty-five years, and been seven years a citizen of the United States, and who shall not, when elected, be an inhabitant of that state in which he shall be chosen.

Clause 3: Number of Representatives

Representatives and direct taxes shall be apportioned among the several states which may be included within this Union, according to their respective numbers, which shall be determined by adding to the whole number of free persons, including those bound to service for a term of years, and excluding Indians not taxed, three-fifths of all other persons. The actual enumeration shall be made within three years after the first meeting of the Congress of the United States, and within every subsequent term of ten years, in such manner as they shall by law direct. The number of Representatives shall not exceed one for every thirty thousand, but each state shall have at least one Representative; and until such enumeration shall be made, the state of New Hampshire shall be entitled to choose three, Massachusetts eight, Rhode Island and Providence Plantations one, Connecticut five, New York six, New Jersey four, Pennsylvania eight, Delaware one, Maryland six, Virginia ten, North Carolina five, South Carolina five, and Georgia three.

Clause 4: Vacancies

When vacancies happen in the representation from any state, the executive authority thereof shall issue writs of election, to fill such vacancies.

Clause 5: Officers and Impeachment

The House of Representatives shall choose their Speaker and other officers; and shall have the sole power of impeachment.

Section 3: The Senate

Clause 1: Numbers

The Senate of the United States shall be composed of two Senators from each state, chosen by the legislature thereof, for six years, and each Senator shall have one vote.

Clause 2: Classifying Terms

Immediately after they shall be assembled in consequence of the first election, they shall be divided as equally as may be into three classes. The seats of the Senators of the first class shall be vacated at the expiration of the second year, of the second class at the expiration of the fourth year, and of the third class at the expiration of the sixth year, so that one-third may be chosen every second year; and if vacancies happen by resignation, or otherwise, during the recess of the legislature of any state, the executive thereof may make temporary appointments until the next meeting of the legislature, which shall then fill such vacancies.

Clause 3: Qualifications

No person shall be a Senator who shall not have attained to the age of thirty years, and been nine years a citizen of the United States, and who shall not, when elected, be an inhabitant of that state for which he shall be chosen.

Clause 4: Role of Vice President

The Vice President of the United States shall be President of the Senate, but shall have no vote, unless they be equally divided.

Clause 5: Officers

The Senate shall choose their other officers, and also a President pro tempore, in the absence of the Vice President, or when he shall exercise the office of President of the United States.

Clause 6: Impeachment Trials

The Senate shall have the sole power to try impeachments. When sitting for that purpose, they shall be on oath or affirmation. When the President of the United States is tried, the Chief Justice shall preside: and no person shall be convicted without the concurrence of two-thirds of the members present.

Clause 7: Punishment for Impeachment

Judgment in cases of impeachment shall not extend further than removal from office, and disqualification to hold and enjoy any office of honor, trust or profit under the United States; but the party convicted shall nevertheless be liable and subject to indictment, trial, judgment, and punishment according to law.

Section 4:
Congressional Elections

Clause 1: Regulations

The times, places and manner of holding elections for Senators and Representatives shall be prescribed in each state by the legislature thereof; but the Congress may at any time by law make or alter such regulations, except as to the places of choosing Senators.

Clause 2: Sessions

The Congress shall assemble at least once in every year, and such meeting shall be on the first Monday in December, unless they shall by law appoint a different day.

Section 5:
Rules and Procedures

Clause 1: Quorum

Each house shall be the judge of the elections, returns, and qualifications of its own members, and a majority of each shall constitute a quorum to do business; but a smaller number may adjourn from day to day, and may be authorized to compel the attendance of absent members, in such manner, and under such penalties as each house may provide.

Clause 2: Rules and Conduct

Each house may determine the rules of its proceedings, punish its members for disorderly behavior, and, with the concurrence of two-thirds, expel a member.

Clause 3: Congressional Records

Each house shall keep a journal of its proceedings, and from time to time publish the same, excepting such parts as may in their judgment require secrecy; and the yeas and nays of the members of either house on any question shall, at the desire of one-fifth of those present, be entered on the journal.

Clause 4: Adjournment

Neither house, during the session of Congress, shall, without the consent of the other, adjourn for more than three days, nor to any other place than that in which the two houses shall be sitting.

Section 6:
Payment and Privilege

Clause 1: Salary

The Senators and Representatives shall receive a compensation for their services, to be ascertained by law, and paid out of the treasury of the United States. They shall in all cases, except treason, felony, and breach of the peace, be privileged from arrest during their attendance at the session of their respective houses, and in going to and returning from the same; and for any speech or debate in either house, they shall not be questioned in any other place.

Clause 2: Restrictions

No Senator or Representative shall, during the time for which he was elected, be appointed to any civil office under the authority of the United States, which shall have been created, or the emoluments whereof shall have been increased during such time; and no person holding any office under the United States, shall be a member of either house during his continuance in office.

Section 7: How a Bill Becomes a Law

Clause 1: Tax Bills

All bills for raising revenue shall originate in the House of Representatives; but the Senate may propose or concur with amendments as on other Bills.

Clause 2: Law-Making Process

Every bill which shall have passed the House of Representatives and the Senate, shall, before it becomes a law, be presented to the President of the United States; if he approves he shall sign it, but if not he shall return it, with his objections to that House in which it shall have originated, who shall enter the objections at large on their journal, and proceed to reconsider it. If after such Reconsideration two-thirds of that House shall agree to pass the bill, it shall be sent, together with the objections, to the other House, by which it shall likewise be reconsidered, and if approved by two-thirds of that House, it shall become a law. But in all such cases the votes of both houses shall be determined by yeas and nays, and the names of the persons voting for and against the bill shall be entered on the journal of each house respectively. If any bill shall not be returned by the President within ten days (Sundays excepted) after it shall have been presented to him, the same shall be a law, in like manner as if he had signed it, unless the Congress by their adjournment prevent its return, in which case it shall not be a law.

Clause 3: Role of the President

Every order, resolution, or vote to which the concurrence of the Senate and House of Representatives may be necessary (except on a question of adjournment) shall be presented to the President of the United States; and before the same shall take effect, shall be approved by him, or being disapproved by him, shall be repassed by two-thirds of the Senate and House of Representatives, according to the rules and limitations prescribed in the case of a bill.

Section 8: Powers Granted to Congress

Clause 1: Taxation

The Congress shall have power to lay and collect taxes, duties, imposts and excises, to pay the debts and provide for the common defense and general welfare of the United States; but all duties, imposts and excises shall be uniform throughout the United States;

Clause 2: Credit

To borrow money on the credit of the United States;

Clause 3: Commerce

To regulate commerce with foreign nations, and among the several states, and with the Indian tribes;

Clause 4: Naturalization, Bankruptcy

To establish a uniform rule of naturalization, and uniform laws on the subject of bankruptcies throughout the United States;

Clause 5: Money

To coin money, regulate the value thereof, and of foreign coin, and fix the standard of weights and measures;

Clause 6: Counterfeiting

To provide for the punishment of counterfeiting the securities and current coin of the United States;

Clause 7: Post Office

To establish post offices and post roads;

Clause 8: Patents, Copyrights

To promote the progress of science and useful arts, by securing for limited times to authors and inventors the exclusive right to their respective writings and discoveries;

Clause 9: Federal Courts

To constitute tribunals inferior to the Supreme Court;

Clause 10: International Law

To define and punish piracies and felonies committed on the high seas, and offenses against the law of nations;

Clause 11: War

To declare war, grant letters of marque and reprisal, make rules concerning captures on land and water;

Clause 12: Armed Forces

To raise and support armies, but no appropriation money to that use shall be for a longer term than two years;

Clause 13: Navy

To provide and maintain a navy;

Clause 14: Regulation of Armed Forces

To make rules for the government and regulation of the land and naval forces;

Clause 15: Militia

To provide for calling forth the militia to execute the laws of the Union, suppress insurrections, and repel invasions;

Clause 16: Regulations for Militia

To provide for organizing, arming, and disciplining the militia, and for governing such part of them as may be employed in the service of the United States, reserving to the states respectively the appointment of the officers, and the authority of training the militia according to the discipline prescribed by Congress;

Clause 17: District of Columbia

To exercise exclusive legislation in all cases whatsoever, over such District (not exceeding ten miles square) as may, by cession of particular states, and the acceptance of Congress become the seat of the government of the United States, and to exercise like authority over all places purchased by the consent of the legislature of the state in which the same shall be, for the erection of forts, magazines, arsenals, dockyards, and other needful buildings; —and

Clause 18: Elastic Clause

To make all laws which shall be necessary and proper for carrying into execution the foregoing powers, and all other powers vested by this Constitution in the government of the United States, or in any department or officer thereof.

Section 9: Powers Denied Congress

Clause 1: Slave Trade

The migration or importation of such persons as any of the states now existing shall think proper to admit, shall not be prohibited by the Congress prior to the year one thousand eight hundred and eight, but a tax or duty may be imposed on such importation, not exceeding ten dollars for each person.

Clause 2: Habeas Corpus

The privilege of the writ of habeas corpus shall not be suspended, unless when in cases of rebellion or invasion the public safety may require it.

Clause 3: Illegal Punishment

No bill of attainder or ex post facto Law shall be passed.

Clause 4: Direct Taxes

No capitation, or other direct, tax shall be laid, unless in proportion to the census or enumeration herein before directed to be taken.

Clause 5: Export Taxes

No tax or duty shall be laid on articles exported from any state.

Clause 6: No Favorites

No preference shall be given by any regulation of commerce or revenue to the ports of one state over those of another; nor shall vessels bound to, or from, one state be obliged to enter, clear, or pay duties in another.

Clause 7: Public Money

No money shall be drawn from the treasury, but in consequence of appropriations made by law; and a regular statement and account of the receipts and expenditures of all public money shall be published from time to time.

Clause 8: Titles of Nobility

No title of nobility shall be granted by the United States: and no person holding any office of profit or trust under them shall, without the consent of the Congress, accept of any present, emolument, office, or title, of any kind whatever, from any king, prince, or foreign state.

Section 10: Powers Denied the States

Clause 1: Restrictions

No state shall enter into any treaty, alliance, or confederation; grant letters of marque and reprisal; coin money; emit Bills of credit; make anything but gold and silver coin a tender in payment of debts; pass any bill of attainder, ex post facto law, or law imparing the obligation of contracts, or grant any title of nobility.

Clause 2: Import and Export Taxes

No state shall, without the consent of the Congress, lay any imposts or duties on imports or exports, except what may be absolutely necessary for executing its inspection laws; net produce of all duties and imposts, laid by any state on imports or exports, shall be for the use of the treasury of the United States and all such laws shall be subject to the revision and control of Congress.

Clause 3: Peacetime and War Restraints

No state shall, without the consent of the Congress, lay any duty of tonnage, keep troops or ships of war in time of peace, enter into any agreement or compact with another state or with a foreign power, or engage in war, unless actually invaded, or in such imminent danger as will not admit of delay.

Article 2: The Executive

Section 1: The Presidency

Clause 1: Terms of Office

The executive power shall be vested in a President of the United States of America. He shall hold his office during the term of four years, and, together with the Vice President, chosen for the same term, be elected, as follows:

Clause 2: Electoral College

Each state shall appoint, in such manner as the Legislature thereof may direct, a number of electors, equal to the whole number of Senators and Representatives to which the State may be entitled in the Congress; but no Senator or Representative, or person holding an office of trust or profit under the United States shall be appointed an elector.

Clause 3: Former Method of Electing President

The electors shall meet in their respective states, and vote by ballot for two persons, of whom one at least shall not be an inhabitant of the same state with themselves. And they shall make a list of all the persons voted for, and of the number of votes for each; which list they shall sign and certify; and transmit sealed to the seat of the government of the United States, directed to the President of the Senate. The President of the Senate shall, in the presence of the Senate and House of Representatives, open all the certificates, and the votes shall then be counted. The person having the greatest number of votes shall be the President, if such number be a majority of the whole number of electors appointed; and if there be more than one who have such majority, and have an equal number of votes, then the House of Representatives shall immediately choose by ballot one of them for President; and if no person have a majority, then from the five highest on the list the said House shall in like manner choose the President. But in choosing the President, the votes shall be taken by States, the representation from each state having one vote; a quorum for this purpose shall consist of a member or members from two-thirds of the states, and a majority of all the states shall be necessary to a choice. In every case, after the choice of the President, the person having the greatest number of votes of the electors shall be the Vice President. But if there should remain two or more who have equal votes, the Senate shall choose from them by ballot the Vice President.

Clause 4: Election Day

The Congress may determine the time of choosing the electors, and the day on which they shall give their votes, which day shall be the same throughout the United States.

Clause 5: Qualifications

No person except a natural-born citizen, or a citizen of the United States at the time of the adoption of this Constitution, shall be eligible to the office of President; neither shall any person be eligible to that office who shall not have attained to the age of thirty-five years, and been fourteen years a resident within the United States.

Clause 6: Succession

In case of the removal of the President from office, or of his death, resignation, or inability to discharge the powers and duties of the said office, the same shall devolve on the Vice President, and the Congress may by law provide for the case of removal, death, resignation or inability, both of the President and Vice President, declaring what officer shall then act as President, and such officer shall act accordingly, until the disability be removed, or a President shall be elected.

Clause 7: Salary

The President shall, at stated times, receive for his services, a compensation, which shall neither be increased nor diminished during the period for which he shall have been elected, and he shall not receive within that period any other emolument from the United States, or any of them.

Clause 8: Oath of Office

Before he enter on the execution of his office, he shall take the following oath or affirmation: —"I do solemnly swear or affirm) that I will faithfully execute the office of President of the United States, and will to the best of my ability, preserve, protect and defend the Constitution of the United States."

Section 2: Powers of the President

Clause 1: Military Powers

The President shall be commander in chief of the Army and Navy of the United States, and of the militia of the several states, when called into the actual service of the United States; he may require the opinion, in writing, of the principal officer in each of the executive departments, upon any subject relating to the duties of their respective offices, and he shall have power to grant reprieves and pardons for offenses against the United States, except in cases of impeachment.

Clause 2: Treaties, Appointments

He shall have power, by and with the advice and consent of the Senate, to make treaties, provided two-thirds of the Senators present concur; and he shall nominate, and by and with the advice and consent of the Senate, shall appoint ambassadors, other public ministers and consuls, judges of the Supreme Court, and all other officers of the United States, whose appointments are not herein otherwise provided for, and which shall be established by law; but the Congress may by law vest the appointment of such inferior officers, as they think proper, in the President alone, in the courts of law, or in the heads of departments.

Clause 3: Vacancies

The President shall have power to fill up all vacancies that may happen during the recess of the Senate, by granting commissions which shall expire at the end of their next session.

Section 3: Presidential Duties

He shall from time to time give to the Congress information of the state of the Union, and recommend to their consideration such measures as he shall judge necessary and expedient; he may, on extraordinary occasions, convene both Houses, or either of them, and in case of disagreement between them, with respect to the time of adjournment, he may adjourn them to such time as he shall think proper; he shall receive ambassadors and other public ministers; he shall take care that the laws be faithfully executed, and shall commission all the officers of the United States.

Section 4: Impeachment

The President, Vice President, and all civil officers of the United States shall be removed from office on impeachment for, and conviction of, treason, bribery, or other high crimes and misdemeanors.

Article 3: The Judiciary

Section 1: Federal Courts and Judges

The judicial power of the United States shall be vested in one Supreme Court, and in such inferior courts as the Congress may from time to time ordain and establish. The judges, both of the Supreme and inferior courts, shall hold their offices during good behavior, and shall, at stated times, receive for their services a compensation, which shall not be diminished during their continuance in office.

Section 2: The Courts' Authority

Clause 1: General Authority

The judicial power shall extend to all cases, in law and equity, arising under this Constitution, the laws of the United States, and treaties made, or which shall be made, under their authority; —to all cases affecting ambassadors, other public ministers and consuls; —to all cases of admiralty and maritime jurisdiction; —to controversies to which the United States shall be a party; —to controversies between two or more states; —between a state and citizens of another state; —between citizens of different states; —between citizens of the same state claiming lands under grants of different states, and between a state, or the citizens thereof, and foreign states, citizens or subjects.

Clause 2: Supreme Court

In all cases affecting ambassadors, other public ministers and consuls, and those in which a state shall be party, the Supreme Court shall have original jurisdiction. In all the other cases before mentioned, the Supreme Court shall have appellate jurisdiction, both as to law and fact, with such exceptions, and under regulations, as the Congress shall make.

Clause 3: Trial by Jury

The trial of all crimes, except in cases of impeachment, shall be by jury; and such trial shall be held in the state where the said crimes shall have been committed; but when not committed within any state, the trial shall be at such place or places as the Congress may by law have directed.

Section 3: Treason

Clause 1: Definition

Treason against the United States, shall consist only in levying war against them or in adhering to their enemies, giving them aid and comfort. No person shall be convicted of treason unless on the testimony of two witnesses to the same overt act, or on confession in open court.

Clause 2: Punishment

The Congress shall have power to declare the punishment of treason, but no attainder of treason shall work corruption of blood, or forfeiture except during the life of the person attainted.

Article 4: Relations Among States

Section 1: State Acts and Records

Full faith and credit shall be given in each state to the public acts, records, and judicial proceedings of every other state. And the Congress may by general laws prescribe the manner in which such acts, records and proceedings shall be proved, and the effect thereof.

Section 2: Rights of Citizens

Clause 1: Citizenship

The citizens of each state shall be entitled to all privileges and immunities of citizens in the several states.

Clause 2: Extradition

A person charged in any state with treason, felony, or other crime, who shall flee from justice, and be found in another state, shall on demand of the executive authority of the state from which he fled, be delivered up, to be removed to the state having jurisdiction of the crime.

Clause 3: Fugitive Slaves

No person held to service or labor in one state, under the laws thereof, escaping into another, shall, in consequence of any law or regulation therein, be discharged from such service or labor, but shall be delivered up on claim of the party to whom such service or labor may be due.

Section 3: New States

Clause 1: Admission

New states may be admitted by the Congress into this Union; but no new state shall be formed or erected within the jurisdiction of any other state; nor any state be formed by the junction of two or more states, or parts of states, without the consent of the legislatures of the states concerned as well as of the Congress.

Clause 2: Congressional Authority

The Congress shall have power to dispose and make all needful rules and regulations respecting the territory or other property belonging to the United States; and nothing in this Constitution shall be so construed as to prejudice any claims of the United States or of any particular state.

Section 4: Guarantees to the States

The United States shall guarantee to every state in this Union a republican form of government and shall protect each of them against invasion; and on application of the legislature, or of the executive (when the legislature cannot be convened), against domestic violence.

Article 5: Amending the Constitution

The Congress, whenever two-thirds of both houses shall deem it necessary, shall propose amendments to this Constitution, or, on the application of the legislatures of two-thirds of the several states, call a convention for proposing amendments, which, in either case shall be valid to all intents and purposes, as part of this Constitution, when ratified by the legislatures of three-fourths of the several states or by conventions in three-fourths thereof, as the one or the other mode of ratification may be proposed by the Congress; provided that no amendment which may be made prior to the year one thousand eight hundred and eight shall in any manner affect the first and fourth clauses in the ninth section of the first article; and that no state, without its consent, shall be deprived of its equal suffrage in the Senate.

Article 6: Supremacy of the National Government

Section 1: Valid Debts

All debts contracted and engagements entered into, before the adoption of this Constitution, shall be as valid against the United States under this Constitution, as under the Confederation.

Section 2: Supreme Law

This Constitution, and the laws of the United States which shall be made in pursuance thereof, and all treaties made, or which shall be made, under the authority of the United States, shall be the supreme law of the land; and the judges in every state shall be bound thereby, anything in the constitution or laws of any state to the contrary notwithstanding.

Section 3: Loyalty to the Constitution

The Senators and Representatives before mentioned, and the members of the several state legislatures, and all executive and judicial officers, both of the United States and of the several states, shall be bound by oath or affirmation to support this Constitution; but no religious test shall ever be required as a qualification to any office or public trust under the United States.

Article 7: Ratification

The ratification of the conventions of nine states shall be sufficient for the establishment of this Constitution between the states so ratifying the same.

Done in convention by the unanimous consent of the states present, the seventeenth day of September in the year of our Lord one thousand seven hundred and eighty-seven and of the independence of the United States of America the twelfth. In witness whereof we have hereunto subscribed our names.

George Washington—President and deputy from Virginia

NEW HAMPSHIRE: John Langdon, Nicholas Gilman

MASSACHUSETTS: Nathaniel Gorham, Rufus King

CONNECTICUT: William Samuel Johnson, Roger Sherman

NEW YORK: Alexander Hamilton

NEW JERSEY: William Livingston, David Brearley, William Paterson, Jonathan Dayton

PENNSYLVANIA: Benjamin Franklin, Thomas Mifflin, Robert Morris, George Clymer, Thomas FitzSimons, Jared Ingersoll, James Wilson, Gouverneur Morris

DELAWARE: George Read, Gunning Bedford, Jr., John Dickinson, Richard Bassett, Jacob Broom

MARYLAND: James McHenry, Daniel of St. Thomas Jenifer, Daniel Carroll

VIRGINIA: John Blair, James Madison, Jr.

NORTH CAROLINA: William Blount, Richard Dobbs Spaight, Hugh Williamson

SOUTH CAROLINA: John Rutledge, Charles Cotesworth Pinckney, Charles Pinckney, Pierce Butler

GEORGIA: William Few, Abraham Baldwin

Bill of Rights: Amendments 1–10

Passed by Congress September 25, 1789. Ratified December 15, 1791.

Amendment 1: Religious and Political Freedom

Congress shall make no law respecting an establishment of religion or prohibiting the free exercise thereof; or abridging the freedom of speech, or of the press; or the right of the people peaceably to assemble, and to petition the Government for a redress of grievances.

Amendment 2: Right to Bear Arms

A well regulated militia, being necessary to the security of a free state, the right of the people to keep and bear arms shall not be infringed.

Amendment 3: Quartering Troops

No soldier shall, in time of peace, be quartered in any house, without the consent of the owner, nor in time of war, but in a manner to be prescribed by law.

Amendment 4: Search and Seizure

The right of people to be secure in their persons, houses, papers, and effects against unreasonable searches and seizures, shall not be violated, and no warrants shall issue, but upon probable cause, supported by oath or affirmation, and particularly describing the place to be searched, and the persons or things to be seized.

Amendment 5: Rights of Accused Persons

No person shall be held to answer for a capital or otherwise infamous crime, unless on a presentment or indictment of a Grand Jury, except in cases arising in the land or naval forces, or in the militia, when in actual service in time of war or public danger; nor shall any person be subject for the same offense to be twice put in jeopardy of life or limb; nor shall be compelled in any criminal case to be a witness against himself, nor be deprived of life, liberty or property, without due process of law; nor shall private property be taken for public use without just compensation.

Amendment 6: Right to a Speedy, Public Trial

In all criminal prosecutions, the accused shall enjoy the right to a speedy and public trial, by an impartial jury of the State and district wherein the crime shall have been committed, which district shall have been previously ascertained by law, and to be informed of the nature and cause of the accusation; to be confronted with the witnesses against him; to have compulsory process for obtaining witnesses in his favor, and to have the assistance of counsel for his defense.

Amendment 7: Trial by Jury in Civil Cases

In suits at common law, where the value in controversy shall exceed twenty dollars, the right of a trial by jury shall be preserved, and no fact tried by a jury, shall be otherwise reexamined in any court of the United States, than according to the rules of the common law.

Amendment 8: Limits of Fines and Punishments

Excessive bail shall not be required, nor excessive fines imposed, nor cruel and unusual punishments inflicted.

Amendment 9: Rights of People

The enumeration in the Constitution of certain rights, shall not be construed to deny or disparage others retained by the people.

Amendment 10: Powers of States and People

The powers not delegated to the United States by the Constitution, nor prohibited by it to the States, are reserved to the States respectively, or to the people.

Amendments 11–27

Amendment 11: Lawsuits Against States

Passed by Congress March 4, 1794. Ratified February 7, 1795. Proclaimed 1798.

Note: Article 3, Section 2, of the Constitution was modified by Amendment 11.

The judicial power of the United States shall not be construed to extend to any suit in law or equity, commenced or prosecuted against one of the United States by citizens of another state or by citizens or subjects of any foreign state.

Amendment 12: Election of Executives

Passed by Congress December 9, 1803. Ratified June 15, 1804.

Note: A portion of Article 2, Section 1, of the Constitution was superseded by the 12th Amendment.

The electors shall meet in their respective states and vote by ballot for President and Vice President, one of whom, at least, shall not be an inhabitant of the same state with themselves; they shall name in their ballots the person voted for as President, and in distinct ballots the person voted for as Vice President, and they shall make distinct lists of all persons voted for as President, and of all persons voted for as Vice President, and of the number of votes for each, which lists they shall sign and certify, and transmit sealed for the seat of the government of the United States, directed to the President of the Senate;—the President of the Senate shall, in the presence of the Senate and House of Representatives, open all the certificates and the votes shall then be counted;—the person having the greatest number of votes for President, shall be the President, if such number be a majority of the whole number of electors appointed; and if no person have such majority, then from the persons having the highest numbers not exceeding three on the list of those voted for as President, the House of Representatives shall choose immediately, by ballot, the President. But in choosing the President the votes shall be taken by states, the representation from each state having one vote; a quorum for this purpose shall consist of a member or members from two-thirds of the states, and a majority of all the states shall be necessary to a choice. And if the House of Representatives shall not choose a President whenever the right of choice shall devolve upon them, before the fourth day of March next following, then the Vice President shall act as President, as in the case of the death or other constitutional disability of the President. The person having the greatest number of votes as Vice President, shall be the Vice President, if such number be a majority of the whole number of Electors appointed, and if no person have a majority, then from the two highest numbers on the list, the Senate shall choose the Vice-President; a quorum for the purpose shall consist of two-thirds of the whole number of Senators, and a majority of the whole number shall be necessary to a choice. But no person constitutionally ineligible to the office of President shall be eligible to that of Vice President of the United States.

Amendment 13: Slavery Abolished

Passed by Congress January 31, 1865. Ratified December 6, 1865.

Note: A portion of Article 4, Section 2, of the Constitution was superseded by the 13th Amendment.

Section 1

Neither slavery nor involuntary servitude, except as a punishment for crime whereof the party shall have been duly convicted, shall exist within the United States, or any place subject to their jurisdiction.

Section 2

Congress shall have power to enforce this article by appropriate legislation.

Amendment 14: Civil Rights

Passed by Congress June 13, 1866. Ratified July 9, 1868.

Note: Article 1, Section 2, of the Constitution was modified by Section 2 of the Fourteenth Amendment.

Section 1

All persons born or naturalized in the United States, and subject to the jurisdiction thereof, are citizens of the United States and of the state wherein they reside. No state shall make or enforce any law which shall abridge the privileges or immunities of citizens of the United States; nor shall any state deprive any person of life, liberty, or property, without due process of law; nor deny to any person within its jurisdiction the equal protection of the laws.

Section 2

Representatives shall be apportioned among the several states according to their respective numbers, counting the whole number of persons in each state, excluding Indians not taxed. But when the right to vote at any election for the choice of electors for President and Vice President of the United States, Representatives in Congress, the executive and judicial officers of a state, or the members of the legislature thereof, is denied to any of the male inhabitants of such state, being twenty-one years of age and citizens of the United States, or in any way abridged, except for participation in rebellion, or other crime, the basis of representation therein shall be reduced in the proportion which the number of such male citizens shall bear to the whole number of male citizens twenty-one years of age in such state.

Section 3

No person shall be a Senator or Representative in Congress, or elector of President and Vice President, or hold any office, civil or military, under the United States, or under any state, who, having previously taken an oath, as a member of Congress, or as an officer of the United States, or as a member of any state legislature, or as an executive or judicial officer of any state, to support the Constitution of the United States, shall have engaged in insurrection or rebellion against the same, or given aid or comfort to the enemies thereof. But Congress may, by a vote of two-thirds of each House, remove such disability.

Section 4

The validity of the public debt of the United States, authorized by law, including debts incurred for payment of pensions and bounties for services in suppressing insurrection or rebellion, shall not be questioned. But neither the United States nor any state shall assume or pay any debt or obligation incurred in aid of insurrection or rebellion against the United States, or any claim for the loss or emancipation of any slave; but all such debts, obligations and claims shall be held illegal and void.

Section 5

The Congress shall have power to enforce, by appropriate legislation, the provisions of this article.

Amendment 15: Right to Vote

Passed by Congress February 26, 1869.
Ratified February 3, 1870.

Section 1

The right of citizens of the United States to vote shall not be denied or abridged by the United States or by any state on account of race, color, or previous condition of servitude.

Section 2

The Congress shall have power to enforce this article by appropriate legislation.

Amendment 16: Income Tax

Passed by Congress July 12, 1909.
Ratified February 3, 1913.
   Note: Article 1, Section 9, of the Constitution was modified by the Sixteenth Amendment.

The Congress shall have power to lay and collect taxes on incomes, from whatever source derived, without apportionment among the several states, and without regard to any census or enumeration.

Amendment 17: Direct Election of Senators

Passed by Congress May 13, 1912.
Ratified April 8, 1913.
   Note: Article 1, Section 3, of the Constitution was modified by the Seventeenth Amendment.

Clause 1

The Senate of the United States shall be composed of two Senators from each state, elected by the people thereof, for six years; and each Senator shall have one vote. The electors in each state shall have the qualifications requisite for electors of the most numerous branch of the state legislatures.

Clause 2

When vacancies happen in the representation of any state in the Senate, the executive authority of such state shall issue writs of election to fill such vacancies: Provided, that the legislature of any state may empower the executive thereof to make temporary appointments until the people fill the vacancies by election as the legislature may direct.

Clause 3

This amendment shall not be so construed as to affect the election or term of any Senator chosen before it becomes valid, as part of the Constitution.

Amendment 18: Prohibition

Passed by Congress December 18, 1917. Ratified January 16, 1919. Repealed by Amendment 21.

Section 1

After one year from the ratification of this article the manufacture, sale, or transportation of intoxicating liquors within, the importation thereof into, or the exportation thereof from the United States and all territory subject to the jurisdiction thereof for beverage purposes is hereby prohibited.

Section 2

The Congress and the several states shall have concurrent power to enforce this article by appropriate legislation.

Section 3

This article shall be inoperative unless it shall have been ratified as an amendment to the Constitution by the legislatures of the several states, as provided in the Constitution, within seven years from the date of the submission hereof to the states by Congress.

Amendment 19: Women Suffrage

Passed by Congress June 4, 1919. Ratified August 18, 1920.

Clause 1

The right of citizens of the United States to vote shall not be denied or abridged by the United States or by any state on account of sex.

Clause 2

The Congress shall have power to enforce this article by appropriate legislation.

Amendment 20: "Lame Duck" Sessions

Passed by Congress March 2, 1932. Ratified January 23, 1933.
  Note: Article 1, Section 4, of the Constitution was modified by Section 2 of this amendment. In addition, a portion of the Twelfth Amendment was superseded by Section 3.

Section 1

The terms of the President and Vice President shall end at noon on the 20th day of January, and the terms of Senators and Representatives at noon on the 3rd day of January, of the years in which such terms would have ended if this article had not been ratified; and the terms of their successors shall then begin.

Section 2

The Congress shall assemble at least once in every year, and such meeting shall begin at noon on the 3rd day of January, unless they shall by law appoint a different day.

Section 3

If, at the time fixed for the beginning of the term of the President, the President elect shall have died, the Vice President elect shall become President. If a President shall not have been chosen before the time fixed for the beginning of his term, or if the President elect shall have failed to qualify, then the Vice President elect shall act as President until a President shall have qualified; and the Congress may by law provide for the case wherein neither a President elect nor a Vice President elect shall have qualified, declaring who shall then act as President, or the manner in which one who is to act shall be selected, and such person shall act accordingly until a President or Vice President shall have qualified.

Section 4

The Congress may by law provide for the case of the death of any of the persons from whom the House of Representatives may choose a President whenever the right of choice shall have devolved upon them, and for the case of the death of any of the persons from whom the Senate may choose a Vice President whenever the right of choice shall have devolved upon them.

Section 5

Sections 1 and 2 shall take effect on the 15th day of October following the ratification of this article.

Section 6

This article shall be inoperative unless it shall have been ratified as an amendment to the Constitution by the legislatures of three-fourths of the several states within seven years from the date of its submission.

Amendment 21: Repeal of Prohibition

Passed by Congress February 20, 1933. Ratified December 5, 1933.

Section 1

The eighteenth article of amendment to the Constitution of the United States is hereby repealed.

Section 2

The transportation or importation into any state, territory, or possession of the United States for delivery or use therein of intoxicating liquors, in violation of the laws thereof, is hereby prohibited.

Section 3

This article shall be inoperative unless it shall have been ratified as an amendment to the Constitution by conventions in the several states, as provided in the Constitution, within seven years from the date of the submission hereof to the states by the Congress

Amendment 22: Limit on Presidential Terms

Passed by Congress March 21, 1947.
Ratified February 27, 1951.

Section 1

No person shall be elected to the office of the President more than twice, and no person who has held the office of President or acted as President, for more than two years of a term to which some other person was elected President shall be elected to the office of the President more than once. But this article shall not apply to any person holding the office of President when this article was proposed by the Congress, and shall not prevent any person who may be holding the office of President or acting as President, during the term within which this article becomes operative from holding the office of President or acting as President during the remainder of such term.

Section 2

This article shall be inoperative unless it shall have been ratified as an amendment to the Constitution by the legislatures of three-fourths of the several states within seven years from the date of its submission to the states by the Congress.

Amendment 23: Voting in District of Columbia

Passed by Congress June 17, 1960.
Ratified March 29, 1961.

Section 1

The district constituting the seat of government of the United States shall appoint in such manner as Congress may direct: A number of electors of President and Vice President equal to the whole number of Senators and Representatives in Congress to which the district would be entitled if it were a state, but in no event more than the least populous state; they shall be in addition to those appointed by the states, but they shall be considered, for the purpose of the election of President and Vice President, to be electors appointed by a state; and they shall meet in the district and perform such duties as provided by the twelfth article of amendment.

Section 2

The Congress shall have power to enforce this article by appropriate legislation.

Amendment 24: Abolition of Poll Taxes

Passed by Congress August 27, 1962. Ratified January 23, 1964.

Section I

The right of citizens of the United States to vote in any primary or other election for President or Vice President, for electors: for President or Vice President, or for Senator or Representative in Congress, shall not be denied or abridged by the United States or any state by reason of failure to pay any poll tax or other tax.

Section 2

The Congress shall have power to enforce this article by appropriate legislation.

Amendment 25: Presidential Disability, Succession

Passed by Congress July 6, 1965.
Ratified February 10, 1967.
Note: Article 21 Section 1, of the Constitution was affected by the Twenty-fifth Amendment.

Section I

In case of the removal of the President from office or of his death or resignation, the Vice President shall become President.

Section 2

Whenever there is a vacancy in the office of the Vice President, the President shall nominate a Vice President who shall take office upon confirmation by a majority vote of both houses of Congress.

Section 3

Whenever the President transmits to the President pro tempore of the Senate and the Speaker of the House of Representatives his written declaration that he is unable to discharge the powers and duties of his office, and until he transmits to them a written declaration to the contrary, such powers and duties shall be discharged by the Vice President as Acting President.

Section 4

Whenever the Vice President, and a majority of either principal officers of the executive departments or of such other body as Congress may by law provide, transmit to the President pro tempore of the Senate and the Speaker of the House of Representatives their written declaration that the President is unable to discharge the powers and duties of his office, the Vice President shall immediately assume the powers and duties of the office as Acting President.

Thereafter, when the President transmits to the President pro tempore of the Senate and the Speaker of the House of Representatives his written declaration that no inability exists, he shall resume the powers and duties of his office unless the Vice President and a majority of either the principal officers of the executive departments or of such other body as Congress may by law provide, transmit within four days to the President pro tempore of Senate and the Speaker of the House of Representatives their written declaration that the President is unable to discharge the powers and duties of his office. Thereupon Congress shall decide the issue, assembling within forty-eight hours for that purpose if not in session. If the Congress, within twenty-one days after receipt of latter written declaration, or, if Congress is not in session, within twenty-one days after Congress is required to assemble, determines by two-thirds vote of both houses that the President is unable to discharge the powers and duties of his office, the Vice President shall continue to discharge the same as Acting President; otherwise, the President shall resume the powers and duties of his office.

Amendment 26: 18-Year-Old Vote

Passed by Congress March 23, 1971.
Ratified July 1, 1971.
Note: Amendment 14, Section 2, of the Constitution was modified by Section 1 of the Twenty-sixth Amendment.

Section 1

The right of citizens of the United States, who are eighteen years of age or older, to vote shall not be denied or abridged by the United States or by any state on account of age.

Section 2

The Congress shall have power to enforce this article by appropriate legislation.

Amendment 27: Congressional Pay

Passed by Congress September 25, 1989.
Ratified May 7, 1992.

No law varying the compensation for the services of the Senators and Representatives shall take effect until an election of Representatives shall have intervened.

Flag Etiquette

The proper way to honor and display the flag comes from Public Law 929, the "Flag Code." Here are some highlights.

Time and Occasions for Display

Times of Display

Outdoors, the flag should be displayed only between sunrise and sunset. However, for a special patriotic occasion, the flag may be displayed 24 hours a day if it is properly illuminated after sunset. It should not be displayed when the weather is bad unless it is an all-weather flag.

Raising and Lowering

The flag should be raised briskly to the top of its pole and lowered slowly and ceremoniously. When flown at half-staff, the flag should first be hoisted quickly to the peak and then lowered to the half-staff position. Before being lowered for the day, it should again be raised to the peak.

Special Occasions for Display

The flag should be displayed every day, but especially on holidays.

Display at Public Institutions

The flag should be displayed on or near the main building of all public institutions, and in or near every polling place on election days. On school days, it should be displayed in or near every school.

Position and Manner of Display

Flagpole Display

The blue field, called the *union*, must always be at the top of the flag. The union hangs from the uppermost point of a flagpole.

In a group of state or local flags, the United States flag should be in the center and at the highest point. When they are flown from the same flagpole, the United States flag should be on top. When they are flown from adjacent flagpoles, the United States flag should be hoisted first and lowered last.

When flags of two or more nations are displayed, they are to be flown from separate staffs of the same height.

Indoor Display

If the flag is hung on a wall or in a window, the union should be on the viewer's left (the flag's right). When displayed with another flag against a wall with their staffs crossed, the United States flag should be to the right and its staff should be in front.

On a speaker's platform, the flag should be displayed either on the wall above and behind the speaker or on a flagpole to the speaker's right.

Special Events Display

In a procession with other flags, the United States flag should be at the marching right (the flag's right) or at the front and center of a line of flags. On a parade float, the flag should be flown from a staff. The flag should not be draped over any vehicle.

When the flag is used to cover a casket, the union should be at the head and over the left shoulder. The flag should not be lowered into the grave nor touch the ground.

Respect for the Flag

The flag should always be carried aloft, never flat or horizontally. It should not:

* be dipped to honor any person or thing.
* displayed with the union down, except as a signal of dire distress.
* touch anything beneath it.
* be used as clothing, drapery, or bedding.
* have anything placed on it, drawn on it, or attached to it.
* be used for advertising purposes
* be printed, sewn, or embroidered on anything disposable, such as paper napkins.

A flag patch or pin may be affixed to official uniforms, and should be worn on the left lapel, near the heart.

Care of Flag

The flag should never be used or stored in a way that would allow it to be easily torn, soiled, or otherwise damaged.

When the flag is no longer fit for display, the flag should be destroyed in a dignified manner, preferably by burning.

Conduct during Ceremonies

When the flag is raised or lowered, and during the playing of the national anthem or recitation of the Pledge of Allegiance, all present should face the flag and stand at attention with their right hands over their hearts. People in military uniform should give a military salute. Men should remove their hats with their right hands and hold their hats at their left shoulders so their hands will rest over their hearts.

Presidents of the United States

I. GEORGE WASHINGTON
1789–1797
No Political Party
Birthplace: Virginia
Born: February 22, 1732
Died: December 14, 1799

4. JAMES MADISON
1809–1817
Democratic Republican
Birthplace: Virginia
Born: March 16, 1751
Died: June 28, 1836

2. JOHN ADAMS
1797–1801
Federalist
Birthplace: Massachusetts
Born: October 30, 1735
Died: July 4, 1826

5. JAMES MONROE
1817–1825
Democratic Republican
Birthplace: Virginia
Born: April 28, 1758
Died: July 4, 1831

3. THOMAS JEFFERSON
1801–1809
Democratic Republican
Birthplace: Virginia
Born: April 13, 1743
Died: July 4, 1826

6. JOHN QUINCY ADAMS
1825–1829
Democratic Republican
Birthplace: Massachusetts
Born: July 11, 1767
Died: February 23, 1848

7. ANDREW JACKSON
1829–1837
Democratic Republican
Birthplace:
     South Carolina
Born: March 15, 1767
Died: June 8, 1845

11. JAMES K. POLK
1845–1849
Democrat
Birthplace:
     North Carolina
Born: November 2, 1795
Died: June 15, 1849

8. MARTIN VAN BUREN
1837–1841
Democrat
Birthplace: New York
Born: December 5, 1782
Died: July 24, 1862

12. ZACHARY TAYLOR
1849–1850
Whig
Birthplace: Virginia
Born: November 24, 1784
Died: July 9, 1850

9. WILLIAM H. HARRISON
1841
Whig
Birthplace: Virginia
Born: February 9, 1773
Died: April 4, 1841

13. MILLARD FILLMORE
1850–1853
Whig
Birthplace: New York
Born: January 7, 1800
Died: March 8, 1874

10. JOHN TYLER
1841–1845
Whig
Birthplace: Virginia
Born: March 29, 1790
Died: January 18, 1862

14. FRANKLIN PIERCE
1853–1857
Democrat
Birthplace:
     New Hampshire
Born: November 23, 1804
Died: October 8, 1869

15. JAMES BUCHANAN
1857–1861
Democrat
Birthplace: Pennsylvania
Born: April 23, 1791
Died: June 1, 1868

19. RUTHERFORD B. HAYES
1877–1881
Republican
Birthplace: Ohio
Born: October 4, 1822
Died: January 17, 1893

16. ABRAHAM LINCOLN
1861–1865
Republican
Birthplace: Kentucky
Born: February 12, 1809
Died: April 15, 1865

20. JAMES A. GARFIELD
1881
Republican
Birthplace: Ohio
Born: November 19, 1831
Died: September 19, 1881

17. ANDREW JOHNSON
1865–1869
Democrat
Birthplace:
       North Carolina
Born: December 29, 1808
Died: July 31, 1875

21. CHESTER A. ARTHUR
1881–1885
Republican
Birthplace: Vermont
Born: October 5, 1829
Died: November 18, 1886

18. ULYSSES S. GRANT
1869–1877
Republican
Birthplace: Ohio
Born: April 27, 1822
Died: July 23, 1885

22, 24. GROVER CLEVELAND
1885–1889, 1893–1897
Democrat
Birthplace: New Jersey
Born: March 18, 1837
Died: June 24, 1908

23. BENJAMIN HARRISON
1889–1893
Republican
Birthplace: Ohio
Born: August 20, 1833
Died: March 13, 1901

28. WOODROW WILSON
1913–1921
Democrat
Birthplace: Virginia
Born: December 29, 1856
Died: February 3, 1924

25. WILLIAM MCKINLEY
1897–1901
Republican
Birthplace: Ohio
Born: January 29, 1843
Died: September 14, 1901

29. WARREN G. HARDING
1921–1923
Republican
Birthplace: Ohio
Born: November 2, 1865
Died: August 2, 1923

26. THEODORE ROOSEVELT
1901–1909
Republican
Birthplace: New York
Born: October 27, 1858
Died: January 16, 1919

30. CALVIN COOLIDGE
1923–1929
Republican
Birthplace: Vermont
Born: July 4, 1872
Died: January 5, 1933

27. WILLIAM H. TAFT
1909–1913
Republican
Birthplace: Ohio
Born: September 15, 1857
Died: March 8, 1930

31. HERBERT C. HOOVER
1929–1933
Republican
Birthplace: Iowa
Born: August 10, 1874
Died: October 20, 1964

32. FRANKLIN D. ROOSEVELT
1933–1945
Democrat
Birthplace: New York
Born: January 30, 1882
Died: April 12, 1945

36. LYNDON B. JOHNSON
1963–1969
Democrat
Birthplace: Texas
Born: August 27, 1908
Died: January 22, 1973

33. HARRY S TRUMAN
1945–1953
Democrat
Birthplace: Missouri
Born: May 8, 1884
Died: December 26, 1972

37. RICHARD M. NIXON
1969–1974
Republican
Birthplace: California
Born: January 9, 1913
Died: April 22, 1994

34. DWIGHT D. EISENHOWER
1953–1961
Republican
Birthplace: Texas
Born: October 14, 1890
Died: March 28, 1969

38. GERALD R. FORD
1974–1977
Republican
Birthplace: Nebraska
Born: July 14, 1913

35. JOHN F. KENNEDY
1961–1963
Democrat
Birthplace: Massachusetts
Born: May 29, 1917
Died: November 22, 1963

39. JAMES E. CARTER, JR.
1977–1981
Democrat
Birthplace: Georgia
Born: October 1, 1924

40. RONALD W. REAGAN
1981–1989
Republican
Birthplace: Illinois
Born: February 6, 1911

42. WILLIAM J. CLINTON
1993–2001
Democrat
Birthplace: Arkansas
Born: August 19, 1946

41. GEORGE H. W. BUSH
1989–1993
Republican
Birthplace: Massachusetts
Born: June 12, 1924

43. GEORGE W. BUSH
2001–
Republican
Birthplace: Connecticut
Born: July 6, 1946

References

CHAPTER 1

Devine, Felice Primeau. *U.S. Citizenship: A Step-by-Step Guide.* New York: LearningExpress, 2001.

The INS Online, http://www.ins.gov

Masi, Mary. *Pass the U.S. Citizenship Exam.* New York: LearningExpress, 1999.

megalaw.com

Points of Light Foundation

ThinkQuest, "Ellis Island History," http://library.thinkquest.org/20619/Eihist.html

"UC Tuition Break OK'd for Some Immigrants," *Los Angeles Times,* January 18, 2002.

CHAPTER 2

"The American Revolution." http://www.historychannel.com.

Carnes, Mark C. ed. *Macmillan Compendium American History.* New York: Simon & Schuster, 1996.

English Bill of Rights.

FindLaw for Legal Professionals. www.findlaw.com

Schwartz, Bernard. *A History of the Supreme Court.* New York: Oxford Press, 1993.

U.S. Supreme Court Cases. www.findlaw.com

CHAPTER 3

Agel, Jerome, and Gerberg, Mort. *The U.S. Constitution for Everyone.* Perigree, 2001.

"Constitution of the United States: Analysis and Interpretation." http://www.access.gpo.gov/congress/senate/constitution/

Jordan, Terry. *The U.S. Constitution: And Fascinating Facts About It.* Oak Hill Publishing, 1999.

Levy, Elizabeth. *If You Were There When They Signed the Constitution.* Scholastic Trade, 1992.

National Archives Exhibit Hall http://www.archives.gov/exhibit_hall/charters_of_freedom/constitution/constitution.html

The United States Constitution Online. http://www.usconstitution.net

Webster, Mary E. *The Federalist Papers: In Modern Language: Indexed for Today's Political Issues.* Merril Press, 1999.

CHAPTER 4

American Civil Liberties Union. http://www.aclu.org/features/f110499a.html

Commager, Henry Steele. *Documents of American History.* New York: Appleton-Century-Crofts, Inc., 1958.

FindLaw, www.findlaw.com

Legal Information Institute, Cornell Law School: http://www.law.cornell.edu/topics/topic1.html

Legal Information Institute, Cornell Law School: http://supct.law.cornell.edu/supct/cases/topic.htm

National Archives and Records Administration, http://www.archives.gov/exhibit_hall/charters_of_freedom/bill_of_rights/bill_of_rights.html

CHAPTER 5

1791–1991 *The Bill of Rights and Beyond,* Bicentennial Commission.

Bernstein, R. B. with Jerome Agel. *Amending America: If We Love the Constitution So Much, Why Do We Keep Trying to Change It?* New York: Times Books, Random House, 1993.

Legal Information Institute, Cornell Law School, http://www.law.cornell.edu/topics/topic1.html

FindLaw, http://caselaw.lp.findlaw.com/data/constitution/amendment09

Helmer, Diana Star. *Women Suffragists.* New York: Facts on File, Inc., 1998.

Legal Information Institute, Cornell Law School, Supreme Court Cases, http://supct.law.cornell.edu/supct/cases/topic.htm

CHAPTER 6

Benjamin, Gerald, "Term Limits in the State legislatures: book review" *Political Science Quarterly,* Winter 2000/2001, Vol. 115, issue 4

Cowley, Geoffrey et al., "The New War on Parkinson's," *Newsweek,* 5/22/2000, vol. 135, issue 21.

Emanuel, Steven L. *Emanuel Law Outlines: Criminal Procedure,* 22nd ed. New York: Aspen Law & Business, 2001.

Hayward, Steven, "Same as the Old Boss?" *Reason,* Dec. 97, vol. 29, Issue 7.

Janda, Kenneth; Jeffrey M. Berry; and Jerry Goldman, *The Challenge of Democracy,* Boston: Houghton Mifflin Company, 2000.

Morrill, R., "Gerrymandering," *Focus on Geography,* Fall 1991, Vol. 41, Issue 3, p. 23.

O'Connor, Karen and Larry J. Sabato, *American Government: Continuity and Change,* New York: Addison Wesley Longman, Inc., 2002.

Patrick Perry, "Michael J. Fox's Challenging New Role," *Saturday Evening Post,* Sep/Oct 2000, Vol. 272, Issue 5.

United States Senate Committee on Appropriations, "Benefits of Stem Cell Research (testimony of Michael J. Fox)," September 14, 2000.

United States Supreme Court, *Shaw v. Reno,* Attorney General et al.

United States Supreme Court, *Wesberry v. Sanders,* 376 U.S. 1, 1964.

Wallison, Ethan, "The Legislative Shuffle," *Washington Monthly,* Sept. 2000, Vol. 32, Issue 9.

CHAPTER 7

About.com government resources http://usgovinfo.miningco.com/blcab.htm

American Memory, Library of Congress http://memory.loc.gov/const/fed/fed_69.html

The White House http://www.whitehouse.gov /government

Legal Information Institute, Cornell Law School. http://supct.law.cornell.edu/supct/cases/topic.htm

Oxford Essential Guide to the U.S. Government. New York: Berkley Books, 2000.

"Presidential succession law" http://www4.law. cornell.edu/uscode/3/19.html

Sherrill, Robert (1978). *Governing America: An Introduction.* New York: HBJ, 1978.

U.S. Marshals. http://www.usdoj.gov/marshals/ missions.html

CHAPTER 8

Farnsworth, Elizabeth. "Interview of Stuart Taylor of the *American Lawyer,*" http://www.pbs.org/ newshour/bb/law/sentencing_2-20.html

"Justice Breyer Denounces Mandatory Sentences," FAMM-gram, Dec. 1998.

Kaminer, Wendy. "Federal Offense," *The Atlantic,* http://theatlantic.com/politics/crime/kaminer2.htm

"Mandatory Sentencing Laws and Drug Offenders in New York State," The Correctional Association of New York, http://www.lindesmith.org/library/ rock3.html

Mann, Judy. "The Harm in Mandatory Sentences." *The Washington Post,* 16 February 2000.

NOLO, Law for All, http://www.nolo.com

"Remarks by Chief Justice William H. Rehnquist, September 27, 2001." Oxford: Oxford University Press, 1993, http://www.supremecourtus.gov/ publicinfo/speeches/sp_09-27-01.html

"Remarks by Stephen Breyer, October 22, 2001." http://supremecourtus.gov/publicinfo/speeches/ sp_10-22-01.html

Schwartz, Bernard. *A History of the Supreme Court.* New York: Oxford, 1993.

U.S. Courts, The Federal Judiciary, http://www.uscourts.gov

CHAPTER 9

Carnes, Michael C., ed. *Macmillan Compendium of American History.* New York: Simon and Schuster Macmillan, 1996.

Law Librarian's Society: State Constitutions http://www.llsdc.org/sourcebook/state-leg.htm

National Governors Association http://www.nga. org/governors

State of Nebraska, http://www.unicam.state.ne.us/ learning/history.htm

Tabulated Information on State Government, http://www.infoplease.com/ipa/A0108309.html

U.S. Dept. of Justice, Office of Justice Programs, Bureau of Justice Statistics, State Court Organization, 1998

CHAPTER 10

Anderson Township, Ohio, http://www. andersontownship.org

Bellah, Robert N.; Madsen, Richard; Sullivan, William M.; Swidler, Ann; and Tipton, Steven M. *Habits of the Heart: Individualism and Commitment in American Life.* Berkeley, CA: University of California Press, 1985.

Carreau, Joel. *Edge City: Life on the New Frontier.* New York: Doubleday, 1988.

Florida Special Districts Handbook, http://www.dca. state.fl.us/fhcd/programs/sdip/Handbook/ handbook.pdf

National Association of Counties, http://www.naco. org/ pubs/research/briefs/dillon.cfm

New York Times, December 28, 2001: Mayor Rudolph Giuliani's farewell speech (excerpts)

Schmidt, Steffen W.; Shelley, Mack C.; and Bardes, Barbara A. *American Government and Politics Today.* Belmont, CA: Wadsworth, 2001.

Schrag, Peter. *Paradise Lost: California's Experience, America's Future.* New York: The New Press, 1998.

Seckler-Husdon, Catheryn. *Our Constitution and Government.* Washington, D.C.: United States Government Printing Office, 1978.

U.S. Census Bureau, http://www.census.gov/govs/ www/estimate99

CHAPTER 11

Bike, William S.: *Winning Political Campaigns.* Juneau, Alaska: The Denali Press, 1998.

Boyers, Sara Jane: *Teen Power Politics: Make Yourself Heard.* Brookfield, Connecticut: Twenty-First Century Books, 2000.

Democratic National Committee, Party Platform, *http://www.democrats.org/about/platform1.html*

Dershowitz, Alan M.: *Supreme Injustice: How the High Court Hijacked Election 2000.* New York: Oxford University Press, 2001. S

Federal Election Commission, http://www.fec.gov/elections.html

GovSpot, Election 2000, http://www.govspot.com/election/

Morin, Isobel V.: *Politics, American Style: Political Parties in American History.* Brookfield, Connecticut: Twenty-First Century Books, 1999. MV

Pascoe, Elaine: *The Right to Vote.* Brookfield, Connecticut: The Millbrook Press, 1997. MV

Reichley, A. James: *The Life of the Parties: A History of American Political Parties.* New York: The Free Press, a Division of Macmillan, Inc., 1992. CM

Republican National Committee, Party Platform, http://www.rnc.org/GOPInfo/Platform/2000platform3

The League of Women Voters: Choosing the President: A Citizen's Guide to the 2000 Election. New York: The Lyons Press, 1999. MV

The Political Staff of the Washington Post: *Deadlock: The Inside Story of America's Closest Election.* New York: Public Affairs, 2001.

U.S. Census Bureau, http://www.census.gov/prod/3/98pubs/cenbr984.pdf

White, John Kenneth and Daniel M. Shea: *New Party Politics: From Jefferson and Hamilton to the Information Age.* Boston: Bedford/St. Martin's, 2000.

CHAPTER 12

AOL-Time Warner. http://www.pbs.org/wgbh/pages/frontline/shows/cool/giants/aoltimewarner.html

Common Cause http://www.commoncause.or/about/fact.htm

Communications Decency Act http://www.cdt.org/speech/cda/

Emily's List http://www.emilyslist.org/el-about/history.asp

Federalist Papers (Number 10) http://memory.loc.gov/const/fed/fed_10.html

Reno vs. *ACLU* http://www2.law.cornell.edu/

Students Against Destructive Decisions, http://www.saddonline.com

The Oxford Essential Guide to the U.S. Government (2000). New York: Berkeley Books, 2000.

The Political Money Line http://www.tray.com

CHAPTER 13

Antonelli, and others. "Unanimous Ninth Circuit Substantially Affirms Lower Court Injunction Against Napster," *Intellectual Property & Technology Law Journal* (May 2001).

Avalon Project at the Yale Law School: "The Code of Hammurabi," http://www.yale.edu/lawweb/avalon/medieval/hammenu.htm.

Chicago v. *Morales* U.S. Supreme Ct., (1999)

Dansby, Andrew. "Napster Fires Off Brief Against RIAA's Injunction," *Rolling Stone,* 7 July 2000.

Friedman, Lawrence M. *American Law.* New York: W.W. Norton & Company, 1984.

Gideon v. Wainright, 372 U.S. 335 (1963).

Greenfield, Karl Taro. "The Free Jukebox.," *Time,* 27 March 2000.

Hall, Kermit L. *The Magic Mirror.* New York: Oxford University Press, 1989.

Horovitz, Bruce. "Authentic Ali: Many Fans, New and Old, Drawn to Spiritual Side," *USA Today,* 8 June 1999.

Lash, Jolie. "Offspring Come to Napster's Aid," *Rolling Stone,* 26 April 2000.

Library of Congress, United States Constitution, http://www.access.gpo.gov/congress/senate/constitution/toc.html.

Saraceno, Christina. "Court Comes Down Hard on Napster," *Rolling Stone,* 27 July 2000.

Stuntz, Jean. "Spanish Laws for Texas Women: The Development of Marital Property Law to 1850," *Southwestern Historical Quarterly* 104 (April 2001)

Wallace, Max. "Today's Athletes Owe Everything to Ali," *New York Times,* 30 April 2000

CHAPTER 14

ABCNews, "The Booming Prison Business," http://abcnews.go.com/sections/us/prison/prison_business.html

ACLU Prison Project, http://www.aclu.org/issues/prisons/npp_mission.html

Abramsky, Sasha. "The Death Row Raiders," *Rolling Stone,* 10/14/99, issue 823 p. 91.

Belli, Melvin M., Sr., and Allen P. Wilkinson. *Everybody's Guide to the Law.* New York: Harper & Row, Publishers, Inc., 1986.

Cole, George F. and Christopher E. Smith. *The American System of Criminal Justice,* 9th ed. Belmont, CA: Wadsworth/Thomson Learning, 2001.

Emanuel, Steven L. *Emanuel Law Outlines: Criminal Procedure,* 22nd ed. New York: Aspen Law & Business, 2001.

Feinman, Jay M. *Law 101: Everything You Need to Know About the American Legal System.* New York: Oxford University Press, 2000.

Gifis, Steven H. *Law Dictionary.* Hauppauge, NY: Barron's Educational Series, Inc., 1996.

Lectric Law Library, *Jane Bronstein vs. David Letterman,* http://www.lectlaw.com/files/cas68.htm

National Criminal Justice Reference Service, U.S. Department of Justice Report, Law Enforcement and Juvenile Crime, http://www.ncjrs.org/pdffiles1/ojjdp/191031.pdf

PBS, Juvenile Justice, http://www.pbs.org/wgbh/pages/frontline/shows/juvenile

Ramsey, Sarah H. and Douglas E. Abrams, *Children and the Law in a Nutshell,* St. Paul, MN: West Group, 2001.

Tucker, Cynthia. "Trying Kids as Adults is the Real Crime," *Denver Post,* 11/20/99.

U.S. Department of Justice, *1999 Juvenile Justice Bulletin,* http://www.ncjrs.org/pdffiles1/ojjdp/178995.pdf

Whittell, Giles, "Snatched from Death's Door," *The Times of London,* 3/19/99.

CHAPTER 15

Black, John. *Oxford Dictionary of Economics.* New York: Oxford University Press, 1997.

Morris, Kenneth M. and Siegel, Alan. *The Wall Street Journal Guide to Understanding Money and Investing.* New York: Lightbulb Press,1993.

CHAPTER 16

Black, John. *Oxford Dictionary of Economics.* New York: Oxford University Press, 1997.

Coal mining songs: http://www.umwa.org/history/hist1.shtml

Consumer Price Index: http://www.bls.gov/cpi/cpifaq.htm#Question%203

Endangered Species Act: http://www.epa.gov/region5/defs/html/esa.htm

Federal Reserve Bank: http://www.federalreserve.gov/pubs/f

Federal Reserve System: http://www.federalreserve.gov/pubs/frseries/frseri.htm

Federal Trade Commission: http:/federalreserve.gov

Janda, Kenneth, Berry, Jeffrey M., Goldman, Jerry. *The Challenge of Democracy.* Boston: Houghton Mifflin Co., 2000.

The Economist Guide to Economic Indicators. New York: John Wiley & Sons, Inc., 1997.

U.S. Bureau of Economic Analysis: www.bea.doc.gov

United Mine Workers of America http://www.umwa.org/history/hist1.shtml

CHAPTER 17

American Red Cross: Youth Services, http://www.redcross/services/youth

Anti-China protests: http://www.commondreams.org/news2000/0412-03.htm

Avalon Project at the Yale Law School, "Monroe Doctrine;" December 2, 1823, http://www.yale.edu/lawweb/avalon/monroe.htm

Biography of Kofi Annan, http://www.un.org/News/ossg/sg/pages/sg_biography.html

The CIA Factbook http://www.cia.gov/cia/publications/factbook/

Current, Richard N.; Williams, T. Harry; Freidel, Frank; and Brinkley, Alan. *A Survey: American History,* 6th Edition. New York: Alfred E. Knopf, 1983.

Department of State Diplomacy: The State Department at Work, http://www.state.gov/r/pa/rls/dos/4078.htm

Director of Homeland Security. http://www.cnn.com/2001/US/09/21/rec.home.land.facts

Director of Homeland Security. http://www.whitehouse.gov/response/faq-homeland.html

FindLaw for Legal Professionals, U.S. Supreme Court, *Dorr v. US,* 195 U.S. 138 (1904)

NATO http://www.nato.int

International Aid. Summary of USAID/OFDA Response in FY 2000.

Magnier, Mark. "$1.5 billion pledged to aid Afghanistan," *Chicago Tribune,* January 21, 2002.

NAFTA Treaty. NAFTA Treaty, Part one: http://www.mac.doc.gov/nafta/ch01.htm

NATO. Welcome to NATO, an Introduction, http://oas.org/en/pINFO/OAS/oas.htm

Red Cross. American Red Cross: International Service Opportunities, http://www.redcross.org/services/intl/opps.html

Schwartz, Bernard. *A History of the Supreme Court.* New York: Oxford, University Press, 1993.

The Peace Corps. "Pierce Couple Joins Peace Corps" *Cincinnati Enquirer,* February 19, 2002.

The UN in Brief, http://www.un.org/Overview/brief.html

"Treaties in Force: A List of Treaties and Other International Agreements of the United States in Force as of January 1, 2000," http://www.state.gov/www/global/legal_affairs/tifindex.html

"U.S. Department of State Strategic Plan (2000)" http://www.state.gov/www/global/general_foreign_policy/2000_dos_stratplan_pta.html

UN Peacekeeping http://www.un.org/News/facts/peacefct.htm

United Nations: UN Peacekeeping Missions
http://In.infoplease.com/ipa/A0862135.html

Viglucci, Andres, and Weaver, Jay. "Elian's Odyssey Ends," *Miami Herald*, June 29, 2000.

Weaver, Jay. "Elian's Fate Unclear," *Miami Herald*, December 1, 1999.

World Bank. "What is the World Bank?" http://www.worldbank.org

World Trade Organization. http://www.wto.org

CHAPTER 18

Aldonas, Grant. "Open Trade: Greater Opportunities for All Countries," http://usinfo.state.gov/journals/ites/0102/ijee/aldonas.htm

"At the Crossroads of Gender and Racial Discrimination," World Conference Against Racism, http://www.un.org/WCAR/e-kit/gender.htm

"Beyond Economic Growth: Meeting the Challenges of Global Development," Appendix II, data tables 1 & 2, World Bank Group, http://worldbank.org/depweb/beyond/beyond/beyond.html

"Bush Opposes Kyoto Protocol," Natural Resources Defense Council, http://nrdc.org/globalWarming/nnego.asp

"Chronology of Terrorist Attacks," Public Agenda, http://www.publicagenda.org/issues/factfiles_detail.cfm?issue_type=americas_global_role&list=8

"Definitions of Terrorism," Political Terrorism Database, http://polisci.home.mindspring.com/ptd/ptd_definition.html

"Economic Growth and Human Development," Sustainable Development Information Service (SDIS), http://www.wri.org/trends/econgrow.html

"Emerging and Re-emerging Infectious Diseases," World Health Organization (WHO), http://www.who.org.int/inf-fs/en/fact097.html

"Global Warming 101," Natural Resources Defense Council, http://www/nrdc.org/globalWarming/f101.asp

Hinrichson, Don. "Putting the Bite on Planet Earth: Rapid Human Population Growth is Devouring Global Natural Resources," http://dieoff.org/page120.htm

Larson, Alan. "A New Negotiating Dynamic at Doha," http://isinfo.state.gov.journals/ites/0102/ijee/larson.htm

"Overview of Poverty Reduction Strategies," The World Bank Group, http://worldbank.org/poverty/strategies/overview.htm

Pechter, Kenneth. "Colloquium: Comparative Policy Analysis Under Innovation-Driven Change: Assessments of the University-Industry Linkage in Japan and the United States," http://glocom.org/special_topics/glocom_colloquium/200201_pechter_comparative/index.html

"Population below the poverty line," *World Factbook*.

"Racial Discrimination and Related Intolerance," *Human Rights Watch World Report 2002*, http://www.hrw.org/wr2k2/print.cgi?racism.html

"Refugee Summit: States Must Reaffirm Commitments," Human Rights Watch, http://www.hrw.org.press/2001/12/recon1211.htm

Rothkopf, David. "In Praise of Cultural Imperialism?" *Foreign Policy*, Number 107, Summer 1997, pp. 38–55.

"Significant Terrorist Incidents, 1961–2001: A Chronology," Office of the Historian, Bureau of Public Affairs, http://usinfo.state.gov/topical/pol/terror/01103131.htm

Sims, ReeseAnne. "The United States vs. the World: A theoretical Look at Cultural Imperialism," http://www.utexas.edu/depts/eems/cultimp.387._.html

Van De Bogart, Willard. "Using the Internet for a Global Information Seeking Approach for the Long Term Survival of Humanity and the Eco-System," http://earthportals.com/monk.html

World Investment Report 2001: Promoting Linkages, United Nations Conference on Trade and Development, New York: United Nations, 2001.

Wallace, Kelly. "Bush to unveil alternative global warming plan," CNN.com, http://www.cnn.com/2002/ALLPOLITICS/02/13/bush.global.warming/index.html

"Undernourishment around the World: Reductions in Undernourishment over the Past Decade," FAO of the UN, http://www.fao.org/docrep/003/y1500e/y1500e03.htm

"Who Is Using Drugs," UNDCP, http://www.undcp.org/drug_demand_who.html

"World Drug Report 2000 – Highlights," UNDCP, http://www.undcp.org/wdr_highlights_2000.html

"World Situation with regard to Drug Abuse," Commission on Narcotic Drugs of the Economic and Social Council of the UN, http://undcp.org/pdf/document_1999-12-23_2.pdf

World Refugee Survey 2001, U.S. Committee for Refugees, http://www.refugees.org/world/worldmain.htm

Credits

Index

Boldfaced numerals tell you where the word or phrase is defined.

D

G

H